for Ray,

with all best wishes,

[illegible]

16/12/2010

UND POTTERY

UND POTTERY –
a History and Comparative Study of the Art Pottery made at the University of North Dakota

KEN FORSTER

MARLIN MEDIA PUBLISHING

First published in the United States of America in 2004
by Marlin Media Publishing
1950 Northgate Boulevard, D6
Sarasota, Florida 34234

Author: Ken Forster
Publication Coordinator: Linda Carrigan
Book Design: Mark Mazzuki
Photo Manipulation: Mark Mazzuki and Rita Ligtenberg
Proofreader: Gail Knight

Printed in Hong Kong

ISBN 0-9740633-1-2
Library of Congress Control Number: 2004104523

In memory of

GENE REYNOLDS

"He was my North, my South, my East and West,
My working week and my Sunday rest,
My noon, my midnight, my talk, my song..."

(excerpted from "Funeral Blues" by W. H. Auden)

CONTENTS

CONTENTS

Appendices

CONTENTS

ACKNOWLEDGMENTS

When, shortly after I arrived in the United States, I first met Lucile Henzke at a flea market in Fort Worth, Texas – at a time when she had begun to research her seminal book *American Art Pottery* – I little knew that I was beginning a journey, as dealer, collector and student, in search of knowledge/ownership of, and commerce in, ceramic artworks, which fascinated me more than any antique or collectible category of design objects I had seen in my early years in Europe and Asia. And when, in the early 1970s, a Californian dealer at an antiques show in Madison, Wisconsin, sold me an assortment of pottery made at the University of North Dakota, I recognized that my interest in the American West had progressed beyond the Hollywood Western movies of my youth. At first, particularly in the Eastern United States, it was difficult to add to this small, wonderful collection and there were very few fellow collectors with whom to discuss it. Then, finally in 1989, along with a growing number of people, who were soon to become friends, I struck "gold." For this reason I extend my first thanks to the Barrs – Jan and Robert – who allowed me to buy so many of their treasures that day so many years ago in Mandan.

In the interim I had made the acquaintance of many people – colleagues and friends – from whom I continue to learn much in my study of late nineteenth and early twentieth century ceramics; and I realize that there is still more to know, since first spending time with David, Jerri, Don, Jen, Mike and those others who participated in the early festivals in Roseville and Crookesville in the 1970s. To them, my thanks for the knowledge, experience and fun-times, as also to Darlene and James Dommel for their kindness and guidance and to such later friends as Tony, Kendall and Cindy. And I extend my gratitude also for the support and encouragement rendered over the years by my dear friends Helen Dougherty, Martin Eidelberg, Jerry Kearns, and the late Dennis Boyd. I appreciate the contributions made by Curt Rustand, Scott Nelson, Dod Stewart, Tony McCormack, Arnie Small and Barbara Gerr, and Richard Risser and David Dilley. I am grateful to Phyllis Richman, for her professional authorial suggestions, and especially so to Dr. David Taylor, whose expert opinion and attention to detail greatly improved the text. Also, without the help and advice of Mark Halvorson, Curator of Collections Research at the State Historical Society of North Dakota in Bismarck; Monroe Warshaw; Tom Lane; and Steve Axtman, Curt Hanson and above all Sandy Slater, Head, of the Elwyn B. Robinson Department of Special Collections at the Chester Fritz Library, University of North Dakota, in Grand Forks, this book would not have been possible.

Finally, I reserve my deepest gratitude to Don Miller, Professor in the Visual Arts Department, College of Fine Arts, at the University of North Dakota, together with my admiration for his devotion to the study of UND pottery.

Plate 1: Vase, 8½" h., marked "North Dakota Products 1926 Made for Gov. A. G. Sorlie by Margaret Cable".
UND Coll. # C-CBL Gift 118-720. (See also fig. 47).

INTRODUCTION

Like love in a cold climate, the Ceramics Department at the University of North Dakota struggled to survive through the first half of the twentieth century. The treasure that is UND pottery – created in what might be considered an unromantically remote location – has somehow managed, over the last 30-40 years, to elude the fame and approbation that it has long deserved. Until recently, only a small cadre of ardent collectors has made the effort to delve into its history and uncover its mystery. It is to be hoped that this book will introduce to a wider audience a subject of artistic accomplishment and success through adversity. Together with a documentation of events in the evolution of the School of Mines at the University, the contributions and achievements of six women dedicated to the study, research and instruction of ceramic art and technique are examined here in order to effect an honest and long-overdue evaluation of both the Ceramics Department's program and its legacy.

Affinities with such potteries as Rookwood, Newcomb, Roseville, Weller, Owens, Marblehead, Walrath, Jervis, University City, Arequipa, Rhead Faience, Overbeck, California Faience, Dedham and Saturday Evening Girls help place the School of Mines among the giants of American art pottery producers in the first half of the twentieth century. The pottery made elsewhere of North Dakota clay (for the St. Louis and Omaha Expositions) -- particularly the striking designs by the Ferock Studios -- reveals the high standards of manufacture and design of its well-known makers, and is both reflective of then-current trends and at the same time innovative and inspiring. It represents today an appropriate prologue to the accomplishments of the Ceramics Department's staff members and the more successful creations of some of the more gifted students. As a result the products of the Babcock-Cable-Mattson years, especially, bear comparison with the better-known examples made by the more celebrated potteries. And an understanding of the theories and practices of Margaret Cable's teachers, Frederick Rhead and Charles Binns, contributes to a greater appreciation of her Department's achievements, which should not be lessened or in any way adversely affected by the lower, "course-souvenir"[1] standard of work by less talented students. Even the slip-cast, plain models, without other hand-applied surface enrichment, usually reveal themselves to be elegant forms, exquisitely finished and invested with beautiful, shaded monochromatic or often blended glazes admirably appropriate to the shape of the vessel.

The University of North Dakota was founded by an act of the Dakota territorial legislature of February 23, 1881, and was originally named the University of the Dakota Territory. As Instructor in Chemistry there, and as State Geologist, Earle Jay Babcock collected, examined and analyzed examples of the various mineral resources of the state, and with the aid of a number of potteries, institutions and individuals in Ohio, Chicago, Minneapolis and New Jersey, he was able to prove the suitability of North Dakota clays for ceramic and brick manufacture. Having successfully exhibited finished products made from the native clays at both a World's Fair and a National Exposition, Babcock encouraged the University administrators to recruit Margaret Cable as Instructor in a new Ceramics Department to be established at the School of Mines in 1910. For the next thirty-nine years, often under very difficult conditions – defined by economics, geography and the prevailing attitudes of the time – Cable carried out the mandate of the Department, which was to prove the viability of North Dakota's native clays and thereby to provide opportunities for commercial development in the state.

Cable's duties included not only experimentation and research but also pottery making, instruction, promotion and administration. The styles and techniques adopted, developed and nurtured by her throughout her career – and continued for at least another decade after her retirement from Grand Forks – resulted in a wide range of art pottery that could be ranked with that of the leading American producers of the time. In this achievement she was helped by a few fellow teachers/potters/technicians/decorators who assisted in the tasks of analysis and research and/or supervised – or collaborated on – the work executed by over two thousand students (including both regular students of the University and also "special" adult students).

At first pottery production was small and limited to conservative designs in tableware, utilitarian items and somber-toned, decorative wares reflective of Cable's training under Ernest Batchelder at the Handicraft Guild in Minneapolis. But after further study with Frederick Rhead at the People's University in St. Louis, Missouri, and with Charles Binns at the New York State School of Clayworking in Alfred, New York, and after the experience gained in working during summer months in the white-ware industry in East Liverpool, Ohio, Cable was not only aware of trends and open to influences within the art pottery community but also in a position to apply her knowledge to her own pottery design and the formulation of her teaching. The early, immediate influences, adding to the design principles promulgated by Rhead and Binns, were those of the Rookwood, Newcomb and Marblehead potteries, as are apparent in work produced in the period 1918-1926 by Cable and Hildegarde Fried.

Having graduated with a degree in chemistry and mathematics and having studied pottery making and ceramic design in Margaret Cable's ceramics class, Fried was both scientist and artist, and as such well qualified to assist Cable in all aspects of ceramic work and instruction in the Department. Her ability is evident in her many vessels and tiles, utilizing both representational and conventionalized design schemes of refined draftsmanship, in subtle color combinations and in glossy and matt glazes. She specialized in producing forms and glazes worthy of her training under Binns, Arts and Crafts designs to equal those of Marblehead and high glaze painted surfaces emulating Rookwood.

Julia Mattson brought to the Ceramics Department her qualifications in art and education together with her experience as "student assistant in ceramics." She, too, was a potter/technician/ decorator as well as being responsible, with Cable, for all instruction in the Department. Her tenure from 1924 through 1963 was instrumental in continuing and furthering, with Cable, the aims of the Department during all of the most difficult years of the Depression and World War II; and her fascination with, and study of, Native American art and design – together with her role in the development of bentonite glazes – were the inspiration for many of the University of North Dakota's most original products from the early 1930s on.

Flora Huckfield, though never a faculty member, joined the staff of the Ceramics Department in the same year as Mattson. Principally a decorator and adept in the use of the airbrush to apply glaze, her contribution to the sustention of the Department during the years when it received no funding and to the active functioning of the program itself through her tireless production of wares for sale during the Spencer era, was indeed vital.

Freida Hammers was a superb resource scientist, responsible from 1926 through the late 1930s for almost all research and formulation of clay mixtures and glaze recipes and for the resolution of other technical problems. She not only introduced the "New Body Mix" which was the staple clay body used most frequently from 1938 on, but also evolved the range of brilliant colors and supervised the development of the bentonite slips most often associated with University of North Dakota pottery.

Plate 2: "The Potter," polychrome mosaic plaque, framed, 27" x 18½", exhibited at the Century of Progress Chicago World's Fair in 1933. UND Coll. # C-CBL 127-934.

During the difficult years of the Depression, Cable wrote to a dealership: "We only carry on because this is a testing laboratory of North Dakota clays and by making pottery in a small way we are proving out their worth and quality in the hope of laying the foundation for and encouraging the future development of a ceramic industry in North Dakota."[2] Economies afforded the Ceramics Department during these years, and beyond, by Hammers' experimentation contributed considerably to the continuance of the program in Grand Forks. And of even greater significance was Cable's realization that the survival of the Department depended on increased revenue from the sale of pottery produced not only to a high standard of craftsmanship but also by easy, quick and relatively cheap methods. When Austin Spencer was hired as salesman in the Upper Midwest for the Department's output, Cable initiated a project whereby Spencer would take orders from dealerships for models represented by samples he carried. These orders could be filled from the Department's regular production of slip-cast wares in multiple copies – some of plain pottery forms, some incorporating in-mold decorations, and others enriched with a limited application of color or enhanced by shading. From 1938 through mid-1949, the relatively large-scale sale of molded production pieces, even more so than student-enrollment fees, helped support the program of the Ceramics Department. The more than 300 items on the "Spencer-list" -- produced continually and in quantity during these years -- account for many of the University of North Dakota models available today to the collector.

By the time of Julia Mattson's retirement in 1963 – fourteen years after Margaret Cable had left Grand Forks – pottery had been produced there, by staff and students, exemplifying all methods of manufacture, decorative technique and stylistic detail. An extensive palette of colors, a great variety of glaze effects and a diversity of imagery had been added to the influences of earlier or contemporary art pottery producers in Ohio, the South, California and the Northeastern United States. The teachings of Frederick Rhead and Charles Binns and the example and advice of Arthur Baggs, Paul Cox and Mary Given Sheerer were the inspiration for the syllabus of the Ceramics Department and for the accomplishments of its staff and students. Techniques, styles, glazes and colors were adopted, adapted and evolved to develop a large body of work, comparable to much of the best of the period produced elsewhere, and in some respects unique to the University of North Dakota.

With the arrival of Margaret Pachl, after Cable's retirement, the University administrators began to make changes affecting the role, plan and syllabus of the Ceramics Department. By the early 1960s, a much greater emphasis was given to instruction and by the mid-1960s – after Mattson's retirement – the "commercial sale" [3] of pottery had been discontinued. Already stylistic trends in American ceramics favored studio pottery of the type designed by Pachl, and not the art pottery of the Cable-Mattson era. Research and experimentation – initially the primary purpose, if not the principal function, of the Department prior to the deprivations and tribulations of the Depression and World War II years – were largely put on hold for at least the twenty years before Pachl's resignation in 1970. In June 1973, the administration of the Ceramics Department, which until this time had remained part of the School of Mines in the College of Engineering, was transferred to the College of Fine Arts.

A knowledge of the history of the Ceramics Department at Grand Forks, particularly in regard to experimentation, curriculum and pottery sales, is essential to an appreciation of the wares produced there. The purpose of this book is, therefore, to explore the steps in the development of Margaret Cable's program and to explain how its artistic reputation came to rank with those of its up-to-now more celebrated contemporaries in the field of American art pottery. University of North Dakota pottery, which has, heretofore, been regarded, undeservedly, as an isolated, regional effort of limited interest must now be rightly regarded as yet another national treasure of American design and craftsmanship.

Endnotes
1 Gauger letter dated August 19, 1931, to Cable.
2 Cable letter dated February 1, 1933, to Mrs. Stella Roseland of the Luger Furniture Co., in Fargo.
3 Cable letter dated May 10, 1927, to Professor Parmelee of the University of Illinois.

RESOURCES / CREDITS

All letters quoted are from the Elwyn B. Robinson Department of Special Collections at the Chester Fritz Library, University of North Dakota.

Archival photographs (UAP #s) are from the University Picture File at the Elwyn B. Robinson Department of Special Collections at the Chester Fritz Library, University of North Dakota.

Archival photographs (SHSND #s) are from the collection of the State Historical Society of North Dakota.

Other archival photographs are from the author's collection.

Archival documentary material (included in Figs. 1-56) is from the Elwyn B. Robinson Department of Special Collections at the Chester Fritz Library, University of North Dakota, where indicated, or from the author's collection.

All pottery photographed (Plates 1-219), unless otherwise indicated, is from the author's collection.

Pottery (UND Coll. #s) is from the collection of the University of North Dakota.

Pottery (SHSND Coll. #s) is from the collection of the State Historical Society of North Dakota.

Other pottery is from the collection of Darlene and James Dommel, and – photographed by unidentified photographers – from the collections of Curt Rustand, Dod Stewart, Tony McCormack, Scott Nelson, Barbara Gerr, and Richard Risser and David Dilley.

All photography of pottery and other items in the author's collection is by Monroe Warshaw or Tom Lane.

All photography of pottery in the collection of the University of North Dakota is by Donald Miller.

All photography of pottery in the collection of the State Historical Society of North Dakota is by Mark J. Halvorson.

All photography of pottery in the Dommel collection is by James Dommel.

PART I

The Early History of the School of Mines; Earle J. Babcock; Ferock Studios

Disregarding the Native American inhabitants of the area, a visitor to the Dakota Territory from the eastern United States wrote, in 1864: "It's a beautiful land but I doubt that human beings will ever live here." [1] Twelve years later the Sioux defeated and decimated the forces of George Armstrong Custer at the Battle of Little Bighorn, and another thirteen years were to pass before the Territory became the states of North and South Dakota, in 1889. At this time the region had none of the cultural traditions or established economic advantages of Massachusetts, New Jersey and Ohio, which became the principal areas of the American ceramics industry at the beginning of the twentieth century. As early as 1877, a year after the Centennial Exposition in Philadelphia, a group of ladies in Cincinnati, of a leisured class unknown in the Northwest, became actively involved in making and decorating ornamental pottery. Even in the southern agrarian economy of Louisiana the port city of New Orleans had already at that time been receptive, for generations, to cultural influences from other parts of the United States and from abroad; and in California there were early signs of a prosperous and productive environment for artists and artisans.

Fig. 1: Postcard, c. 1910, showing the campus of the University of North Dakota.

But North Dakota was essentially a blank page. In the region to the west of Minneapolis, access to museums, libraries, institutions of higher learning and opportunities for artistic education hardly existed. Other than the indigenous Woodlands people, the population was sparse, and contained in a very few small communities scattered across the state. Development and change were very slow, and brought about by only a few determined and hardworking individuals. Even as late as 1934, Margaret Cable, the central figure in the story of University of North Dakota pottery, lamented: "This business of being stuck way off up here in the middle of a wheat field with no other potters to talk things over with, or museums to inspire, gets me." [2]

While North Dakota was poor in cultural resources for many years, it was rich in natural resources. Its soil, in many areas, was extremely fertile and the state became a center of wheat production and sugar beet culture in the U.S.A. The land was also rich in lignite coal as well as a high grade of clay. With regard to the latter, centuries earlier "clay made the region a center of that form of Indian art through many generations." [3] During the prehistoric period a substantial ceramic tradition developed that included pottery making by the Northwestern Plains villages in eastern North Dakota, and the Missouri Valley villages (populated by ancestors of the Hidatsa and the Mandan) to the west. This indigenous tradition had long since died out by the end of the nineteenth century, however. At that time, a new era was beginning, and it can be traced to 1895, when the North Dakota Geological Survey was created in order to investigate the state's mineral resources. Shortly thereafter, the Survey was led by Earle Jay Babcock who remained State Geologist until 1902.

Earle Jay Babcock (fig. 3) was born June 11, 1865, in St. Charles, Minnesota. He graduated with a B.S. degree from the University of Minnesota in 1889, in which year he was appointed Instructor in Chemistry at the University of North Dakota. The University had been established in Grand Forks in the period 1881-1883. By 1889 there were 24 students of college rank in the University; over the next ten years the number grew substantially, and it was during this period that a School of Mines (fig. 2) was established.

Fig. 2: School of Mines Building. SHSND # A 6006.

Before obtaining his doctorate in 1914, Babcock had become Professor of Industrial Chemistry, Metallurgy and Mining, Director of the School of Mines and the North Dakota Mining Experiment Station, and then Dean of the College of Mining Engineering from 1898. During the summers of his first years in North Dakota, Babcock took trips – at his own expense – through the state, on horseback, by buckboard or by bicycle, gathering mineral examples for later analysis. He sought to determine purposes and products for which they might best be used. In 1892, the University published his *Clays of Economic Value in North Dakota*, which was followed fourteen years later by the North Dakota Geological Survey's *Fourth Biennial Report*, co-authored by Babcock and Charles H. Clapp, geology instructor at the University of North Dakota. The *Fourth Biennial Report* was considered to be "the single most comprehensive report on the clay resources of North Dakota." [4] Throughout his career Babcock, who was to become known as the "Dean of Lignite," worked industriously conducting research into geological, mining and engineering problems, and contributing widely to scientific and industrial publications and reports. In 1906, after many years of investigation and analysis of clay resources, Babcock wrote: "For several years I have made a study of these clays, first in the field, as state geologist, and later in the laboratories and testing rooms, as dean of the School of Mines. I have done an immense amount of practical work on them and feel thoroughly familiar with their peculiar characteristics and the uses to which the different deposits may be put." [5]

After successful experimentation with the clays he had gathered, Babcock's next step was to attempt to capitalize on this research by publicizing widely, on a national stage if possible, the ceramic viability of North Dakota clay. Such an opportunity arose with the Louisiana Purchase Exposition which was held in St. Louis, Missouri, in 1904. Babcock envisaged a display of North Dakota clays and finished products made from them, such as "sewer pipe, paving brick, enameled brick, roofing tile, drain tile, ornamental building brick, hollow terra cotta lumber," [6]

Fig. 3: Earle Jay Babcock. SHSND # C 1817.

Plate 3: "Flowered" tableware; large plate 8½" dia., small plate 5¼" dia. UND Coll. # C-MSC 179-771 & 772.

as well as tableware and decorative pottery. To this end, in 1903 and 1904, he wrote letters to the Beaver Falls Art Tile Co. and the Mayer Pottery Co., in Pennsylvania; Edwin Bennett's Tile Works, in Baltimore; the National China Co. and the Homer Laughlin China Co., in East Liverpool, Ohio; the Brockman Pottery Co., in Cincinnati; the Cook Pottery Co. and the Trenton Potteries Co., in New Jersey; S. A. Weller, the Ohio Pottery Co. and the Roseville Pottery Co., in Zanesville, Ohio; and the Art Institute of Chicago. For example, in his letter to Weller [7] he wrote: "I am anxious to have some of our fine white clay made up into some samples of Art Pottery…I should be glad to pay you liberally for making up quite a lot of such art pieces from ND clay. You will find that the clay will give you no trouble in working." On the same day he wrote to Roseville asking for a selection of jardinières and pedestals in various sizes "hand decorated/fancy glaze/special underglaze," and umbrella stands in "A-finish Iris Decoration" and "B-finish Rose," as well as tankard sets. Replying to Babcock, the Ohio Pottery Co. reported that it had tested "some ND clay with excellent results" but was unable "to make and finish vases, pitchers, etc., as you request, on account of our inability to do that class of work." [8] The firm referred Babcock to the J. B. Owens Pottery Co., also in Zanesville. Babcock subsequently wrote to Owens and requested pieces made up "in the Utopian glaze effect but should like some in the Utopian dull finish too." [9]

Many of the companies approached were sent quantities of clay, which Babcock wanted them to test and then use as the body for many of their usual designs. Several of them were unable, or unwilling, to acquiesce to his request, most notably S. A. Weller who replied: "…for business reasons alone it would be impossible for us to undertake it. We feel it would hardly be interesting to you for us to enumerate these reasons." [10] But some of the companies were able to comply. The Mayer Pottery Co. reported completion of "2 teacups of each of the trial bodies" for tea sets and "about 20 pitchers of various shapes and sizes and a dozen platters." [11] Mr. George F. Young of Roseville wrote to Babcock: "…the 100 lbs. of clay has arrived and we have made several jardinières. They have gone through the kilns once and will be out the second time within a very few days. The 1200 lbs. have not yet arrived but we will be in position to rush it through without delay. So far we have experienced no difficulty whatever." [12] Mr. G. S. Brush of Owens wrote to Babcock: "we are pushing your pieces as fast as possible and will have same ready for shipment in a short time…and can assure you clay works very well." [13] The Owens invoice for the "special pieces… from your clay" lists 25 pieces "Mat Finish," 3 Venetian table sets, and 50 pieces "Glaze Finish, Vases," at a total cost of $415.50. [14]

At the end of May 1904, Babcock sent Owens and Roseville instructions for delivery – to the Mines and Metallurgy Building, North Dakota Booth, World's Fair Grounds, St. Louis, Missouri – of, respectively, "the assortment of Utopian Art Vases and special pieces of Venetian Art Ware" and "the jardinières and special pieces which you are making for me from N. Dakota clay." [15]

In addition to the tableware made and decorated by the Mayer Pottery Co. that consisted of "Purple Flowered Ware" (40 pieces) and "Pink Flowered Ware" (45 pieces), [16] other items were supplied by the Art Institute of Chicago. [17] In the considerable correspondence of this time between Babcock and Judson T. Webb of the Art Institute, reference is made to vases and tableware, including tea services, which were to be glazed and decorated at the Art Institute, and also to pieces which were to be shipped, in bisque state, to North Dakota for decoration and firing by a local china painter, Mrs. C. C. Schmidt of Jamestown, North Dakota.

In his initial contacts with his suppliers, Babcock had requested that all pieces be marked "Made of North Dakota clay." It is not known to what extent this requirement was fulfilled. Some ware was certainly delivered unmarked, and the University collection includes only a couple of Owens Utopian vases (plate 129), and a small variety of the "Flowered" tableware (plate 3) which are marked with an incised "ND".

In a letter he wrote in 1906, Babcock stated: "when I set up the St. Louis exhibit it was necessary for me to select in person each lot of material as I found no one else knew the difference in the layers (of the clays), which appear to the eye nearly identical but which give entirely different results. After having selected the material it was analyzed, properly prepared, made into dishes, and otherwise variously tested here at the School of Mines under my personal direction. I then selected and prepared the raw material which was sent to several of the best eastern potteries and after a great deal of difficulty I arranged to have some of it made into wares. The results astonished even the pottery people...I found it an extremely difficult matter to get any eastern pottery to make up this clay, for two reasons. First because they did not wish to stop their regular work and clean out their machines to run a small lot of clay, with which they were entirely unfamiliar, through the various stages of mixing, tempering, moulding, bisque burning, glazing, decorating, and glaze burning, operations which required the services of one of their expert men. But besides this, most of the concerns did not wish to prove the value of clay products which might be developed into competing industries, and in many cases it was only through personal effort and acquaintance that I succeeded, and after assuring the potteries that I was absolutely in no way financially interested in any of the clay but that my interest was purely from a scientific standpoint." [18]

After this effort, and the subsequent success of his display at the World's Fair, Babcock had clearly resolved to exhibit examples of the pottery made from North Dakota clays in a museum setting at the University. Presumably for this purpose, he ordered and received, throughout 1905, further shipments from Roseville – tankard sets, both "special underglaze" and "hand-decorated" [19] – and from Owens – "a few more pieces of the Utopian Ware...mat finish, the color being very rich dark brown shades." [20] Babcock agreed that Owens should "make up a few other finishes to show the possibilities of the clay," adding "please scratch on the bottom of each piece (or otherwise mark permanently) 1905." [21] The same instruction was given to Roseville. In August of that year he inquired of Owens regarding shipment of his order of ware marked "N.D. 1905". [22]

In September 1909, Babcock traveled in the eastern United States visiting the potteries with which he had established contact prior to the St. Louis Exposition. In Trenton, New Jersey, he arranged for the Cook Pottery Co. to ship to Grand Forks "a number of moulds and some samples of clays, glazes, segars, etc., to use in my clay working and for museum purposes." [23]

Plate 4: Small, handled, green leaf dish with iridescent glaze pooling; marked "N.D. Clay". UND Coll. # C-MSC Gift 96-690. Another example in the University's collection is marked "Bisbee 1904".

During his visit to Zanesville, Ohio, he ordered from J. B. Owens eighteen old molds, segars and tile set samples "for use in my museum and experimental work." [25]

In October, 1907, a Revelation Pottery Kiln ordered from H. J. Caulkins & Co. of Detroit, Michigan, was installed, and with the testing laboratories, research apparatus and a small mines museum in place, Babcock was able to introduce some ceramic instruction into the School of Mines curriculum. In 1909, students in the Chemistry and Engineering Departments were offered courses taught by Babcock and Miss Marcia Bisbee, a chemistry instructor, who, five years earlier, had been the first person to attempt the making and firing of pottery at the University (plate 4).

At first, the students' efforts were concentrated on the production of structural tiles, building blocks, bricks, insulators and sewer pipes, which were to be featured that year, along with coal, lignite briquettes and other mineral resources, at the National Corn Exposition in Omaha, Nebraska. And in this, his second endeavor to promote widely, on a national stage, the suitability of North Dakota clays for ceramic purposes, Babcock contracted to have pottery items made from the native clay by the Handicraft Guild, in Minneapolis, and by the Ferock Studios, in Zanesville. He renewed his acquaintance with Judson T. Webb, formerly of the Art Institute of Chicago and from whom he had ordered tableware for the display at the St. Louis Exposition. Webb had, in the interim, moved to Minneapolis to assist in establishing the pottery program at the Handicraft Guild. There he directed an assistant, Miss Margaret Cable, to arrange the supply of Babcock's order of "a few small pieces of various forms and glazed with various colors, say about 15 or 20 pieces in all" [26] needed by the end of November 1909. This was the beginning of a professional relationship between Babcock and Margaret Cable, which developed into one of great importance to the School of Mines.

Another woman assisting Babcock in the Corn Exposition endeavor was Maude Sibyl Pollock, of the Ferock Studios, whom he had met in Zanesville on September 4, 1909. Most of his correspondence with the J. B. Owens Co. during the past six years had passed through the hands of Miss Pollock, (fig. 4) at that time an employee of the Owens company. In late 1909, perhaps motivated by changes in the Owens business operation, and possibly to derive advantage from Babcock's search for a production source for his pottery display in Omaha, Maude Pollock formed the Ferock Studios, in Zanesville, in partnership with Frank Ferrell. By that time Ferrell had already spent some twelve years in the ceramics industry in Zanesville, first with Weller, then with J. B. Owens, and afterwards with Peters & Reed. In 1919, he became art director of the Roseville Pottery. Ferrell was familiar with all aspects of pottery manufacture and was soon to be considered one of the foremost designers of pottery in the United States.

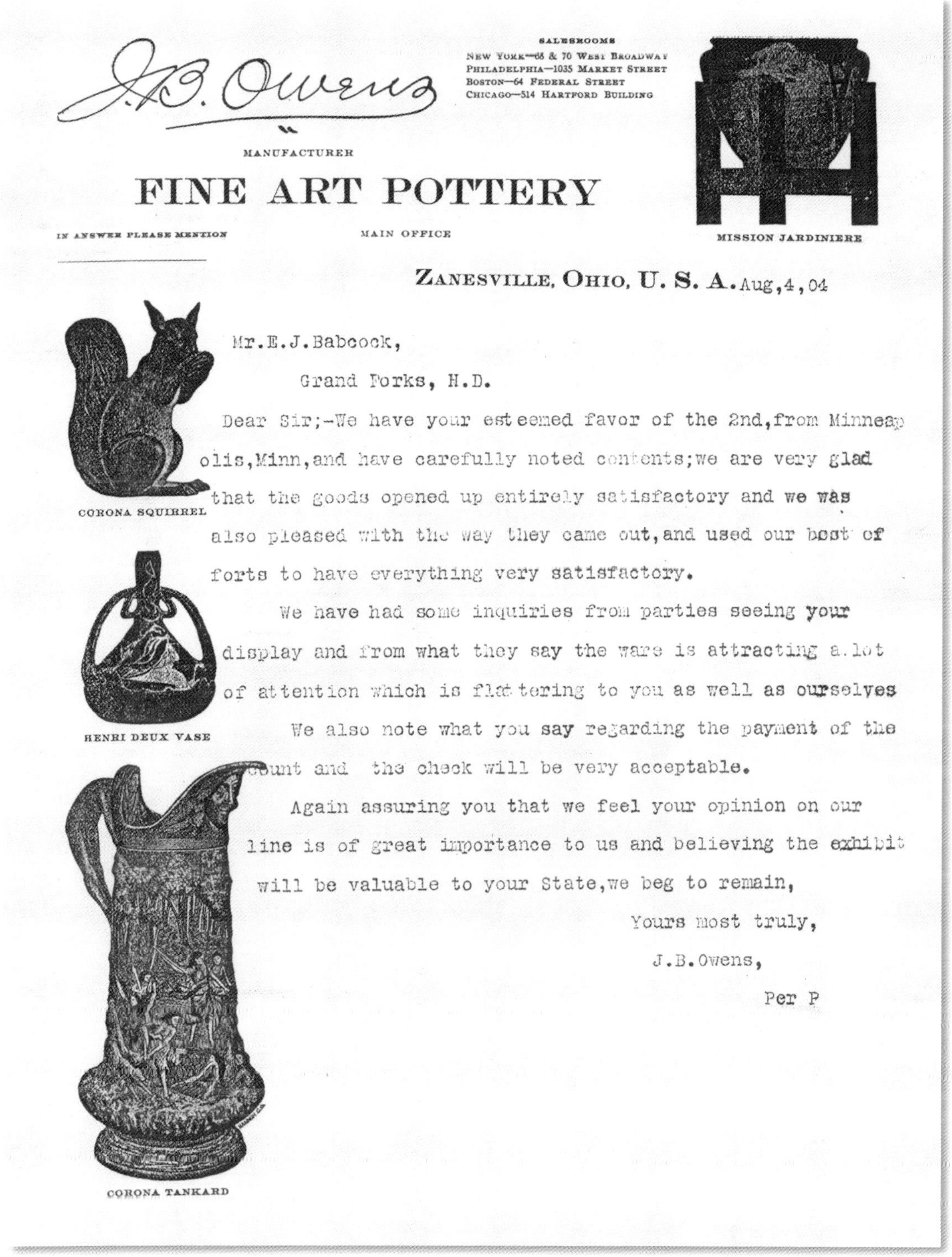

J. B. Owens

SALESROOMS
NEW YORK—68 & 70 WEST BROADWAY
PHILADELPHIA—1035 MARKET STREET
BOSTON—64 FEDERAL STREET
CHICAGO—514 HARTFORD BUILDING

MANUFACTURER

FINE ART POTTERY

IN ANSWER PLEASE MENTION

MAIN OFFICE

MISSION JARDINIERE

ZANESVILLE, OHIO, U. S. A. Aug,4,04

CORONA SQUIRREL

HENRI DEUX VASE

CORONA TANKARD

Mr.E.J.Babcock,

Grand Forks, N.D.

Dear Sir;-We have your esteemed favor of the 2nd,from Minneap olis,Minn,and have carefully noted contents;we are very glad that the goods opened up entirely satisfactory and we was also pleased with the way they came out,and used our best ef forts to have everything very satisfactory.

We have had some inquiries from parties seeing your display and from what they say the ware is attracting a lot of attention which is flattering to you as well as ourselves

We also note what you say regarding the payment of the count and the check will be very acceptable.

Again assuring you that we feel your opinion on our line is of great importance to us and believing the exhibit will be valuable to your State,we beg to remain,

Yours most truly,

J.B.Owens,

Per P

Fig. 4: J. B. Owens Co. letter dated August 4, 1904, written by Maude Sibyl Pollock.

Plate 5: Ferock vase, 12"h.; with reticulation.

Designs from Ferrell's Ferock Studios that were executed in North Dakota clay are arguably the most original, sophisticated and yet subtle samples of art pottery commissioned by Babcock for the expositions in St. Louis and Omaha. Their shapes, surface modeling and glaze colors manifest an affinity with some of the Arts and Crafts-style lines being made in Cincinnati and Zanesville during the period 1900-1910. They are more closely related to Rookwood's Modeled Matt, several Owens lines and even some of the early Van Briggle designs in matt green, yellow and brown, and have little in common with the "structural naturalism"[27] of Grueby or the stylized shapes of Teco, though there is an undeniable resonance of the contemporary Chicago art and design in some of the more dramatic Ferock examples. Most of the Ferock decoration is characterized by interesting, muted colors in matt or semi-matt glazes, often streaked and flowing, that highlight sparse, conventionalized floral, abstract and even geometric motifs, which are modeled or incised (plates 5; 6).

Plate 6: Ferock vases.

Babcock ordered and received from Ferock Studios an assortment of vases -- small, medium and large -- in a range of "beautiful new shapes"[28] and in "a wide variety of colors showing what can be produced from the clays in the matt effect, which is the most talked of in Pottery today,"[29] – all bearing the Ferock name and with an incised or penciled "ND". Later he requested an additional delivery of "a little variety of small dishes, glazed, white or cream tint, made from North Dakota clay, say about 20 small forms which could be hand-decorated... a few white tiles also."[30] Again, as it had been in St. Louis, Babcock's display of pottery in Omaha was highly successful.

The future of the Ferock Studios was not bright, however. Maude Pollock wrote to Babcock: "For health reasons the writer is compelled to dispose of her business...too much of a strain on my nervous system and have at last deemed it advisable to retire permanently." (fig. 5) She continued by offering him "very low for cash" all molds and glazes of the Ferock Studios, and in doing so played to Babcock's hand in writing: "This would be an ideal chance for your capitalists to start a small pottery right in your city where you have clays in abundance and it would be ready to begin work so soon as a kiln could be built."[31] But Pollock's offer was declined by Babcock.[32]

Whether the Ferock Studios ever actually delivered to other enterprises their "rare creations of the Potter's craft...Tiles," as advertised in their letterhead, is not known, though there is one example of a low vase produced by Clewell which replicates the design of one made for the School of Mines.[32] But the examples in the university and other collections, which bear the Ferock name, are also marked "ND clay", and most of those in private collections throughout the United States are known to have emerged originally from the Upper Midwest.

The success of the displays in St. Louis and in Omaha (fig. 6) helped provide the impetus for the establishment, in 1910, of a ceramics department at the University of North Dakota. Margaret Cable, recruited from the Handicraft Guild, was appointed Instructor in Ceramics in

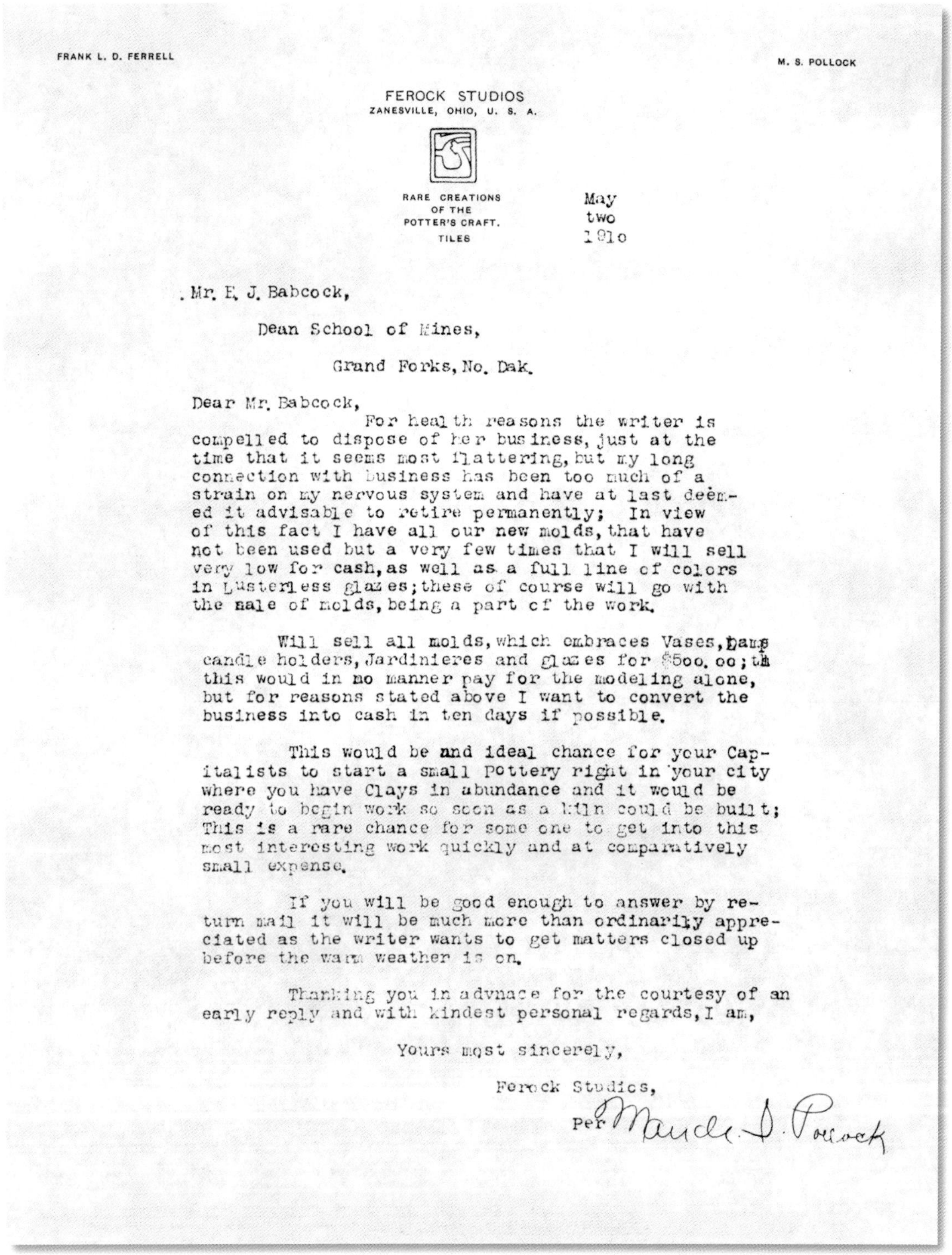

FRANK L. D. FERRELL

M. S. POLLOCK

FEROCK STUDIOS
ZANESVILLE, OHIO, U. S. A.

RARE CREATIONS
OF THE
POTTER'S CRAFT.
TILES

May
two
1910

. Mr. E. J. Babcock,

Dean School of Mines,

Grand Forks, No. Dak.

Dear Mr. Babcock,
For health reasons the writer is compelled to dispose of her business, just at the time that it seems most flattering, but my long connection with business has been too much of a strain on my nervous system and have at last deemed it advisable to retire permanently; In view of this fact I have all our new molds, that have not been used but a very few times that I will sell very low for cash, as well as a full line of colors in Lusterless glazes; these of course will go with the sale of molds, being a part of the work.

Will sell all molds, which embraces Vases, lamps candle holders, Jardinieres and glazes for $500.oo; th this would in no manner pay for the modeling alone, but for reasons stated above I want to convert the business into cash in ten days if possible.

This would be and ideal chance for your Capitalists to start a small pottery right in your city where you have Clays in abundance and it would be ready to begin work so soon as a kiln could be built; This is a rare chance for some one to get into this most interesting work quickly and at comparatively small expense.

If you will be good enough to answer by return mail it will be much more than ordinarily appreciated as the writer wants to get matters closed up before the warm weather is on.

Thanking you in advnace for the courtesy of an early reply and with kindest personal regards, I am,

Yours most sincerely,

Ferock Studios,

Per Maude S. Pollock

Fig. 5: Ferock Studios letter of May 2, 1910, signed by Maude Sibyl Pollock.

Grand Forks. She saw to the day-to-day running of the Department under the supervision of Dean Babcock at the School of Mines. This arrangement allowed Babcock to devote himself to research on other aspects of mining engineering, metal assays, lignite coals and other mineral resources. It also gave him more time and opportunity to develop a "technical museum of our School of Mines" and to collect pottery samples and raw materials from "the principal potteries in this country and abroad." [33] In 1912 and 1913, he dispatched letters (fig. 7) to many of the companies with which he had previously had contact, and also to others, including Brush-McCoy, in Roseville and Zanesville, Ohio; Buffalo Pottery, in Buffalo, New York; Warwick China Co., in Wheeling, West Virginia; Gates Potteries, in Terra Cotta, Illinois; and Moravian Pottery and Tile Works, in Doylestown, Pennsylvania seeking samples, descriptive catalogs, price-lists and discount sheets for the museum's collection.

Fig. 6: The University of North Dakota exhibit at the National Corn Exhibition in Omaha, Nebraska, 1909.

Babcock wrote to Roseville [34]: "What I want for the collection is samples of the clays, flint, feldspar, etc., entering the body and a sample of the raw ware and the burned bisque," the latter two items to illustrate the change in color and the degree of shrinkage in firing. Most of these approaches resulted in compliance, probably because the firms were persuaded by Babcock's explanation that "this is for a museum in an educational institution, and second, because it will serve as a valuable advertisement for your ware." [35] From the Vase Kraft Studio of the Fulper Pottery Co., in Flemington, New Jersey, for the total price of $10.00, Babcock ordered four pieces: "one #16 Rose Bowl...flambé; one #37 low pear shaped bowl in mirrored glazes; one #23 two-handled jardinière...Café Au Lait, one #57 straight vase...leopard skin, crystals...," and he received, also, three pieces: "one #105 single light lamp; one #5 Elephant Vase; one piece of Famille Rose Ware," offered at no charge by Fulper, together with samples of all raw materials. In reply to William H. Grueby of the Grueby Faience and Tile Co. of Boston, Babcock suggested that they "send as good a collection as you can for $30.00, pieces not too large. Include one or two sample tiles and 1 lb. samples of the raw materials used in the body," [36] which Grueby acknowledged on May 20, 1913.

Babcock's last active participation in a national display of finished products from North Dakota clays was at the Panama-Pacific Exposition held in 1915, in San Francisco (fig. 8). With the assistance of Margaret Cable, he organized an exhibit of 208 items of pottery – with a total estimated value of $481.00 – as well as a variety of the same kind of utilitarian and architectural

The College of Mining Engineering and Experimental
Station of the University of North Dakota
Grand Forks, N. Dak.

The Mining Experimental Sub-Station
Hebron, N. Dak.

The Mining Sub-Station at Hebron, North Dakota
Established to aid the development of the mining and allied manufacturing industries of the state by providing practical tests on a commercial scale to supplement the research work of the laboratories of the School of Mines

THE UNIVERSITY OF NORTH DAKOTA

COLLEGE OF MINING ENGINEERING
E. J. Babcock, Dean

GRAND FORKS
Post Address, University, North Dakota

April 17, 1912.

The Roseville Pottery Co.,
Zanesville, Chio.

Gentlemen:

We are desirous of securing a collection of typical pottery and clay wares for the technical museum of our School of Mines. We want to get a few characteristic pieces of pottery, tiles, etc., together with small samples of the raw materials used in the body of the ware. We are getting these samples from the principal potteries in this country and abroad. You understand that this collection is not for commercial purposes, but for our technical museum.

In order to help us select samples, would you kindly send us complete illustrated and descriptive catalogues of your designs in the various wares and products, and would you also send us a discount sheet, making a special price to us for this museum purpose? No doubt you will be willing to do so for two reasons, first, because this is for a museum in an educational institution, and second, because it will serve as a valuable advertisement for your ware. We usually get for such purposes extremely low rates and frequently the material is donated.

In any event, kindly give us your lowest possible special discount on your catalogue numbers and prices, and also, if you have any suggestions as to a few special designs and styles of wares which are particularly representative of your manufacture, would you kindly suggest these to us? Cur purpose is, as you will understand, to get as accurate representatives as possible of the various products from different potteries and at the lowest possible price.

Any suggestions you can make aiding us in making this technical collection of clay products, will be much appreciated.

Very truly,

EJB/IU

Address:

Fig. 7: Babcock's form-letter of April 17, 1912, to potteries regarding the School's museum.

Fig. 8: North Dakota Pavilion at the Panama-Pacific Exposition in San Francisco, 1915. SHSND # D 0120-01.

ware as was shown in St. Louis and Omaha, comprising 110 items. [37] This latter category included electrical ware, matt-glazed and enameled hollow bricks (plate 7), small bricklets, tile, cooking and baking items, molasses jugs, drain tile, hollow brick, paving brick, fire brick, roof tiles, ornamental brick and muffles.

The art pottery in the exhibit consisted of tea services, both white and decorated; some pieces "decorated downtown" -- possibly by local china painters not affiliated at this time with the Ceramics Department at the University -- others decorated by Mrs. Schmidt or slip-painted by students Mrs. Chandler and Mrs. McVey. Additional pieces of tableware and other items of artware, made in the Ceramics Department, including tankard sets, hair receivers, vases, bowls, fern dishes, tobacco jars and jardinières, were thrown or molded in shapes by Margaret Cable, student Hildegarde Fried, and a number of other women students, such as Jessie Budge, Helen Barnes, Rena Parizek, Ethel Halcrow, Bessie Campbell, Cora Elwick, and one male student Mr. Hitchcock; for some items molds acquired from Zanesville sources were used. Different clay bodies, listed as white fire clay, and #1, #2, #14-D, #16-D, and #119-C, were fired with painted, transfer-printed or stenciled decoration of roses, pinecones, grapes and leaves, crab apples, "Colonial pattern," etc., and covered in clear, high-gloss, matt and blended glazes.

As with previous exhibits of pottery made with North Dakota clays, the reception accorded this display (figs. 9; 10) was very satisfying. National magazines took note of the remarkable

Plate 7: Six enameled hollow bricks, matt-glazed, approx. 8"x 4"x 2½", all with stamped seal mark: (left to right) SHSND Coll. # 1997.34.17/34.10/34.19/34.14/34.9/34.13. One enameled solid block brick, high-glazed, approx. 8"x 3¾"x 2", unmarked: SHSND Coll. # 1989.324.2 (right).

variety and quality, and *Pottery and Glass* requested photographs for publication "in order to give this the greatest significance." [38] Mr. Will Holbein, Secretary of the North Dakota State Commission, Panama-Pacific Exposition, wrote from San Francisco to the Governor of North Dakota endorsing Babcock's view that the entire exhibit should be returned, at the end of the show, to the University – presumably for addition to the collection – rather than disposing of it "out here." [39]

Regrettably, very few examples of these exhibits, purchases and early donations survive today in the University collection. The few that are in the collection include a Weller Jap Birdimal creamer (plate 153), a Paul Revere pitcher, a Clifton Pottery Indian Ware vase and a Weller Matt Green paneled vase (which may have been a separate, and later, alumnus donation, and which was quite certainly not made of North Dakota clay by Weller at Babcock's request [40]) in addition to the "Flowered" tableware and the Owens Utopian vases already mentioned. The whereabouts of Babcock's early collection for the "technical museum" is unknown. However, it is acknowledged that some pieces from the expositions in St. Louis, Omaha and San Francisco -- and possibly from the University collection -- which had remained on exhibit in Bismarck, were destroyed in the fire at the North Dakota Capitol Building on December 28, 1930.

Earle Jay Babcock was appointed Dean of the College of Engineering in 1916, when the name of that faculty was changed from the School of Mines, and in 1917 he served as Acting President of the University of North Dakota. After thirty-six years of service he died, in 1925, of heart failure while swimming at Lake Bemidji in Minnesota.

Fig. 9: Art pottery exhibited in the North Dakota Pavilion. SHSND # D 0120-05.

Fig 10: Industrial and utilitarian pottery exhibited in the North Dakota Pavilion. SHSND # D 0120-03.

Endnotes

1 *The National Geographic Magazine*, Volume C, No. 3, September, 1951: "North Dakota Comes Into Its Own," by Leo A. Borah.
2 Cable letter dated April 25, 1934, to Arthur Baggs at Ohio State University.
3 *The New York World*, June 19, 1927.
4 *North Dakota History, Journal of the Northern Plains*, Volume 65, No. 2 & 3, Spring/Summer, 1998: "A Brief History of Clay Resources in North Dakota," by Edward C. Murphy.
5 Babcock letter dated June 18, 1906.
6 Babcock letter dated July 18, 1903.
7 Babcock letter dated March 22, 1904.
8 Ohio Pottery Co. letter dated February 17, 1904.
9 Babcock letter dated March 24, 1904.
10 Weller letter dated February 29, 1904.
11 Mayer letters dated February 17 and 27, 1904.
12 Roseville letter dated April 12, 1904.
13 Owens letter dated May 4, 1904.
14 Owens invoice dated July 13, 1904.
15 Babcock letters dated May 30, 1904.
16 Undated, handwritten notation on letterhead of the St. Louis World's Fair Commission, North Dakota.
17 Invoice dated September 1, 1904.
18 Babcock letter dated June 18, 1906, to Mr. James C. Young, regarding the North Dakota display of pottery at the World's Fair.
19 Babcock letter dated May 18, 1905.
20 Babcock letter dated May 18, 1905.
21 Babcock letter dated June 5, 1905.
22 Babcock letter dated August 26, 1905.
23 Babcock letter dated October 22, 1909.
25 Babcock letter dated December 10, 1909.
26 Babcock letter dated November 8, 1909, to Cable.
27 *American Art Pottery* (Wilmington: Delaware Art Museum, 1978) by Kirsten Keen.
28 Pollock letter dated November 20, 1909.
29 Pollock letter dated November 10, 1909.
30 Babcock letter dated October 22, 1909.
31 Pollock letter dated May 2, 1910.
32 Babcock letter dated May 7, 1910.
32 During the very brief existence of the Ferock Studios, Babcock did put Pollock in touch with Mr. Joseph Bell DeRemer – at that time the most prominent architect in Grand Forks – to whom samples were submitted. Pollock was, as she explained to Babcock in her letters dated February 7 and 19, 1910, "especially anxious to make up a mantel or two for his clients," since, cognizant, as she was, of the building boom in the city in those years, she felt that "in that prosperous country there should be a great demand for handmade pieces, both in tiles and pottery." She also traveled in "the east... several weeks seeing trade in that vicinity" – as she wrote in another letter to Babcock dated January 1, 1910 – presumably promoting and offering the services and products of the Ferock Studios to potential client firms.
33 Babcock letter dated April 17, 1912.
34 Babcock letter dated May 20, 1913.
35 Babcock letter dated May 10, 1913.
36 Undated, handwritten note by Babcock on Grueby letter dated June 24, 1912. It is interesting to note from this letter by William H. Grueby the following appraisal of the problems of the contemporary art pottery business, at least as far as the Grueby company was concerned: "Some few years ago we started in making pottery with our dull finished enamel on it making it in the old fashioned way of every piece being made on the wheel and then modelled by hand afterwards. We took medals in every place we exhibited and also received gold medals in Paris, but we found that although we made between six and seven hundred different designs and they varied in price from 50 cents to $100.00 each that it was not a paying proposition and a year ago we decided to discontinue the making of pottery."
37 Utilitarian/architectural ware with a value of $22.00.
38 Letter dated June 15, 1915, from *Pottery and Glass*.
39 Letter to Babcock dated September 11, 1915.
40 As suggested by Marion Nelson: *Art Pottery of the Midwest*, catalog #159, fig. 75.

PART II

The Personalities of the Ceramics Department

A. Margaret Kelly Cable

Margaret Kelly Cable -- variously referred to in early Census documentation and city directories as Marguerite and Margaret B. -- was born in 1884 of Scottish-Irish ancestry on her mother's side of the family, and "good New England Yankee" on her father's. [41] Her parents had both been educated at Oberlin College, in Ohio. Her father practiced medicine in Cleveland, where he was also a minister of religion, before succumbing to his pioneering spirit and missionary zeal and moving the family to Crookston, Minnesota, where Margaret was born. The family returned to Minneapolis by the mid-1890s. There Margaret attended, and graduated from, Minneapolis Central High School, having completed a manual-arts training course. Already at that time interested in handicrafts, she continued her studies in design and composition under Ernest A. Batchelder in the Pottery Shop of the Handicraft Guild, a School of Normal Art, Craftwork and Design, in that city, for two years -- the first as an apprentice and the second as an assistant -- before being asked to teach there. Additionally, at the Guild, she studied metalwork (under James Winn of Chicago and Douglas Donaldson of Pasadena, Calif.), jewelry making under Mrs. Ida Pell Conklin (of the Guild) and photography. In 1910, she was awarded the photography prize of the Minnesota State Art Society. By this time she felt she was "familiar with the teaching of pottery, both hand-building and wheel work; and with the more commercial side – the making and cast of moulds, the making of glazes and the firing of kilns"; and considered herself adept at the designing of shapes and the application of decoration. [42] After her father's death the family was unable to finance Margaret's further education through college and the attainment of a degree, and, furthermore, it was necessary for her to help support the family. Though for the first six months of her career at the Handicraft Guild she worked without remuneration, "the next six months I got $2.00 a week. After that $3.00..." [43]

Fig. 11: Margaret Cable at the wheel in the Ceramics Department. UAP # 2365.

In 1910, having already made the acquaintance of Dean Babcock and having been of service to him in providing pottery for the exhibition in Omaha the previous year, she was appointed Instructor by him in the newly established Ceramics Department at the University of North Dakota, and took up residence in Grand Forks. There she continued Babcock's practical investigations of the native higher-grade clays, such as analyzing and combining them, and firing them at different temperatures, and examining reactions with a variety of glazes. Also she initiated instructional work that would prove advantageous to the University for both technical and economic reasons.

Fig. 12: Tableware with decal decoration. UAP # 2342.

Since she had not completed a college course, Cable compensated in other ways to broaden her knowledge in both the practice and theory of pottery making. She spent several vacations working in the potteries of East Liverpool, Ohio, where her mother had family connections, and also attended summer schools under Frederick H. Rhead at the People's University in St. Louis, in June-August, 1911, and under Charles F. Binns, in 1918, at the New York State School of Clayworking, Alfred University, in Alfred, New York. She corresponded with Rhead and Binns throughout her career, as also with Arthur E. Baggs, of Ohio State University, and Paul Cox, of Iowa State College. All of these men were giants in the field of ceramics. Cable approached them frequently for advice regarding characteristics of clay and glaze, and also sought assistance and support from Mary Given Sheerer of Newcomb College during the years of the 1920s. Through the Ceramics Department's subscription to such magazines as *Clay Worker, Ceramic Age, Pottery Gazette, Pottery and Glass*, and especially *Keramic Studio* and *The Potter*, Cable was able to add to her technical knowledge and expertise and gain significant information on ceramic design.

Exceptionally adept at the potter's wheel (fig. 11) and highly skilled in other methods of pottery making and most aspects of decoration, Cable stayed abreast of the latest trends in technique, glaze and design initiated by other potteries. As Instructor in the Ceramics Department she recognized that "one must not only know how to pot but to impart this knowledge to students ranging in age from the youngest freshman in the regular University classes to the little gray haired grandma in the special adult group."[44] This latter assembly, referred to in the Department as "special" students, was particularly significant to the development of the program from the early years on. Many of these students were wives of faculty members and other women of the town and surrounding area, who soon filled the "special" classes to the extent that there was always a waiting list of applicants. The objective of these classes was threefold: firstly, to offer instruction in pottery making, decoration and design; secondly, to earn funds from enrollment fees to aid in the financing of the Department's program; and thirdly -- and very importantly -- to have a greater number of hands employed in the effort to promote the viability of North Dakota clays. Enthusiastic, imaginative and indefatigable in her teaching as in other duties, Cable very soon had her students making "really artistic and beautiful products… created by the application of technical methods combined with careful design and manipulation."[45]

At the request of schools and clubs she traveled extensively in the state, and beyond, with her kick-wheel, to lecture and to demonstrate, all the time emphasizing and publicizing the effective use of North Dakota clay. She prepared the exhibit for the Panama-Pacific Exposition in 1915, and in 1919 she sent a selection of the Department's pottery -- 10 of 21 items submitted -- to the Art Institute of Chicago for inclusion in the juried Exhibition of Applied Arts there in October of that year. When requests and invitations became so great that she could not find the time to pack up her wheel and materials and travel so often, she would send a lecture script together with photographs and samples of pottery. Her "Possibilities of Pottery Making from North Dakota Clay," prepared in 1923 for the North Dakota Federation of Women's Clubs, together with twenty-one illustrations, incorporated not only explanations of clay preparation and the process of pottery making but also historical references and quotations from the *Bible*, the *Rubaiyat of Omar Khayyam* and Longfellow's poem "Keramos." Her travels took her as far as San Antonio, Texas, in 1928, where she was named chairman of the Industrial Arts Division at the national convention of the General Federation of Women's Clubs.

Between 1910 and 1920, [46] Cable collected information on techniques and designs used by other potteries in the United States and Europe, and requested samples from many, including, most notably, Marblehead. The material she collected, and the articles she read in *Keramic Studio* and *The Potter* helped expand her knowledge. In addition, she sought illustrations of suitable motifs, ordered stencils and decals, and requested molds, particularly from Knowles, Taylor & Knowles Co. (plate 120). As a result, she was able to report that, by 1921, "besides the art wares...we are making an ivory colored tableware (figs. 12; 13; also plate 8) similar in color and quality to the famous Royal Doulton." [47]

Fig. 13: Display of tea services and other ware at an exposition or fair.

Guided by Charles Binns' book *The Story of the Potter*, which had become the inspiration for her work, she was teaching, by 1921, "some sixty students in ceramic work." [48] In that year she was named Assistant Professor, and was able, in the summer, to visit Frederick Rhead at the American Encaustic Tile Works, in Zanesville. In 1922, the *Grand Forks Daily Herald* twice published articles drawing attention to work at the Ceramics Department. The first, published in its edition of June 10, commented in glowing terms on the "underglaze painting" to be viewed at the "Annual Exhibition of Ceramic Work at University." The second article of July 18, titled "U.N.D. Pottery Exhibits are Given Praise" described the acclaim accorded the University's display, along with pottery by Niloak, at the convention of the National Federation of Business and Professional Women, in Chattanooga, Tennessee. By 1925 -- the year of Dean Babcock's death -- there were almost seventy names on the ceramics class waiting list. The next year, even though by that time Cable was supported by three assistants -- Julia Mattson, Freida Hammers and Flora Huckfield -- she wrote to Professor E. F. Chandler: "I have never... had to work as hard, or put in such long hours as this year. What I need more than anything else is more help." [49]

In that same year the Governor of North Dakota, A. G. Sorlie, requested that Cable select two pieces of University pottery for presentation to H. M. Queen Marie of Romania, on the occasion of her visit to the state. Acknowledgment of this gift was received in June and Cable

Plate 8: Low bowl with decal decoration.

later noted: "It is interesting to see how a Queen takes care of such matters. The fact of her commanding her Secretary to express her grateful thanks gave me an envious feeling. Think of the detail we could escape if only some of the busy people could so command." [50] The Governor also commissioned Cable to design and make a vase – later to be called the "North Dakota Products Vase," or sometimes the "Sorlie Vase," – whose decoration would consist of imagery representative of the state. The prospect of incorporating so much varied decoration on one pot left Cable "quite breathless," [51] but the commission was successfully executed, and the result remains to this day one of Margaret Cable's greatest achievements (plate 1; fig. 47).

The following year, on being appointed North Dakota Outstanding Woman of the Year by Gov. Sorlie, Cable attended the Women's World Fair in Chicago -- "a vivid and far-visioned exposition of the progress and achievements of the women of many centuries and races." [52] For ten days there she demonstrated pottery throwing on her wheel, lectured to the crowds of appreciative spectators and exhibited a large collection of University of North Dakota pottery, to considerable acclaim for herself, the University and the state. Such local and national publications as the *UND Alumni Magazine, Great Northern Semaphore, Christian Science Monitor, Milwaukee Journal* and *Independent Woman* reviewed Cable's achievement at the 1927 Women's World Fair. [53] As well, the *Chicago Daily Tribune* [54] twice published photographs of Margaret Cable at her wheel and in the North Dakota booth, together with references to her accomplishments and those of her Department. Similar accolades were to be found in the *New York World* article -- "Dakota Revives Pottery Making" -- focusing on the School of Mines' use of the same clay beds as had been used by "native potters through many generations, but following now modern methods." [55]

In May, 1929, Cable sent forty-two items, including ornamental ware, cooking items and tiles to the Northern Pacific Railway Co., for exhibit in their New York City office. However she was not only interested in displaying the Ceramics Department's pottery in distant places. She also sought to acquaint her students, her University and her community with other potteries' production. Always receptive to outside influences and eager to keep pace with developments in the art pottery field, Cable persuaded the University to mount a traveling exhibition organized by the American Federation of Arts, in Washington, DC. The exhibition -- #604, *American Pottery* -- took place in Grand Forks in March 1932, and comprised ninety-six pieces selected by the Jury of the Society of Arts and Crafts, Boston. Among the twenty-one exhibitors were Binns, Clewell Studios, Cowan, Russell Crook, Dedham, Jugtown, Marblehead, Moravian, Newcomb and Paul Revere. The show was very well received by the staff of the Ceramics Department, students past and present and many visitors from Grand Forks and other parts of the state. Cable

Fig. 14: Pottery with bentonite decoration exhibited at the Chicago World's Fair, 1933. UAP # 2619.

wrote a letter for the purchase, for the University's permanent collection, of "Binns vase #3 @ $30.00, Cowan green bowl #13 @ $12.50 and Paul Revere pitcher #93 @ $3.50." [56]

Cable, who had been an associate member of the American Ceramics Society since 1913, attended many of the Society's conventions. She presented several papers at the conventions including "The Development of Ceramic Work at the University of North Dakota," in Columbus, Ohio, in 1921; "Colored Glazes and Indian Design on North Dakota Pottery," in Atlantic City in 1924; "Pots and Pines, a Decorative Problem for the Artist Potter," in Columbus, Ohio, in 1925. She also exhibited twenty-three pieces of University pottery, including one of the three duplicates of the "North Dakota Products Vase," in Detroit in 1927; and assortments of other pieces, in Atlanta, Georgia, in 1926; and Atlantic City, in 1928. In the February 11, 1931, edition of the *Grand Forks Herald* under the heading "Three Will Attend Ceramics Meeting," it was announced that William E. Budge, Associate Professor of Ceramic Engineering, would accompany Margaret Cable and Freida Hammers to the ACS convention in Cleveland, Ohio, on February 27-28, where papers would be read by Budge and Cable and a display of the University's pottery would be shown. Her justification for her regular attendance at ACS meetings was that "I feel very strongly the value of getting before this technical organization the fact that North Dakota contains a variety of clays of very high character which can be used in the production of many types of clay products and also that North Dakota possesses a Ceramic Department which is testing and proving out the use and value of the clays found within the State. This sort of publicity and advertising is very well worthwhile." [57] In this she was correct, for national attention was being brought to her work by such magazines as *Ceramic Industry* which published a review of the School of Mines display at the American Ceramic Society convention that year. The Columbus, Ohio, meeting was attended by amongst others, the heads of ceramics departments in twelve schools, along with pottery experts and executive heads of ceramic firms,

Fig. 15: Margaret Cable at the wheel in the Ceramics Department, early 1940s. (Photo presently in the possession of the Art Department, University of North Dakota.)

who also brought displays of their wares. But "the exhibition from North Dakota was by far the most beautiful exhibit in the room. The exquisite shadings and treatment made possible by delicately applied decoration was evidenced by this striking exhibit." [58]

In 1932, Cable requested endorsement of her application for Fellowship of the Society from Charles Binns, Paul Cox, Mary Sheerer and Harold S. Nash (of the University of Cincinnati School of Applied Arts.) Her nomination was also supported by, among others, important ceramics instructors Prof. E. de Forest Curtis and Prof. Myrtle Merritt French, and by Frederick H. Rhead. Despite her concern that her application might be deferred due to her lack of a degree, her application was successful.

For the Century of Progress Exposition in Chicago, in 1933, Cable selected almost two hundred pieces for display in the North Dakota booth. [59] Included were a number of pieces with bentonite decoration (fig. 14); also, eleven -- of fourteen originally planned -- mosaic tile panels (plate 2) representing various scenes of life in the state. The panels, which were designed by students in the Art Department and executed by members of the Ceramics Department, illustrated the dairy, grain, livestock and mining industries, and incorporated regional motifs, such as an oxcart, an Indian smoking a peace pipe, and farm animals and buildings. Cable herself attended the Exposition from June 20 through August 20, and lectured and demonstrated "until my voice cracked and my knees gave way, but it was great fun." [60] In an article by Professor William G. Whitford, of the University of Chicago, the University of North Dakota's display was described as "the outstanding exhibit of United States Pottery at the 1933 Centennial." Professor Whitford continued: "At the University Miss Cable has developed a ceramic department and a type of pottery of great interest. Sgraffito and polychrome decoration have been perfected." [61]

After her appointment as Associate Professor in 1934, Cable accepted the invitation, extended to the Ceramics Department, to participate in the Third Annual Robineau Memorial/National Ceramic Exhibition, and sent fifteen items (comprising twenty-two pieces) to Syracuse, New York. These included four of her own pieces, two by Mattson, two by Huckfield, and one by Laura Taylor. Competition at the prestigious Ceramic Nationals was always prodigious, and the invitation, alone, to the Ceramics Department of the University of North Dakota lent it considerable honor. [62]

Throughout the Depression, Cable and her assistants continued to work tirelessly, and in spite of budgetary austerity and inadequate facilities, the Department was able to survive. Already in 1931, Cable had complained that "Twenty years in the basement of an old building is a long time;" [63] supplies were limited due to cost, and equipment was apt to break down. Production delays were common and the kiln was out of repair. Replacement parts were not quickly available, and when they did appear and were ready for installation, there was "no mason or even a helper that can be hired in Grand Forks, and it will be at least a month to six weeks before we can get one." [64] For Cable it was also a time of personal hardship. Salaries were cut throughout the University. The funding of the Ceramics Department was withdrawn. Cable sold her house after only six years of occupancy, and, in 1933, moved, with her sister, to a small rental apartment nearby, before returning, in 1935, to the Hamline Street apartment where they had lived prior to Thanksgiving, 1927.

Plate 9: Pottery marked "Huckie Maggie Santa Barbara". Dommel Coll.

During these years, Cable turned her attention to experiments with more economical materials and methods of production. A simpler line of attractive ware called Prairie Pottery was introduced, and the reception of this cheaper, and more easily produced item inspired Cable to further research that would in turn reward her long-held desire to assist and train less advantaged students. In the summer of 1935, she had visited Maria Martinez in New Mexico, to study her methods of forming, decorating and firing her famous black and red wares. In the following two years, she spent considerable time at Indian schools in the Dakotas, teaching students, training teachers and offering advice on clay bodies and methods of firing. These experiences led her to extend her vocation beyond the University and the Indian reservation at Pine Ridge to include considerations on the teaching of schoolchildren. By 1935 she had already begun to conduct experiments "in an attempt to find a method of firing colored pottery in a manner inexpensive and simple enough for use in North Dakota rural schools," [65] but felt that "our work along this line has not progressed sufficiently for us to feel capable of giving advice." [66]

During the war years, when enrollment in all classes at the University of North Dakota was lagging, Cable was able, by dint of her engaging personality and the popular appeal of her teaching, to continue to capture the attention of special students. She believed that "...as a teaching potter I work not only with the dull, earthy material men call clay but also with the living plastic stuff of young pliable minds and fingers. What greater interest could one want than the satisfaction of bringing the two together – clay, and the student, imbued with the divine urge to create, for pottery is truly a creative art." [67] She included in her instruction the history of pottery making and a study of contemporary ceramics that illustrated how an understanding of

Plates 10–13: Designs by Cable

Plate 10: Vase, marked "MKC 1917". UND Coll. # C-CBL 5-115.

clays, glazes, techniques, styles and motifs could aid in identifying origin, ensure appreciation of craftsmanship, determine artistic worth and contribute to commercial success. Cable rendered assistance wherever it was required, including, in the years 1944-1946, to the Civilian Public Service camp near Williston, where Hal Riegger, an Alfred graduate, former master's program student under Baggs at Ohio State University and teacher at the Pennsylvania Museum School of Industrial Art, was instructing fellow conscientious objectors in the making of pottery as a recreational activity.

Plate 11: Slip-painted covered jar, marked "MKC". UND Coll. # C-CBL 59-229.

Cable's success in her career and vocation was built on her intelligence, enthusiasm, generosity, kindness, persistence, and capacity for serious study and hard work. Her teaching methods were based on competence, confidence and empathic encouragement, and her writings are clear, straightforward and often lyrical; in fact her prose style is far superior to her poetry. In 1945, she was elected to membership in the National Society of Arts and Letters. To the attributes of scientific knowledge, technical skill, aesthetic sense, tireless service and love of teaching must be added her political astuteness; every year she prepared and selected pottery for Christmas gifts to the Governor, state officials and their wives, and other recipients she felt might be in a position to advance the effectiveness and popularity of the Department's program.

In 1949, Margaret Cable retired, and, after spending the summer at the cabin at Lake Bemidji, moved with her sister, Flora Huckfield, to Los Angeles, California, to be near other family members. In December of the following year, they were living in Tujunga, California, but later moved to an address in Santa Barbara. During the 1950s, Cable and her sister made, decorated and fired pottery in Santa Barbara (plate 9); it is possible that she had the use of a small kiln at the State College (now University of California Santa Barbara) as a perquisite for teaching duties. Here another connection is drawn to Frederick Rhead, her much-admired teacher, who had taught and exhibited pottery at the Santa Barbara State Normal School of Manual Arts and Home Economics (as it was then known) in 1913-1914.

Cable died in a hospital in Santa Barbara on October 31, 1960, at the age of seventy-six. In the last decade of her life she received the highest honor awarded by the American Ceramics Society – the Charles Fergus Binns Medal for High Achievement in the Field of Ceramic Art – at its annual meeting in Chicago in 1951. Since Binns had been her first and foremost mentor, this was for her the best and most appropriate national recognition of her devotion to widening the appreciation of ceramic art not only in the Upper Midwest but throughout the United States.

Plate 12: Vase, 9½"h., marked "MKC 1923 T.311". UND Coll. # C-CBL 31-201.

Plate 13: Vase, 7¾"h., marked "MKC 1925 T.495". UND Coll. # C-CBL 18-188.

The Song of the Pot

I am a lucky little lump of North Dakota clay.
My heart is filled with gladness
And I sing a song all day,
For a potter found me worthy of his very finest ware,
And fashioned me upon his wheel
With tender loving care.
With the magic of his fingers gave me form and life and soul,
Transformed me from a shapeless clod
Into a flower bowl.
As I hold within my arms a prairie rose bouquet
I bless the hand that made me
All from North Dakota clay.

– Margaret Kelly Cable, c. 1926.

Plates 14 – 18: Designs by Fried

Plate 14: Vase, marked "H. Fried UND XMAS 1923". UND Coll. # C-HLD 12-640.

B. **Hildegarde Fried**

Plate 15: Covered jar, 1918, made at Alfred, marked "Fried AU 18".

In 1918, five years after her graduation, with a degree in chemistry and mathematics, from the University of North Dakota, where she had enrolled in Margaret Cable's ceramics class, Hildegarde Fried was appointed as Assistant in Ceramics. Since she shared Cable's interest in pottery making, design and poetry, she must have proved a congenial companion to Cable, when they both visited the New York School of Clayworking in Alfred, New York, to study for the summer of 1918 under Charles Binns. Her background in chemistry stood her in good stead in her studies with Binns, whose classes in the scientific constitution of glazes were legendary. While she was in Alfred, she was also able to advance her facility at the wheel, while furthering her study of design (plate 15).

Plate 16: Vase, marked "H. Fried". UND Coll. # C-HLD 18-646.

Plate 17: Bowl, 8" dia., marked "H. Fried". Nelson Coll.

At the end of that summer, Cable and Fried visited the Marblehead Pottery, in Marblehead, Massachusetts, where both were delighted and influenced by that pottery's special concern with stylistic decoration in the Arts-and-Crafts manner. During the next six years in the Ceramics Department, in addition to her decoration of vessels and tiles, Fried occupied much of her time with experimentation in glaze chemistry and its application. She was named Instructor in Ceramics in 1920, and four years later resigned to marry Dr. Joseph A. Dreps, who also taught at the University. Although she was no longer included in the faculty, Hildegarde Fried Dreps continued to make and decorate forms, perhaps as an honorary member of the Department, through at least the summer of 1926. According to the March, 1963, issue of the *Alumni Review*, a book of her poems, entitled *Oars in Silver Water*, had been recently published.

She died in Maryville, Missouri, in 1977.

Plate 18: Vases, marked "HF" and (left to right) "338" and "341". UND Coll. # C-HLD 44-672 and # C-HLD 1-423.

C. **Julia Edna Mattson**

Hildegarde Fried was replaced in the Department by Julia Edna Mattson who was to remain there for thirty-nine years. She was born in Kensington, Minnesota, in 1893, and, after several years teaching school, she enrolled, in 1919, at the University of North Dakota to study art, serving "as part-time student assistant in ceramics." [68] On graduating in 1924 with a B.A. in art and education, she was given her appointment as Instructor in Ceramics at a salary of $1,400.00 per year, which was increased to $1,500.00 two years later. After her appointment to the Ceramics Department, Mattson continued to live at a hall of residence prior to moving, in 1926, to the YWCA. There she remained during the first Depression years through 1934, after which she boarded at the Sigma Kappa sorority. She rented her own apartment on 4th Street in 1938-1940, and on University Avenue from 1940 until her retirement.

Fig. 16: Julia Mattson at the wheel, c. 1927. UAP # 2533.

Like Cable, Mattson was an all-rounder in the Department; she prepared clay, experimented in the fields of clay, glaze and design, constructed molds, stacked kilns and taught most of the courses with Cable. She also had "her own specialty, 'building,' which she taught," and which Cable "rather scoffed at…as a way of making pottery" (plate 123). Mattson was a rather quiet person, "but the students crowded her classes." [69] Again like Cable, she was extremely hard working, efficient and conscientious. The pottery she designed was seen in many exhibitions and displays, and also, later, sold well.

Between 1927 and the beginning of 1938, she made more than 4,400 models and in one nine-month period from September, 1932, through May, 1933, her output was 1,056. She produced medallions and souvenir items, executed special commissions and designed many western motifs including coyote, bison, wheat, covered wagon, oxcart and Indian travois. Her cowboy vases, such as the "Why Not Minot" models (plate 22), and her Indian images (plate

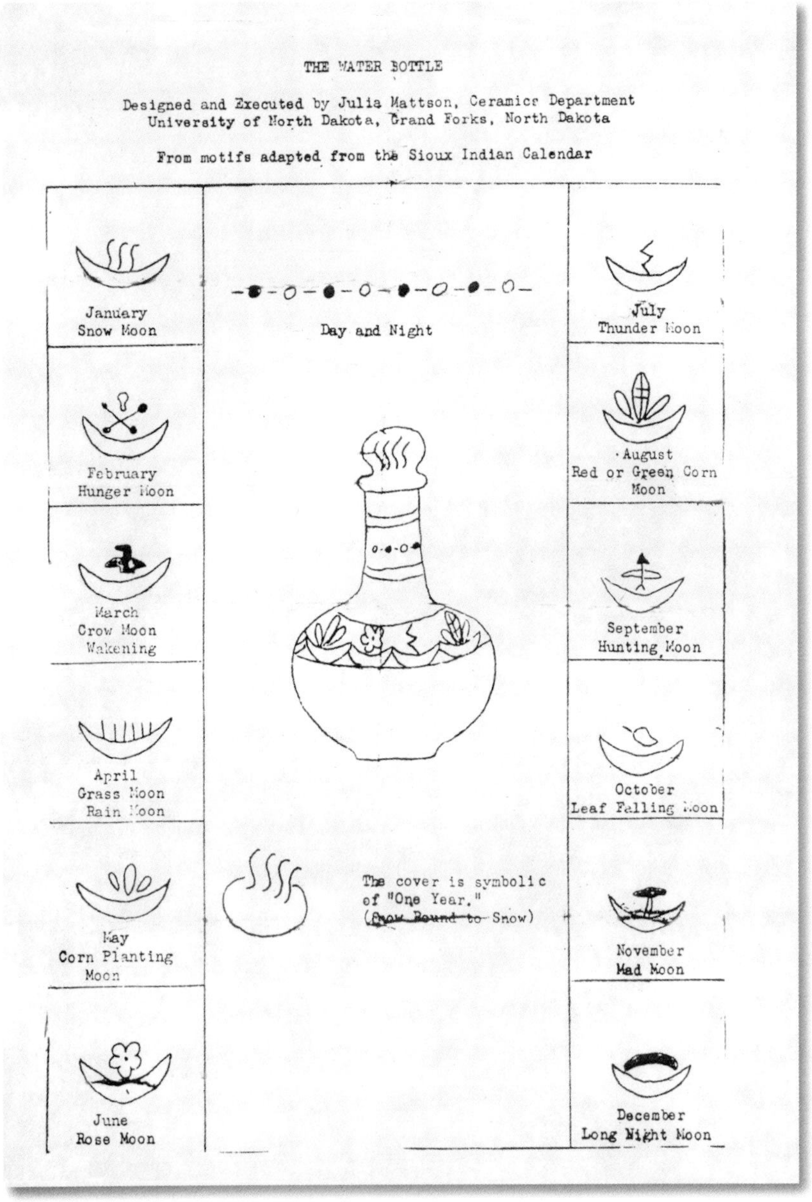

Fig. 17: Explanatory document accompanying the sale of Julia Mattson's "Sioux Calendar" Water Bottle, (see plate 110 left).

110) are today amongst her most well-known designs. She studied art and design at summer school at the Art Institute of Chicago; Indian art at the University of New Mexico; and drawing and painting at the Taos School of Art, in 1937. Her interest in Native American craft and design (fig. 17) resulted in the completion of her thesis "A Survey of Indian Pottery, Arts and Crafts and Symbolism, West of the Mississippi River," in 1951, when she was awarded a Master's degree in educational psychology and ceramics at the University of North Dakota.

She gave lectures and demonstrations both within and outside the state, and traveled in Europe. She drew upon museum and gallery sources for inspiration for her later works in ceramics, oil painting and watercolor, and studied current pottery trends. In 1930, when in Germany, she purchased several items from Anton Lang, as Hildegarde Fried had done in 1922, and ordered pieces from other potters and companies as well.

Mattson's name, along with Cable's, joined those of stellar American ceramists Binns, Henry Varnum Poor, Adelaide Alsop Robineau, and Frederick Rhead and also those of such illustrious companies as Rookwood and Van Briggle, at the 1927 exhibition at the Memorial Art Gallery, in Rochester, New York. At the 1933 Chicago World's Fair, three of the mosaic plaques shown were made by Mattson, and the following year she submitted work, along with Cable, to the Third Annual Robineau Memorial/National Ceramic Exhibition, held at the Syracuse Museum of Fine Arts, where all the best-known American ceramic artists of the time were represented.

Mattson was appointed Assistant Professor in 1950 and was honored by the American Artists Professional League in 1957. At this stage in her career, aspects of her work reflected the influence of the modernistic trends prevalent in ceramic design of the post-war years. For example, she successfully produced pottery with abstract decoration -- mainly colorfully painted patterns composed of dots, splotches, lines and spirals -- and also experimented with asymmetry of form, particularly in a range of vessels with irregularly shaped necks and rims (plates 221; 222). She retired from the University of North Dakota in 1963. In that last year a vase with red, black and

Plates 19 – 22: Designs by Mattson

Plate 19: Vase (left), 5"h., marked "T.505 JM". UND Coll. # C-MTT 93-280. Vase (right), 5¾"h., marked "JM. 507 U.N.D. 1925". UND Coll. # C-MTT 51-151.

yellow decoration by Mattson was selected by the Grand Forks Teen Democrats for presentation to President John F. Kennedy to commemorate his visit to the city in 1963. Also, after that year, it was decided that the cobalt blue seal would no longer be used to identify the origin of University of North Dakota pottery. This decision, Mattson's retirement, and the preference for a new style effectively brought to a close not only the Babcock-Cable-Mattson era but also the making of art pottery in the Ceramics Department at the University of North Dakota.

At the age of 74 years, Julia Mattson died in Los Angeles, California, on December 16, 1967.

Plate 20: Two hand-made and hand-decorated roundels, each marked "JM".

Plate 21: Two vases, 1944: (left) "Harvesting Wheat" (Spencer-list item #188); (right) "Duck Hunter" (Spencer- list item #181 – shape by Bessie Devins).

Plate 22: Two "Why Not Minot" vases, marked (left) "JMATTSON 175" (Spencer-list item of 1943); and (right) "3 JM 4045", c. 1937.

D. **Flora Cable Huckfield**

Fig. 18: Flora Huckfield decorating a vase. UAP # 2524.

Flora Cable Huckfield,[70] the widowed, elder sister of Margaret Cable, joined the staff of the Ceramics Department in 1924, where she stayed until her sister's retirement in 1949. In that year she moved with Cable to California, where she died in 1960.

"Huck," as she was known, was first paid on an hourly basis, which was increased in the fall of 1925 to 60 cents per hour. "Mrs. Huckfield will probably give us about a full day's work (for 20 days) most months, and this will probably amount to an average of about $95.00 per month."[71] The following spring Cable recommended "that the rate per hour be increased from 60 cents to 70 cents," especially since such an increase in Huckfield's pay "can be taken care of from the Pottery Sales Fund."[72] It is not known whether or not her entire salary had previously come from this Fund, but during the Depression and later years it certainly did.

Fig. 19: Flora Huckfield at Iron Mountain. (Photo presently in the possession of the Art Department, University of North Dakota.)

Huckfield was "an expert in applying glazes," sitting "for hours at her little glazing booth, while an electric motor buzzed away to keep up the air pressure in her spray."[73] Many of the pieces made by students were glazed by her. She was responsible for the "wares which are made for sale,"[74] including convention medallions and souvenir items, producing, for example, in the academic year 1931-1932, five hundred and sixty-two items at a price of $1,800.00, and, in the year 1937-1938, five hundred and forty items, four hundred and seventy of which were marked at a total price of $900.00.

Plates 23 – 26: Designs by Huckfield

Plate 23: Sgraffito-decorated vase, c. 1931, marked "King-Huckfield 1329" (shape by King). UND Coll. # C-HCK 56-363.

Plate 24: Vase, c. 1925, marked "Huck 557". UND Coll. # C-HCK Gift 69-560.

Plate 26: Vase, c. 1936, marked "JM2-HUCK-4507" (shape by Mattson). UND Coll. # C-MTT 8-108.

Plate 25: Vase, c. 1936, marked "NYHOUSE-HUCK 4446" (shape by Nyhouse).

Fig. 20: Decorating session in the Ceramics Department with 3 male students and 4 staff members (including -- possibly -- second from right, Freida Hammers). UAP # 2530.

E. **Freida Louise Hammers**

A native of North Dakota, Freida Louise Hammers was born on December 27, 1903. She studied chemistry and physics at the University of North Dakota, where she received her Bachelor of Science and Master of Science degrees in 1923 and 1925, respectively. She studied later at Iowa State College under Paul Cox; and at the University of Minnesota; and at the University of California in Los Angeles, under Glen Lukens. Her interests included ceramics, art and design. She was a proficient sketcher. Margaret Cable wrote of her: "It is rare, indeed, that the person of scientific attainments is also endowed with artistic talent...she has also acquired, during the two years she has been working in the Department, a splendid technique as a potter and decorator."[75] As a student assistant in 1924 and 1925[76], Hammers was expected to devote "about half her time and this will probably average...to about $75 per month."[77] Well qualified to assist in the Department's experimental work, she was appointed Research Assistant in Ceramics and Fuel Testing in 1926, at a salary of $1,500.00. She was named Instructor in 1937, and Assistant Professor of Ceramics in 1939. While initially she had no teaching duties, during the mid-1930's she did teach several classes. When she made pottery, she often used molds by Cable, Huckfield and Mattson and by students – so marked. Her own decorating techniques were primarily incising, excising and sgraffito (fig. 20).

Plates 27 – 30: Designs by Hammers

Plate 27: Vase, marked "FLH T.490". UND Coll. # C-HMM 3-372.

However, "more and more as time went on the pieces I made were used to test glazes,"[78] until by the end of her active presence in the Ceramics Department she had accumulated a list of 1370 pieces, accompanied by precise details of clay content, glaze and firing instructions. She was principally responsible for clay analyses, glaze composition, and solving special technical problems. "Her specialty was mixing glazes, which had to be done with meticulous care, using a gram scale." [79] On November 29, 1938, Hammers glazed her last pot, and shortly afterwards was absent from active participation in the Department's work, for the health reasons which prompted her retirement from the University in 1941. The next year she joined the staff of the Soils Department, Institute of Agriculture, at the University of Minnesota, as Research Chemist, where she remained until her marriage to Merton C. Rich in 1954. She died in Yucaipa, California, in 1977, and committal services were held in Grand Forks, North Dakota attended by many friends and former classmates and students.

Plate 29: Vase, 10½"h., 1925, marked "FLH MKC 1925 T.520". Rustand Coll.

Plate 28: Vase, 11¼"h., 1925, marked "T.516 FLH MKC 1925". Rustand Coll.

Plate 30: Vase, marked "T.506 FLH". UND Coll. # C-HMM 2-371.

F. Margaret Pachl

When Margaret Cable retired in 1949, William H. McKenney was named to head the Ceramics Department. Assisting McKenney was Mrs. Margaret Pachl, who had been appointed Assistant Professor of Ceramics the same year. With both Bachelor and Master of Fine Arts degrees from the New York State College of Ceramics at Alfred University, Pachl had previously headed the ceramics department at the Kalamazoo Institute of Fine Arts, in Michigan. When McKenney left the University of North Dakota in 1952, Pachl took over the direction of the Ceramics Department. Her summer school studies with Marguerite Friedlander Wildenhain (formerly of the Bauhaus and later operating her own Pond Farm workshop in Guerneville, California), and also with Bernard Leach and Shoji Hamada, added to the training she had previously received from Alexander Archipenko, in Woodstock, New York, and Boardman Robinson, in Colorado Springs, Colorado. She exhibited her work throughout the Midwest and beyond, and in 1948 and 1953, she submitted entries to the National Ceramics Exhibitions, in Syracuse.

Plates 31 – 32: Designs by Pachl

Plate 31: Pachl items, modeled and carved, c. 1960. UND Coll. # C-PCH 51-482/90-521/78-509.

During Pachl's tenure at the University of North Dakota, instruction in the Ceramics Department was greatly diversified, individualistic techniques were developed, and modernistic styles were introduced. All this was very much at odds with the more traditional designs favored by her predecessors on the faculty of the Ceramics Department. Pachl's own production of asymmetrical and biomorphic forms has much more in common with American and European studio work of the post-war years – reflecting the influence of Japanese pottery – and her students, in keeping with the modern attitude, were encouraged to approach pottery making as a creative manifestation of self-expression. The popularity of her courses increased dramatically over the twenty-one years she spent at the University of North Dakota. For example, she wrote that at the time of "the 1969-70 first semester registration, by actual count in the fieldhouse alone, there were 273 requests for ceramics classes. I was able to take 105. At second semester registration I took 130 and turned away even more." [80]

Pachl resigned in 1970 to move to Arkansas, where she set up a studio and sold her pottery in Eureka Springs, until her death there in 1982.

Plate 32: Pachl items, c. 1960.

Post–1970

In its search for a competent replacement for Pachl, in June of 1970, the University of North Dakota focused on recruiting both a ceramist with "a strong orientation towards practical aspects," and a ceramic engineer with an interest in clay minerals and their development. These instructors/researchers were necessary to "redeveloping the department's past emphases on industrial-commercial development of North Dakota's clay resources." [81] In turning for help to the College of Ceramics at Alfred University, it was stressed that suitable applicants should possess "initiative and imagination" and a liking for "working independently." [82]

Endnotes

41 Undated Cable letter of 1923/4 to Bertha R. Palmer, chair of the Art Division of the North Dakota Federation of Women's Clubs.
42 Cable letter dated July 16, 1910, applying for the position at the University of North Dakota.
43 Cable letter dated April 9, 1936, to Charles Grantier.
44 Cable letter dated January 27, 1939.
45 Undated Cable letter of 1923/4 to Bertha R. Palmer.
46 In 1920, Cable's salary was raised to $2,000.00 per year, roughly doubling what she had earned two years earlier.
47 Cable letter dated January 23, 1921.
48 Cable letter dated April 5, 1921.
49 Cable letter dated April 21, 1926, to Prof. E. F. Chandler.
50 Cable letter dated November 22, 1926.
51 Cable letter dated March 11, 1927, to Ralph Budd.
52 *Grand Forks Herald,* of May 16, 1927.
53 In July, June, May, June and June, respectively.
54 Final editions of May 19 and May 25.
55 June issue.
56 Cable letter dated March 22, 1932.
57 Cable letter dated January 23, 1926, to President Thomas F. Kane.
58 March, 1925, issue.
59 One hundred and thirty-one items, packed in twelve boxes, and an additional fifty-five pieces were shipped from Grand Forks in May and June-July, respectively.
60 Cable letter dated January 27, 1939.
61 *School Arts Magazine,* Century of Progress edition, October, 1933.
62 That year the prizewinners included Edgar Littlefield, Russell Barnett Aitken and Waylande Gregory; work by the Overbeck sisters - Elizabeth G., and Mary F. - was awarded an Honorable Mention.
63 Cable letter dated January 19, 1931.
64 Cable letter dated October 17, 1939, to Charles Grantier.
65 *Grand Forks Herald,* of March 10, 1935.
66 Cable letter dated April 1, 1935, to the Turtle Mountain Indian School.
67 Cable letter dated January 27, 1939, to the State Chairman of the North Dakota Federation of Women's Clubs.
68 Student assistants, most frequently from the Engineering Department, were employed to mix and grind clay and glaze, and to fire and monitor the kilns; they were paid at an hourly rate (for instance 40 cents in 1926).
69 Letter dated October 26, 1977, from John E. Howard (1936-1939 student assistant).
70 Referred to in early Census documentation and city directories as Flora M. John E. Howard's reference (in his letter of October 26, 1977) to her middle name being Adora may have resulted from a practical joke played on him and her sister by Margaret Cable.
71 Cable letter dated September 25, 1925, to President Thomas F. Kane.
72 Cable letter dated April 21, 1926, to Prof. E. F. Chandler.
73 Letter dated October 26, 1977, from John E. Howard.
74 Cable letter dated April 21, 1926, to Prof. E. F. Chandler.
75 Ibid.
76 From 1924 through 1932, Hammers resided at Davis Hall. During her time at the University of North Dakota Ceramics Department, she developed a close friendship with Margaret Cable, who, in 1939, took her into the Cable-Huckfield home during the time of Hammers' serious health problems.
77 Cable letter dated September 25, 1925, to President Thomas F. Kane.
78 Letter dated July 7, 1976, from Hammers to Darlene Dommel.
79 Letter dated October 26, 1977, from John E. Howard.
80 Pachl's letter of resignation to President Starcher, of May, 1970.
81 Memorandum from Dean A. G. Fletcher, dated June 9, 1970.
82 Fletcher letter dated June 12, 1970, to Prof. Robert Turner.

PART III

Instruction

A. Enrollment, Curriculum, Schedule

Under the heading "Instructor for Pottery at U," the *Grand Forks Herald*, on September 15, 1910, announced the establishment of a Department at the University of North Dakota offering "3 new courses in the practical work connected with the clay industries," which would have both an artistic and a technical focus for women as well as for men. The article continued: "The courses are elective to all in the College of Arts, Teachers College, and the College of Mining Engineering, and full semester credit is given them" and the classes "may be taken for one or both semesters." Practical courses and lectures were added over the years, as Margaret Cable broadened the scope of her teaching to accommodate and fulfill the needs and wishes of her students. One example of this was "a new course in ceramic appreciation and history," that was added in 1931. [83]

Fig. 21: Mattson supervising student in "Throwing" class. UAP # 2371.

Commenting on the Ceramics Department in 1922, Cable wrote: "Although its primary purpose was to afford better research facilities in ceramics, it soon became evident that this, both for technical and economic reasons, could be coupled advantageously with instructional work, utilizing thereby the equipment, the technical force and later, the contributions of advanced students in securing a larger volume of research work, while at the same time affording an opportunity for instruction and training to young people interested in the great field of ceramic technology." [84] Soon after the establishment of the Ceramics Department, in 1910, courses, taught by Cable, were offered to students in the School of Mines and in several other colleges of the University of North Dakota, as well as to such "special," non-credit students as relatives of faculty members and other adult residents of Grand Forks. For many years thereafter many of these special students -- limited to twenty-four per year [85] -- were women with available free time and an interest in handicrafts. Later this offer of instruction was extended to include adult students from the outlying area. "The fee charged is $5.00 a semester. This covers the cost of all materials and firing. Outside of this tuition fee there is no additional charge of any kind." [86] After World War II ceramics courses were also recommended as occupational therapy for returning veterans.

In 1916, Cable's schedule as Instructor in Ceramics included, in number of hours per week: Office work – 5; Lecture – 3; Recitation – 2; Laboratory – 14; Research and Experimentation – 8. Official working hours in the Department were: Monday through Saturday, 9-12 noon, and Monday through Friday, 1-5pm. In that year she taught six courses attended by a total of forty-eight students: Ceramics III – 8 students; Ceramics V – 4 students; two Special Ceramics classes, each with 8 students; and two Special Ceramics classes, each with 10 students. Prior to the Depression the number of "regular" students grew steadily, and by the time of the Fall semester of 1928, Cable's class attendance ranged from 6 to 20 students of the University, and Mattson's from 7 to 13; classes for special students, averaging 10 per class, were held on Tuesday, 2-5pm, and Thursday, 7-10pm. The following year, with 10-12 special students per class, Special Ceramics courses were held on Wednesday, 9-12 noon, and Friday, 2-5pm.

By the Fall semester of 1931, when the class enrollment of University students ranged from 3 to 10, special classes, averaging 10 students per session, took place Thursday, 2-5pm, and Friday, 9-12 noon and 2-5pm. Later in the 1930s, as the Depression deepened, special adult classes for 7-12 students per class were held on Monday, 2-5pm, and Saturday, 9-12 noon; and for male special students on Tuesday, 7-10pm. During these years Cable worked as many as 42-45 hours per week, including between 17 and 24 hours of teaching and office work and between 15 and 21 hours of clayworking and research.

During the Fall semester of the 1935-6 academic year, the schedule for the "Special Ceramics" students and the number of such students (both women and men) were as follows:

Course	Students	Hours	Days	Instructor
S-101 – **ELEMENTARY CLAY WORKING**				
Section I	(9 women)	2-5	Mon.	Cable
Section II	(9 women)	9-12	Fri.	Mattson
Section III	(7 men)	7-10	Tues.	Cable
S-201 – **ELEMENTARY CLAY WORKING**				
Section I	(3 women)	1-3	Tues./Thurs.	Mattson
Section II	(4 women)	3-5	Wed./Fri.	Cable
S-203 – **BUILDING AND MODELING**				
	(6 women)	3-5	Tues./Thurs.	Mattson
S-301 – **ADVANCED CLAY WORKING**				
	(5 women)	10-12	Tues./9-11 Thurs.	Cable
S-309 – **THROWING**				
	(1 woman)	1-3	Wed./Fri.	Cable

By the late 1930s, courses which were elective -- and for which they could earn credit -- were open to all students in the University. "Students taking a broad training in Ceramics are then ready to teach the complete course in schools or go to work in potteries engaged in the manufacture of commercial pottery." [87] "Elementary Clay Working" covered the preparation of clay through crushing, soaking, screening and partial drying to storing, as well as the hand-building of vessels. "Advanced Clay Working" included the "surface enrichment of clay" by incising, carving, sgraffito and slip-painting, as well as instruction in glazing and mold construction. For special students at this time there were six courses taught by Cable and Mattson, including "Building and Modeling," "Throwing," and "Claycraft for Teachers." The class on "Throwing" [88] progressed from centering on the wheel and shaping a cylinder to making bowls and flared and globe-shaped vases.

During the years of World War II, greater numbers of special students offset the low enrollment of University students. In the spring semester of the 1942-3 academic year, Cable's regular students numbered 2-6 per class, and Mattson's 1-4. Two years later, 15 hours of Cable's time were devoted to special classes, 2 hours to regular classes, and not less than 21 hours to duties other than teaching.

In the busiest years of their careers in the Ceramics Department at the University, Cable's and Mattson's classes could attract as many as 20 University students per session, in the worst years as few as 1 or 2.

By 1948, the Department had "an enrollment of 112, many of whom are enrolled in the special adult classes, which meet for a three-hour period once a week." [89] This represented an increase of more than thirty students over the previous ten years. The adults enrolled in the special program remained non-credit students. And by 1972, as evidenced in a letter from Administrative Assistant Mrs. Mildred L. Koth to Mrs. Darlene Dommel: "...the Department's primary function now is undergraduate instruction," [90] and, consequently, both the initial mandate of research and experimentation and the production of pottery for sale played a much lesser role, if any at all, than previously.

In June of 1973, the Ceramics Department, which up until then had remained a part of the College of Engineering, was transferred to the College of Fine Arts. The program was no longer strictly elective, and as Prof. Donald Miller had proposed in 1971, the future direction of the Department necessitated "ceramics becoming a requirement in several areas." [91]

22 UNIVERSITY OF NORTH DAKOTA

CERAMICS

Junior Division Courses

101-102. **Clay-Working Laboratory.** No credits. Three hours a week. First and second semesters. Miss Cable and Miss Mattson. This course is open to adult special students interested in ceramics.

201-202. **Elementary Clay-Working Laboratory.** Four credits. Four hours a week. 201 is prerequisite to 202. First and second semesters. Miss Cable and Miss Mattson.

203-204. **Building and Modelling With Clay.** Four credits. Four hours a week. First and second semesters. Miss Mattson.

Senior Division Courses

301-302. **Advanced Clay-Working Laboratory.** Four credits. Four hours a week. First and second semesters. Prerequisites, Ceramics 201 or 203. Miss Cable.

309-310. **Throwing.** Four credits. Four hours a week. First and second semesters. Miss Cable.

311-312. **History and Appreciation.** Two credits. One recitation a week. First and second semesters. Miss Cable.

313-314. **Claycraft for Teachers.** Four credits. Two hours laboratory a week. First and second semesters. No prerequisite. Miss Cable.

405. **Glazes.** Two credits. Four hours a week. First semester. Prerequisite, Ceramics 201-202. Miss Hammers.

CERAMIC ENGINEERING

Senior Division Courses

303-304. **Elements of Ceramic Engineering.** Six credits. Six hours a week. First and second semesters. Mr. Budge.
Prerequisites, Chemistry 105-106.

306. **Building Materials and Heavy Clay Products.** Two credits. One recitation, two hours laboratory a week. Second semester. Mr. Budge.
Prerequisites, Chemistry 105-106.

309. **Ceramic Bodies.** Three credits. Two recitations and three hours laboratory a week. First or second semester. Mr. Budge.
Prerequisites, Chemistry 105-106; Ceramics 201-202.

401. **Refractories.** Two credits. Two recitations a week. First or second semester. Mr. Budge.
Prerequisites, Chemistry 105-106.

403. **Ceramic Analysis and Testing.** Three credits. One recitation and six hours laboratory a week. First or second semester. Mr. Budge.
Prerequisite, Chemistry 109.

Graduate Division Courses

501-502. **Research in Clays.** Hours and credits to be arranged. Mr. Harrington and staff.

Fig. 22. Ceramics and Ceramic Engineering Department curriculum, mid- to late 1930s

B: **Texts**

As Chairman of the Art Division of the American Ceramic Society, Frederick H. Rhead was very conscious of the need for "a Pottery Text Book... for use in schools, studios, and art potteries," together with a "companion volume to the practical book" on "decorative processes."[92] He considered the need for such published work to be "obvious" since no such comprehensive source of this information was up to this time extant. The "skeleton outline" suggested by him for the "Pottery Text Book" consisted of seventeen chapters, to be compiled by responsible, volunteer members of the Art Division and to appear serially in the *Journal of the American Ceramic Society.* He proposed that these chapters should consider: general history, clay and its preparation, built pottery, throwing and turning, modeling, mold making, casting, pressing, jiggering, the biscuit kiln, glaze preparation, glaze application, the glost kiln – placing, the glost kiln – firing, the glost kiln – drawing, school and studio equipment, and technical and general information – tables, ceramic calculations. The outline for the "textbook on Ceramic Decorative Processes," also with seventeen chapters, should cover: ceramic shape construction, incised processes, sgraffito, slip processes, glaze processes – monochromes, glaze processes – decorations, underglaze processes, majolica processes, mechanical processes – printing, mechanical processes – decalcomania, and mechanical processes – photography on pottery.

That Frederick Rhead's plea for collaboration should be so urgent and his opinion on the importance of this project so profound, speaks to the non-availability of suitable and comprehensive instructional material at that time. For example, up to that time, Margaret Cable could not reach for a ready-made manual of instruction for her classes. Consequently, she was obliged to draw upon her own studies with Batchelder, Rhead and Binns, her reading of the latter's *The Potter's Craft* and of Rhead's articles in *The Potter,* and the contents of such magazines as Robineau's *Keramic Studio,* to facilitate preparation of her own instructional material. Other sources were *Transactions of the American Ceramic Society* – particularly a technical article by Rhead on matt glazes [93] – Rhead's handbook *Studio Pottery,* of 1910, and also an article of his entitled "How to Build a Piece of Pottery." [94] She voraciously collected and absorbed information from a variety of sources wherever published and read, ranging from *Little Romances of China* by the Onondaga Pottery Co., through "America's Most Ancient Art," by Kenneth M. Chapman, [95] *Design Made Easy* by Pedro J. Lemos, *Pueblo Pottery Making* by Carl E. Guthe, *Clays* by Heinrich Ries, to the geological survey work by C. H. Clapp and E. J. Babcock (including chapters headed "The Chemistry of Clay" and "The Physical Properties of Clay").

Cable's own research and experimentation, her correspondence with potters, teachers and respected figures in the ceramics field, her familiarity with the procedures and products of other schools and potteries, her gleanings from the specialized studies of Mattson and Hammers, and her knowledge of Biblical, literary and poetic references to the history of pottery making all contributed also to the formulation of her own "textbook."

She lectured frequently, consistently and persuasively both at the University and outside, at conventions, exhibitions and World's Fairs; she addressed the American Ceramic Society on numerous occasions; and she provided information wherever it was sought -- by other schools, pottery companies, the WPA Project, the Indian Service at Large, and other applicants. Instruction sheets [96] were prepared for every class, and addresses for presentation to every audience.

Endnotes

83 Cable letter dated October 27, 1931, addressed to the American Federation of Arts in Washington, DC.

84 Booklet *The Development of Ceramic Work at the University of North Dakota*, by Margaret Cable, reprinted from the *Journal of the American Ceramic Society*, Volume 5, No. 3, March 1922.

85 Cable letter dated April 30, 1927.

86 Cable letter dated September 23, 1931, to prospective, special students.

87 As announced in a university booklet (fig. 22).

88 Based on Charles Binns' book *The Potter's Craft*.

89 *North Dakota Engineer*, May, 1948.

90 Letter dated April 4, 1972.

91 Proposal dated March 8, 1971.

92 Rhead letter dated October 28, 1922, to the Members of the Art Division, regarding the necessity of their collaborating in the writing of the "Pottery Text Book."

93 *Transactions of the American Ceramic Society*, issue XI, 1909.

94 *Palette and Bench*, II, 1910.

95 Article in *School Arts Magazine*, Volume XXX, #7, March, 1931.

96 For instance, the 16-page, typed booklet, prepared by Cable, as Associate Professor of Ceramics, entitled "Instruction sheets for the making and firing of simple unglazed primitive pottery suitable for rural schools, camp and club projects;" these sheets included precise and clear "Directions for Polishing Red and Black Primitive Pottery," "Directions for Outdoor Firing - Pueblo Method," "Outdoor Firing Making Use of a Closed Container (As practiced at the Ceramic Department, UND)," and "Directions for Glazing with Low Fired Transparent Glaze."

Air View of Grand Forks, N. D.
GRAND FORKS HERALD PHOTO
3B-H1411

PART IV

Clay and Glaze

Dean Babcock's collection of and research on native clays were conducted in a manner designed to produce ultimately -- in addition to material intended for structural and industrial use -- a clay body for use in the projected Ceramics Department. In the early years, many different mixes of clay were tested to prove their suitability for pottery working and firing. The first sufficiently satisfactory result appears to have been a mixture of clays, in equal measure, from the Hebron and Dickinson areas, which was to become known as "Dickinson Potter's Clay," or "Potter's Clay." This body, which burned to an ivory-tinted white or cream color, was used extensively from 1918 through the time of Freida Hammers' assignment to continue and refine the earlier efforts at clay- and glaze-testing. Margaret Cable's directive to Hammers was to discover a combination of clays which, for reasons of economy and aesthetics, would produce a material, which could be used in all methods of pottery making, and which could be fired at a lower temperature to effect a warmer-colored body than had previously been attained. Between 1926 and 1938, clays designated Hettinger, Weigel, Mandan, McCurdy, Ross and Beulah were fired alone or in various combinations to produce different results. Hettinger clay, for example, "works very well in both hand building and casting. It burns to a light cream color and a fairly hard body at cone 1 to 2."[97]

In a letter of May 31, 1946, Cable listed the locations of these beds as follows:

> "Mandan Clay – Morton County.
> Butte 8 miles west of Mandan on Highway No. 10. Big butte. Left hand side of road going west.
>
> Beulah Clay – Mercer County.
> Four to five miles south and west of Beulah on the farm of John Raszler.
>
> Hettinger Clay – Adams County.
> Near the town of Hettinger on the William Hanson farm.
>
> Ross Clay – Mountrail County.
> About 12 miles south and 3 miles west of the town of Ross."

Finally a "New Body Mix" was developed using clays from the counties of Adams, Morton, Mercer and Mountrail, in western North Dakota. Clay from the first of these areas contributed porosity, from the second and third plasticity and from the fourth hardness and densification.

Plate 33: Hammers bowl, 4" dia., c. 1928, marked "3 (in a square) FLH-259 S (in a circle) Ball G682-D"; shape by Ball; glaze # G682-D. UND Coll. # C-HMM 13-382.

On the bottom of many test pieces, the clay body is identified by origin, with the appropriate percentage proportions used. Identification is facilitated by means of initial letters or abbreviations of clay names, such as:

D: Dickinson	**B:** Beulah	**H:** Hebron	**M:** Mandan
W: Weigel	**R:** Ross	**McC:** McCurdy	**Hett:** Hettinger

Ross clays were further designated as to color:

LGR for light gray **DGR** for dark gray **RR** for red

Potter's Clay/ Dickinson Potter's Clay was marked **1** (in a circle), and Dickinson Fire Clay **DFC**. The use of Dickinson clay, dug from a location "three miles west of Dickinson in the big butte of the Dickinson Brick Company," was discontinued in 1938.

During Mrs. Pachl's tenure, the 2-2-3-1 combination, by parts, for Hettinger, Mandan, Beulah and Red Ross clays, was still regarded as "the mixture we use most commonly." [98] It fired to a buff color at a temperature of cone 01, approximately 2030 degrees F. Mrs. Pachl, in answer to an inquiry in 1954, described admirably the properties and requirements of ingredients for clay working: "a clay should be plastic enough to model easily; should dry without undue shrinkage, cracking, warping; and should fire safely at the desired temperature." To achieve these results necessitates the making of a clay body by the addition to the clay of "other plastic or non-plastic materials." "If a clay is too sandy and does not hold together and model well, some stickier or more plastic clay such as ball clay may be added. If the clay tends to crack while drying, some pulverized fired clay, which is called 'grog,' might be added...If the pots are too porous after firing, and the glaze crazes on them, some clay which matures at a lower temperature or some non-plastic materials such as Talc, Feldspar, Nepheline Syenite might be added." [99]

After assembling the various clays to be used, the clay ingredients were ground and mixed with water in a rotating, vibrating hopper, and afterwards excess water was removed by means of a "blunger," leaving "slabs of clay for throwing or building." [100] Clay body, when mixed with water, could also form a slip for pouring into molds, and, in even more diluted form, with pigments added, could be used for slip-painting or slip-trailing.

Plate 34: Vase, c. 1932, marked "DHB 32". UND Coll. # C-MSC Gift 105-699.

Clay from a different area than the body clays -- Stark County -- was used in the formulation of glaze, along with a variety of chemicals for color effects. Glaze materials were very carefully assembled and precisely weighed, since any variance in the weight of any one ingredient could result in failure to achieve the correct shade of color or degree of transparency. Once prepared, the glaze materials would then be ground in a rotating stone barrel through tumbling with granite stones and water to effect a thorough mixing. The chemistry of glazes and the development of formulations were subjects of advanced, technical study, and Margaret Cable was frequently obliged to seek advice from such experts as Charles Binns, Paul Cox and Arthur Baggs, particularly in the late 1920s and the 1930s, when assisting Freida Hammers in her experiments with turquoise blue -- to achieve "Egyptian or Persian effects" [101] -- and copper red (plates 33; 34). Hammers, and also Mattson (plate 67, right), combined glaze elements, in various ratios, with chemical colorants to provide a material for testing, i.e. spraying on different clay bodies and firing at different temperatures, in their search for reliable, effective glazes for use in the Department.

At the University, once a glaze compound was chosen and prepared, that finished glaze, when used, could be poured on to the pot, or the pot could be dipped in glaze (fig. 23), but the preferred method was spraying glaze (fig. 24) on to the pot with the aid of compressed air. Through such use of a spray gun -- or airbrush -- the glaze could be applied thinly and evenly, which was the recommended procedure, since a pot, so treated, could, if necessary (i.e. in the case of an unsatisfactory initial glazing/firing), be reglazed and refired.

For firing in the Department there were two kilns, one for biscuit and one for glazed ware. In the glazing kiln high temperatures had to be achieved, maintained and controlled by regular,

Fig. 23: Glaze dipping. UAP # 2391.

scheduled monitoring and recording of pyrometric cones – progressing in the heat through various stages from erect, then shrinking to bent and collapsed – which could be seen in the kiln. These operations were the duties of student assistants working under the supervision of Julia Mattson, who was also responsible for the careful loading of the kiln and the removal of the fired products (fig. 25).

When, during the Depression, and also the later war years, the funds available to the Department were drastically reduced and fuel supplies severely limited, it was deemed essential to achieve lower firing temperatures, which would be less expensive. Further experimentation was conducted along these lines and one result was the development of a particularly fine bentonite resource. Deposits of bentonite, "an amorphous material resembling clay and possessing many characteristics of a colloid," [102] were discovered in 1930 during survey fieldwork carried out by the College of Engineering in the western part of North Dakota. It was found to contain feldspar, iron compounds, silica and alumina, and to be suited to many varied purposes such as water-softening and medical dressings. One particular bentonite, developed by Hammers and favored by Cable and Mattson, produced, on firing, an exceptionally rich red color, and proved economical to work with, though the procedure for preparation was complex. Differing from previous methods, it involved pulverizing the bentonite, soaking it in water, grinding it and

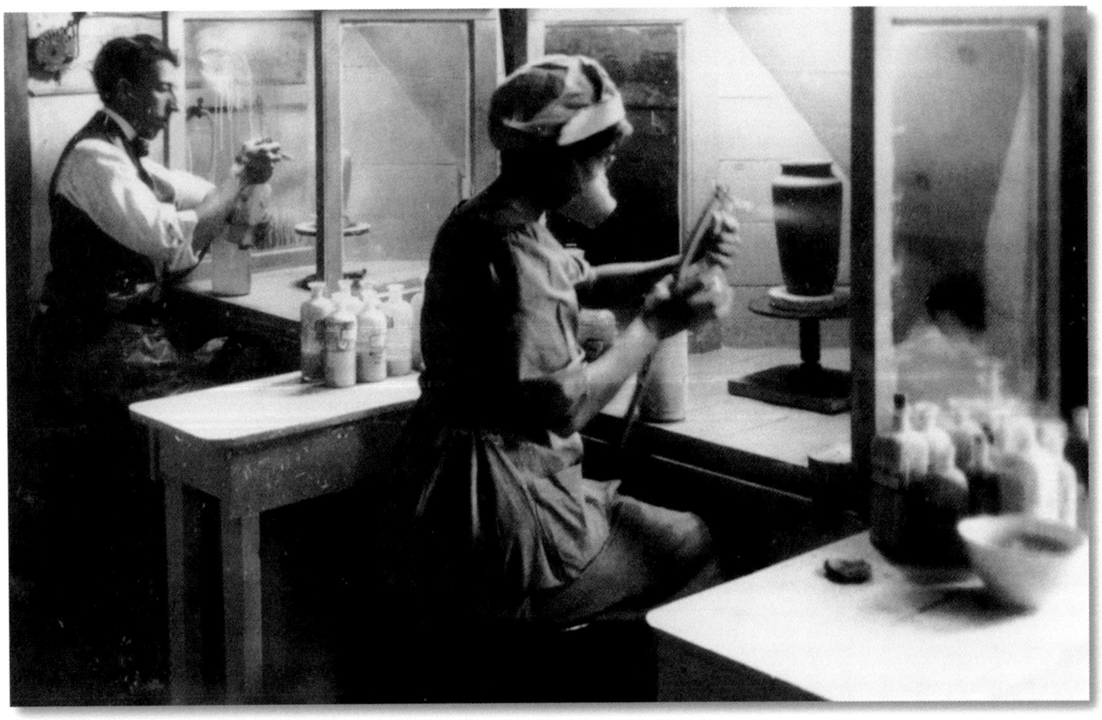

Fig. 24: Glaze spraying; (Seymour Anderson, left). UAP # 2394.

Fig. 25: Cable removing pots from the kiln, c. 1925. UAP # 2396.

Plate 35: Bentonite vase, 1943, by Rhoda Ford.

screening it to achieve a quality of uniform thickness. Addressing the Academy of Science in 1932, Hammers emphasized that the "great advantage of the bentonite slips and glazes is that they may be applied to the raw ware and matured in one firing." [103] Colors ranging from cream through yellow, orange-red to a rich dark red, brown and finally black (plates 35; 36; 37) could be obtained by the addition of small amounts of oxides – mainly zinc, manganese and uranium – to produce unique effects. This bentonite, a readily accessible resource of North Dakota, "is inexpensive and will materially reduce the cost of the finished ware," and is "something that's all North Dakota." [104]

The technique of applying this special material involved spraying on three or four coats of red bentonite, allowing five minutes for drying between each coat, after which the design would be painted in black or other-colored bentonite slips. The vessel was then fired in the glaze kiln to cone 03 (2000 degrees F). "The design must be gone over at least three times and there is no way to correct a line once it is laid on," and great care and expertise must be employed to eliminate the "risk that the result will be unsatisfactory in the fire as the bentonite will blister if too heavy and not register if too thin." [105]

Plate 36: Bentonite vase, 1946, by Ruth Schnell. Rustand Coll.

Plate 37: Three bentonite vases by students, marked (left to right) "GUST" (probably a member of the Gustafson family), c. 1946; "JELLIFF", c. 1949; "SCOTT '48", 1948.

Endnotes

97 Cable letter dated February 23, 1928.

98 Pachl letter dated January 13, 1954.

99 Ibid.

100 Letter dated October 26, 1977, from John E. Howard.

101 Cable letter dated January 25, 1934, to Arthur Baggs.

102 Class information sheet for "Building and Modelling - Bentonite," by Julia Mattson, drawing on "Properties of Some North Dakota Bentonite," by Hammers and Professor Budge, reprinted from the *Journal of the American Ceramic Society*, Volume 14, No. 10, October, 1931.

103 "Bentonite in Ceramic Decoration," by Freida L. Hammers.

104 Cable letter dated December 5, 1932.

105 Cable letter dated July 11, 1940, to Russel Wright.

PART V

Clayworking and Decoration

A. **Shapes**

Adelaide Alsop Robineau wrote: "The artist has no time to waste on experimenting with clays."[106] Cable, later, without the mandate-imposed requirement of her position at the School of Mines, would probably have preferred to devote her energies entirely to making and decorating pottery, to teaching its history, and to elucidating ceramic technique and design. But that luxury was not allowed her. In addition to teaching, she was also responsible for testing and proving North Dakota clays, and demonstrating their suitability for pottery making. Neither the evolution of innovative, complex form nor the seemingly endless attention to extravagant stylistic detail was in her purview, and her own taste, conforming to her personality, tended toward clarity and straightforward simplicity. In this, like Baggs, Cox, Frederick Walrath and other Alfred alumni, Cable showed the influence of Charles Binns, who preferred classic, refined forms. Frederick Rhead, too, favored distinctively simple shapes as the bodies to carry the designs and exhibit the decorating techniques, which were his primary concern, and had, even in his early years in Zanesville, substantially simplified the vessel forms used at Roseville. Marblehead, Rookwood and Newcomb Potteries were all more interested in decoration than shape, and Cable, having proved the viability of a clay body, could follow their lead. Some occasional, later forms made at the University during the Cable/Mattson years reflect a student's idiosyncrasy (plate 38), but, by and large, the Ceramics Department followed a tradition of simplicity in form prior to the studio pottery innovations of the Pachl era (plates 31; 32).

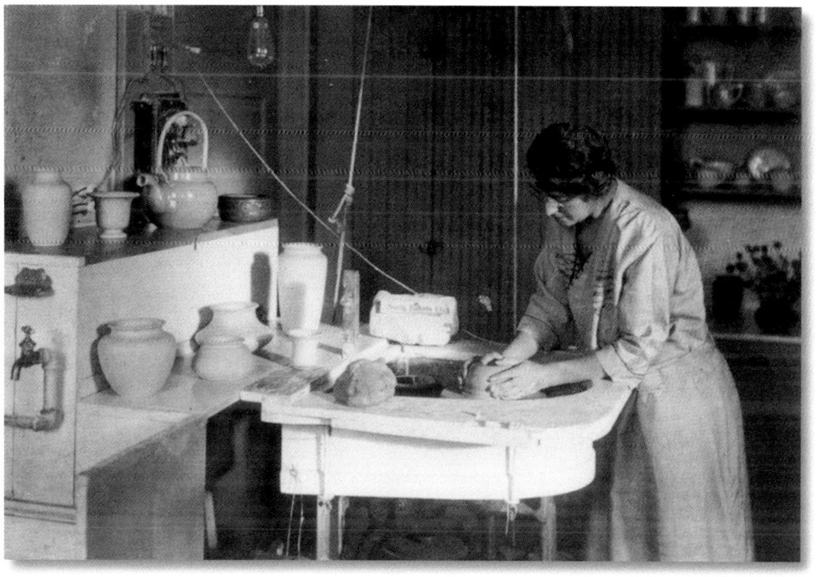

Fig. 26: Cable throwing a pot at the wheel. UAP # 2525.

Rhead's design principles, as propounded in *The Potter* and *Keramic Studio*, and as evidenced in his work in Zanesville, at University City, and more notably in California, concerned the application of a decoration organized to articulate the shape of the pot. At Arequipa, particularly, he utilized modest, understated designs, which were adapted to complement the basic form, or else he considered the glaze, without applied ornament, to be sufficient embellishment. Cable, the attentive disciple, likewise believed that the simple form of a vessel could be enriched by the strategic placement of a conventionalized design or by the glaze treatment alone.

Plate 38: (Left to right) thrown pitcher with hand-built handle and hand-formed rigaree; slab-formed ornament of modernistic form by A. Hillman; carved, hand-built candle-lantern by M. Dowhower.

The methods of producing forms, learned and taught by Cable at the Handicraft Guild, and continued by her at the University of North Dakota, were throwing (fig. 26), hand-building (plate 38) and slip-casting (fig. 31). Cable was so adept at working at the wheel, and so renowned for this facility displayed at schools, clubs, shows, exhibitions and World's Fairs, that she became known as the "Lady of the Wheel." This method of pottery production was superior, she felt, to hand-building. Accordingly, Cable had installed, in the new Ceramics Department at the School of Mines, pottery wheels powered by sewing machine treadles, in order that her students should not be deprived of facilities necessary to their gaining experience in throwing at the wheel. The origin of this innovation appears to be in dispute, as well as the date when it was first put to use. It has been reported that such wheels were developed in response to the high cost of professional power wheels, and initially used both at the School of the Art Institute of Chicago and at the Handicraft Guild of Minneapolis prior to Cable's appointment at the University of North Dakota. [107] In spite of her predilection for throwing, Cable also taught hand-building -- a technique which consists of winding and coiling long ropes of clay to build a pot. Hand-building also includes slab work which achieves the construction of a piece by assembling a flat base and walls of clay (plates 38, middle; 123).

In the early 1920s, a small number of "lamp-vases" (plate 39) were made and decorated, together with appropriately conforming, pierced, ceramic covers and supportive stands (of usually simplified, Chinese shape), to form a 3-part lamp base to be equipped with electrical fittings (fig. 27). From the mid-1920s on, bases with hand-carved decoration (infrequently), or with simplified in-mold design schemes (sometimes), or in molded, plain shapes (often) -- with monochromatic or blended glazes -- continued to be produced for electric lamps. Some of these later lamp bases were in the form of an inverted vase. Otherwise, the closed underside of the lamp base would be recessed and would incorporate a molded hole to accommodate the fittings; a second molded hole, low in the side of the vessel, would allow for entry of the electrical cord. An integral or separate ceramic cap, of suitable shape and with matching glaze treatment, to cover the top of the lamp base would be similarly pierced (plate 40) and, if separate, would probably be also artist-marked and possibly dated and/or numbered on its underside (plate 41).

Other than vases, bowls, tableware and lamp bases, the Ceramics Department's output also included paperweights (plate 63, left), figurines (plates 42; 55), bookends (plate 216), candlesticks, tiles (plates 61; 62; 79; 170), roundels (plates 58; 59; 179), ashtrays and pin-trays (plate 53), souvenir items (plate 63, right), awards (plates 43; 177), medallions (plate 54), pendants and curtain pulls (plates 64; 65; 66).

Plate 39: Lamp base, with cover and supporting stand, 11¾"h., 3 pattern repeats (peacock in arch-type design), peacock in dark blue and green with pink feather-eyes, on background shading from light purplish blue at the top to royal blue at bottom; marked (black base only) "Made by H. Fried Feb 12. 1923. at U.N.Dak." Rustand Coll.

Plate 40: Lamp base with integral cover, marked "N. Dak Flikertails (sic) & Wheat M. Cable 1927". UND Coll. # C-CBL 38-208.

Plate 41: Lamp with separate cover, 1933, both pieces marked with "BT" or "TB" monogram and " '33".

Fig. 27: Lamps exhibited in the Ceramics Department. UAP 2347.

Plate 42: (Left to right) high-glazed elephant figure, marked "L T STALEY 1934". UND Coll. # C-MSC 279 860. Semi-matt running fox or coyote figure, by Laura Taylor, marked "108 LAT (M)". UND Coll. # C-MSC Gift 294-875.

Plate 43: Northern Interscholastic Press Association, 8½"h., "1939 AWARD PRESENTED BY DAKOTA STUDENT U.N.D. WON BY THE AURORA BOREALIS, AURORA, MINN. BEST MIMEOGRAPH PAPER". UND Coll. # C-MSC 122-716.

Fig. 28: Cable preparing a mold. UAP # 2376.

B: **Slip-Casting**

Slip-casting, or molding, to produce multiple copies of plain pottery forms for decoration or in-mold decorated forms for enhancement, which was taught from the very beginning, became more and more dominant during Hammers' time at the University, and was vital to the survival of the ceramics program in the late 1930s and the 1940s. Both plain and ornamented pieces could be produced by molding. Some 20-30 minutes after pouring liquid slip into a plaster mold, the water from the clay would have been drawn into the plaster, at which time the remaining slip could be poured out, and the resultant clay form, while drying, would shrink, thereby pulling away from the sides of the mold, allowing its removal after the dismantling of the various sections of the mold. The form could then be "fettled," or finished by trimming and smoothing seam lines.

At the University of North Dakota prototypes -- "master pots" -- were thrown/ built from which molds were constructed (figs. 28; 29). Slip was then poured into these molds (fig. 30) by instructors and students to produce plain pottery forms (fig. 31) for decorating. Alternatively, a master pot might be given a decorative treatment by carving or modeling, thereby incorporating decoration into the mold. Later the resulting slipcast vessel could be refined with a minimum of handwork. The relief of a raised design could be enhanced, using a carving or excising tool to remove the background of the motif. Colors could then be simply and easily applied to these designs, using a brush, sponge or spray gun, by people with little artistic expertise or formal training -- a method introduced previously by Frederick Rhead at Weller and Roseville, in Zanesville, Ohio.

Interestingly, techniques were employed that imparted a handcrafted, and even hand-decorated effect to the pottery, without an abundance of expensive and time-consuming work by highly skilled artists. Mattson, in particular – never as competent or as confident in throwing as Cable – became extremely adept at producing a ridged effect on the exterior surface of a model, so that the molded item would appear to have been thrown (plates 223; 224). A comparison of several such pieces of the same shape and size would prove them to be too identical to have been hand-thrown. The absence of finger marks on the interior vessel wall would also confirm that they were molded pieces.

At the upper end of the spectrum of American molded ware is Tiffany pottery, which was, through careful embellishment and detailed refinement, by hand, of vibrant organic designs, given its unique and brilliant Art Nouveau distinction. At Tiffany, as at Grueby and Rookwood, philosophical compromises were reached in adapting handcraft techniques to large-scale production.

Molded plain forms, including some of those produced during the Spencer years (1938-1948), were also used by instructors and students alike for decorating by hand – by painting, incising and/or excising – to produce an original design. Molded decorated forms (those incorporating incised/excised design already in the mold) could also receive hand-treatment through the addition of polychrome painting, just as other pieces could be enhanced by the use of background-inlaid color (either of a darker shade, for instance, of the overall glaze stain or a contrasting hue).

In 1997-8, Kathryn McCleery, Professor of Ceramics for over 30 years at the University of North Dakota, designed and began to produce, in limited edition, a porcelain vase named "Prairie Rose", the first slip-cast work made at the University since the Cable/Mattson years.

Fig. 29: Cable withdrawing the master pot from a mold. UAP # 2380.

Fig. 30: Cable filling a mold. UAP # 2382.

Fig. 31: Cable removing ware from a mold. UAP # 2388.

C. **Decorating Techniques**

The principal decorating techniques used at the University of North Dakota -- foreshadowed by artists and potteries in other areas of the United States -- were incising, low-relief carving or excising, sgraffito and stain- or slip-painting. Incised design was achieved by means of an ice pick or orangewood stick (or possibly some needle-type implement) piercing the body of the vessel and leaving an impressed outline of the motif in the surface. In carving/excising, a chisel, in addition to the ice-pick or orangewood stick, could be used to remove the background and produce a shaped motif in relief. In Cable's Department, the sgraffito technique (fig. 32) consisted of applying a wash of color to the vessel before creating the design by scratching through the colored surface to the natural-colored clay beneath (plates 124 through 127). In the "North Dakota Products Vase," for example, the wealth of decorative motifs was outlined in surface relief against a background of contrasting color, achieved by incising through a thin layer of slip stained with cobalt oxide to reveal the natural creamy color of the clay beneath (for the Sorlie, Budd and Milloy versions) and through a brown-stained slip surface (for the Kane presentation). Cable insisted that in sgraffito the corners of the orangewood stick used should be rounded a little so that the incised line would be U- and not V-shaped.

Fig. 32: Sgraffito bisque ware. UAP 2505.

Carving was also used to shape relief decoration added to the surface of the pot, or in an intaglio technique to produce an image beneath the pot's surface. An underglaze colored stain could then be applied to the raw ware -- inlaid in incised outlines or in the background areas of a relief image -- then fired, before being overall glaze-fired with a final, complementary or possibly contrasting, colored glaze, to accentuate a carved or intaglio design (plates 119, right; 165). In both carving and sgraffito Cable recommended the appearance of tool marks in the background (plates 49; 121; 155), in line with Rhead's teaching, to afford an interesting texture as in "fine wood carving, or the tooling of leather, or the hammer marks in (beaten) metal," as she explained in her instruction sheet "Advanced Clay Working – Cable, The Surface Enrichment of Clay – Sgraffito."

Painting in colored stains would essentially result in flat design, whilst painting in colored slip would allow a slight relief in the design and produce greater depth. In applying stains, the approved procedure was, at the "green" stage, to trace the design or draw it freehand, using a pencil or brush.[108] After this, the prepared mineral colors could be painted in with a thin and even application with a watercolor brush (plate 105). Painting with slip (plates 45; 190) involved the same technique to apply liquid clays rather than colored stains. After the painting was completed

Plate 44: Painted vessels (left to right): bowl, marked "MKC Jan. 16 – 1926 T.600"; vase, 1927, by Huckfield on Mattson shape; bowl, c. 1927, "Pasque Flower" by Huckfield.

in either manner, a transparent colorless glaze, a colored glaze, or glazes of blended colors could be applied (plate 44).

Slip-trailing, or tube-lining -- a decorative technique in which lines of clay are pressed through a squeeze-bag onto a vessel's surface; the lines contain a colored glaze and prevent intermingling and running of colors -- was employed by Cable (plates 56; 57; 61; 170), but rarely, if ever, by students. In her "Advanced Clay Working" instructions on slip-painting, Cable writes "as the tube-line is somewhat difficult to control, we had better use a brush." The Department's production clearly reflects this thinking since there is a scarcity of slip-trailed decoration.

Shaded and blended grounds, achieved by the use of an airbrush, were used in the production of ceramic artwares in Cincinnati, Zanesville and New Orleans before the beginning of the twentieth century; softened contours and blurred outlines provided illusions of atmosphere. Similar effects were achieved, shortly thereafter, at the University of North Dakota by the use of a colored glaze to deepen shades and produce pleasing variations suggestive of mood and atmosphere or to give the impression of a time of day particularly in scenic representation. The application of a green glaze would darken the green already painted on the surface of a vessel and create the effect, for example, of a dark green pine tree blending into a lighter background. The use of a blue or brown glaze on such a green design might give the impression of a twilight or evening scene, whereas a colorless glaze might reflect morning light. Firing

Plate 45: Slip-decorated vase; hand-painted seal-mark on base in same slip as decoration. UND Coll. # C-MSC 12-996.

with semi-transparent matt glazes at the appropriate temperature, Cable noted, would result in "a soft, silky" effect[109] (plates 10; 48; 158), reminiscent of Rookwood's misty landscapes and the rhythmic lyricism of Newcomb's matt-glazed botanical studies. In addition to these glaze effects, the use of soft pastel colors imparted an Art Nouveau resonance to some of the vases and bowls produced by Cable and Fried around 1920. In the School of Mines' emulation of Newcomb's moonlit landscapes and Rookwood's twilight snow scenes can be found an echo of the atmospheric tonalism evident in early twentieth century American painting (plates 143; 192; 194).

During the 1930s, in-the-mold relief decoration with applied color – in imitation of slip-painting – and blended grounds achieved by airbrush, became increasingly more standard procedures at the University of North Dakota, and were to prove during the Spencer years, 1938 through 1948, the saving grace of the Ceramics Department's program (plate 151, left; 212 through 214).

The American fascination with the matt-green glaze at the turn of the century, originating in Ohio and the Northeast, and spreading into the Midwest, also found a later echo in North Dakota, in both ornamented and plain forms (plates 25; 119, left). At Wheatley, Grueby, Hampshire and Teco, with varying degrees of success, attempts had been made to produce a ware in which the glaze alone would reinforce the form, and by the 1920s, even at Rookwood, the application of glaze suited to form – without any other type of surface enrichment – had assumed an increased importance, possibly in an attempt to compete with Fulper. At the University of North Dakota too, after the initial conservatism that stemmed from the Handicraft Guild influence, outstanding glaze effects, alone, enhanced many a turned or molded form (plate 109). New colors, color combinations, and color gradations were constantly examined, tested and added to the palette available to decorators (plate 67, right). Mattson's flowing glazes of the 1930s are comparable to those of Frederick Rhead at Arequipa in the period 1911-1913 (plate 205). In addition, the products of Hammers' experiments with crystalline effects (plate 204), though few, have the same appeal as those of University City, Teco and Norweta, in the first decade of the twentieth century, and her red glazes (plates 34; 202, second from right) compare favorably with those of Roseville, Fulper and Newcomb Pottery.

Endnotes

106 *Keramic Studio*, Volume V.

107 *Art and Life on the Upper Mississippi, 1890-1915*, edited by Michael Conforti: "Art for Life's Sake: the Handicraft Guild of Minneapolis," by Marcia Anderson. (Other sources attribute this innovation to the young ceramist Glen Lukens, who, having supposedly built such an effective, low-cost pottery wheel, was asked, as a result, to develop a program of ceramics as occupational therapy for wounded World War I soldiers throughout the country).

108 Included in the documentary material at the Elwyn B. Robinson Department of Special Collections at the Chester Fritz Library in Grand Forks are two large books, one containing outlines of pottery shapes -- some dated up into the 1930s and some annotated with the designer's name; the other contains design tracings, of mainly Arts and Crafts patterns from the teens and the 1920s – many drawn on the curved profile of the appropriate form and bearing Cable's initialed approval.

109 "Pots and Pines, a Decorative Problem for the Artist Potter," by Margaret Cable.

PART VI

Styles, Influences and Motifs

In the early years of Cable's appointment, when clay testing was still of paramount importance in the School of Mines, the production of utilitarian items, such as had been displayed in St. Louis and Omaha, continued, but soon an emphasis on the making of tea services (plate 46) and ornamental art pottery (plate 137) began to assert itself. At first these wares, as could be expected given Cable's background and training in Minneapolis, reflected the Handicraft Guild's simplicity of functional design in an Arts and Crafts manner. The elementary, usually plain forms, heavy bodies, somber colors and handmade appearance of vessels clearly reflect Batchelder's teaching, which incorporated the philosophy and tenets of the Arts and Crafts movement.

But soon this conservative, straightforward and by no means aesthetically or technically innovative production gave way to influences from other areas of art pottery manufacture, particularly the work of Marblehead Pottery, in Massachusetts, Rookwood and the Zanesville potteries, in Ohio, Newcomb Pottery, in Louisiana, and those locations where Frederick Rhead taught and operated.

Plate 46: Tea set, 1914, by Martha Barnes. UND Coll. # C-MSC Gift 77-600.

The history of American art pottery is replete with examples of influences derived by one concern from another by "creative borrowing," [110] and also from design and technical publications, summer school studies, etc. This led inevitably to parallels and affinities between, particularly, Rookwood, the Zanesville firms, Newcomb, Marblehead, Walrath, Arequipa, Rhead Pottery, and Iowa State College on the one hand, and the University of North Dakota on the other. Margaret Cable's familiarity with the designs and techniques employed by the leading American art pottery producers is evident in her teaching and in her own pottery, particularly in the late teens and the 1920s.

Plate 47: Tea set, c. 1923, by Ruth Rudser. SHSND Coll. # 1981.9.1-.3.

In 1918, she visited Marblehead, which she ranked as the finest American pottery of its time. This meeting marked the beginning of her acquaintance with Arthur Baggs. During the second week of February, 1926, she visited Newcomb College, in New Orleans, where she saw first-hand

Fig. 33: Pottery in the Arts and Crafts manner, some with Art Nouveau overtones. UAP #2500.

the product which was being "sold in all the leading cities of the United States," and discovered, probably erroneously or at least questionably, that the decorators "receive a handsome return for their work. Some of the most successful decorators, I understand, receive a compensation of between $3,000. and $4,000. a year." [111] The styles Cable adapted from the products of Marblehead and Newcomb, as well as those of Rookwood, reflected, in essence, the principal trends in American art pottery during the previous two decades. For example, several of her Department's achievements, particularly from the period 1915-1926 (plates 141; 143; 188; 194), emulated Rookwood's use of a glossy glaze highlighting naturalistic representation -- in their Standard, Aerial Blue, Sea Green (plate 142) and Iris (plate 140) lines -- the matt glazes of the turn of the century, and the atmospheric effects of the Vellum line (plate 193). She especially admired Rookwood's color transitions and the almost-Japanese concept of positive and negative space -- apparent in the early Rookwood output -- determining the placement of the motif on the surface of the vessel.

At Marblehead, Arthur Baggs, a former student of Binns', as was Frederick Walrath, [112] also specialized in sparse, static designs, which were vertically oriented or arranged in horizontal bands. Baggs' and Walrath's design ethos, which was characterized by the use of muted colors and matt glazes, appealed to Cable's aesthetic sensibility at a time when she wished to separate her thoughts and ideals from the fustian traditions of nineteenth-century ceramic manufacture and also free herself from the conservative strictures of her early training, though without running the risk at that time of being too innovative or adventurous in her own practice and teaching (plates 11; 15).

In New Orleans, an appreciation of the Rhead aesthetic influenced Newcomb's predilection for horizontal and vertical patterns which was, in time, to be favored by Cable. In addition,

Plate 48: Matt-glazed vase, 13¾"h., marked "M. Cable 1917". Rustand Coll.

Fig. 34: Pottery with regional themes, in incised, carved and sgraffito techniques. UAP # 2470.

Newcomb College's earliest technique -- of incised design outlines sometimes inlaid with dark underglaze, for flat, naturalistic painting, often framed in bands and borders -- contributed to Cable's scheme of decoration at the School of Mines. Soon, however, Newcomb's innovation of low-modeled relief patterning sparingly applied on a plain ground, with soft contours and muted colors in matt glaze -- which was developed by Paul Cox in 1911, and which was to become the signature style of Newcomb -- was adopted as a style-standard for similar attainment in Grand Forks (plates 158; 159; 168). From the 1920s on, Cable's work -- and that of some of her colleagues and students -- clearly reveals her wish to equal Newcomb's consistent, high level of craftsmanship, applied to both conventionalized and abstract ornament, in a decorative style with Art Nouveau associations (plates 93; 104; 141).

In seeking to re-create, in the Ceramics Department, the Arts-and-Crafts look of the Marblehead, Walrath and Newcomb products, Cable and Fried taught that this two-dimensional, illustrational scheme of decoration could be painted freehand on vessels or applied by the use of stencils such as those shown in *Keramic Studio.* Trivets, tea tiles and art tiles could also be decorated in this manner and by these methods. Particularly at Rookwood, the Saturday Evening Girls, in Boston, and California Faience too, trivets and tiles, comparable to those at the University of North Dakota (plates 58; 59; 179), were produced by various techniques, sometimes similar to those in use at Grand Forks. In her essay "Pots and Pines, a Decorative Problem for the Artist Potter," the Arts-and-Crafts look is exemplified by the "effects...obtained by painting a design of bare trees upon the pot, the interlacing branches of which form a semi-conventional border, while the upright trunks serve as a pleasing perpendicular breaking of the background space."

The cross currents of influence in American art pottery were also manifested in an interest in regionalism to assert a distinction and identity designating a "native" origin. In this regard, many potteries vaunted their use of local clays. That not all of their claims were, in fact, true can be seen in the use of clays, at times, from Tennessee, Mississippi and New Jersey by, respectively, Rookwood, Newcomb and Grueby. Also the use of indigenous flora, fauna and other scenic motifs was not always restricted, as the makers would lead the witness to believe. Mary Sheerer called Newcomb pottery "a southern product, made of southern clays, by southern artists, decorated with southern subjects," [113] and the majority, though not all, of their decorative motifs, including magnolia, oleander, gardenia, alligators, and those most recognizable southern images of pines, cypresses and moss-laden live oaks seen by moonlight, reveals a southern inspiration. Marblehead borrowed "something of the gay little gardens and the gray old streets, something of the rocks and the sea" [114] to incorporate in their designs of sailing ships, seagulls, and New England flora and fauna in "espaliered" [115] patterns. Van Briggle was inspired by the flowers and shrubs, particularly poppies and yucca, seen in the colors and light of the

Colorado mountains. Arequipa portrayed madrono, eucalyptus, grapevine, manzanita and Indian paintbrush, while the Roblin Pottery, also in California, depicted lizards, lichens and ferns.

Plate 49: Huckfield vase, c. 1936, 4¼"h., with carved decoration on textured background (shape by Wolff). UND Coll. # C-HCK 25-333

Margaret Cable, in turn, waxed poetic in her listings of such North Dakota state symbols as the wild prairie rose, the Western meadowlark, the Northern pike, Western wheatgrass and the American elm, along with other native flowers and animals and the various prairie motifs used in the decoration of University of North Dakota pottery. In her design for the "North Dakota Products Vase," the motifs used [116] were wheat, Dakota Maid Flour, corn, flax, sweet clover, cow, hog, sheep, hen, duck, turkey, potato, sugar beet, the cream can (symbolic of the dairy industry), pumpkin (symbolic of vegetable products), coal, clay, bee (representing honey output), the prairie rose (state flower), and flickertail or striped gopher (state animal) – (plate 1; fig. 47).

Plate 50: Huckfield vase, c. 1932, marked "FLH 9 – HUCK 1682 Covered Wagon", (shape and clay-body by Hammers).

Though this vocabulary of western motifs symbolizing the prairie landscape is not entirely unique to the University of North Dakota – Paul Cox and Mary Yancey at Iowa State College made use of many of the same images in the 1920s – the School of Mines enjoyed a much greater output of pieces decorated in this way. Some motifs such as wheat, the prairie rose, the pasque flower, the meadowlark, the bison, the coyote, the flickertail, the prairie schooner and the Red River oxcart were a constant inspiration for over three decades. At different times these motifs were treated in different ways. In the late teens and early 1920s the Arts-and-Crafts stylizations were more abstracted than later; flowers and leaves were conventionalized to the point where they all but became geometric shapes, and trees were represented by upright outlines without detail, in the manner of Baggs, Walrath, Rhead and Jervis. Later, at the University, motifs became more representational, if not totally naturalistic, except when a deliberate naiveté of design and execution, more in the manner of the Overbeck sisters in Indiana, was the intent. But, no matter how these motifs were

Fig. 35: Pottery exhibiting a range of techniques and motifs. UAP # 2471.

Fig. 36: Promotional photograph, undated, of University of North Dakota pottery.

Fig. 37: Pottery exhibiting a range of techniques and motifs. UAP # 2472.

seen, by March 1930, Margaret Cable could rightly claim to Conde Nast Publications of New York City: "this colorful ware, made from local clays, decorated with the plant and animal forms indigenous to the state seems literally to breathe the spirit of the pioneer and the prairie." [117]

Plate 51: Vase by Mattson (Spencer-list item # 133A, 1942).

The Ceramics Department's range of motifs, styles and techniques was expanded by every instructor/decorator hired to assist Margaret Cable. Whether through inventive artistry, technical knowledge or willingness to experiment, Mattson, Huckfield and Hammers, as Fried before them, were able to make considerable contributions. This resulted in a class of colors, techniques, glazes, styles and images (figs. 35; 36; 37), which eclipsed, in range, almost all other contemporary potteries in America with the exception of Rookwood.

It was not the concern of the women of the Department's staff to reproduce the wizardry of George Ohr or the fantasy of Robineau; nor were they apparently interested in competing with the iridescent glazes of Sicard at Weller, the lusters of Pewabic, the flambé and volcanic effects of Dedham or the "fire painting" of Theophilus Brouwer at the Middle Lane Pottery. But all other aspects of ceramic production and decoration using the native resources of their state and the technical knowledge they had acquired were the focus of their artistic endeavors.

The brilliance of the new colors and glazes developed by Hammers accelerated the progress made by the Department since the days of the Handicraft Guild's conservative influence. At the University of North Dakota's neighbor, Iowa State College, Professor Paul Cox, who had wanted to leave behind him the soft tones introduced by him at Newcomb Pottery, initiated, in 1920, the use of brightly colored, high-gloss tin-enamel glazes to effect a livelier, cleaner and more distinctive look providing "color emphasis rather than...harmony." [118] The impulse behind the establishment of Cox's program at Ames was in one way similar to, and in another way different from, that instigated ten years earlier in Grand Forks – namely to explore the viability of the state's native clays in an effort to create economic opportunities for development; and through pottery sales to promote and support the program in the Ceramic Engineering Department. At Ames, designs using prairie motifs and indigenous plants in abstract and realistic patterns, carved or incised, glazed-dipped and with inlaid painting in bright colors in challenging combinations

Plate 52: Medallions – commemorating (top left) UND founding (1883); (top right) Parents Day, 1939; (bottom) Lions International Fifth District Annual Convention, 1930.

Plate 53: Pin-trays/ashtrays: (top left) for Catholic Daughters of America; (top right) by Huckfield, c. 1927, later (1938) produced as Spencer-list item # 16; (bottom right) commemorating the Golden Jubilee, 1955, of Tolley, ND.

Plate 54: Sgraffito vase, c. 1932, by Marie Thormodsgard.

and contrasts, were given a final high-gloss overall glaze by spray gun. Mary Yancey visited the University of North Dakota shortly after being recruited by Cox from Newcomb to be the decorator at Iowa State College, and, no doubt, eagerly discussed matters of style and technique with Margaret Cable. Cable, never as restricted in her taste or range of interests as the New Orleans artists, welcomed the Ames initiative and Yancey's innovative color schemes in her own wish for an expansion of her own pottery's appeal, and with greater success.

This wish, or rather determination, of Cable's was greatly helped towards fulfillment by the intensity of Mattson's interest in Native American art and the larger availability of regional decorative motifs it provided for inclusion in the Department's portfolio, marking a noticeable shift in surface embellishment at the University in the mid- to late 1920s. American Indian design had long been popular in Mission-style interiors in the United States. Its geometric simplicity and handcrafted appearance had earlier appealed to followers of the Arts and Crafts Movement in America, and several potteries such as Rookwood, the Zanesville companies and Clifton Art Pottery of Newark, New Jersey, with its Clifton Indian ware of 1906 (plate 184), had availed themselves of Indian imagery and symbolism. At the University of North Dakota, Mattson introduced many new images from American Indian life and art (fig. 51), such as Indian travois, thunderbird, Sioux calendar (plate 110, left), tobacco (plate 110, right), and many decorative, geometric and often symbolical patterns, along with innumerable other western scenes including rodeo activities and cowboy figures (plate 51).

Together, Mattson and Hammers, with Cable's support, adapted the concept of bentonite pottery for use with this imagery to produce a distinctively striking and harmonious styling, unique in the field of American art pottery in the 1930s. Presented to Crown Princess Martha of Norway, in 1939, was a bentonite vase decorated by Mattson with a buffalo motif. Gifts of Mattson bentonite vases with geese, cowboy, Indian or other regional decoration were made at Christmastime in 1932, and later years, to the Governor and other state officials, emphasizing that "this use of bentonite as a glaze for pottery is an entirely new and original idea with us." [119]

However, the University of North Dakota's vocabulary of decorative motifs in the 1930s and the 1940s was not limited exclusively to indigenous phenomena, scenes and images and Indian geometry. Viking ships (for the many purchasers of Norwegian heritage), giraffes, swans, dragons, mermaids, sea-horses, flamingos, cactus, and palm trees (plates 54; 97, left; 108; 117, right; 125; 212, right; 217) were among many devices which found their way from creative minds in Grand Forks to the surfaces of the University's pottery.

Plate 55: Animal figurines: (left) horse by Mattson, Spencer-list item # 48 (1938); (right) coyote.

Such motifs, along with emblems and commemoration legends, were also used in the adornment of souvenir paperweights and pin-trays/ashtrays (plate 53), and convention and school medallions (plate 52). For example, the buffalo-decorated pendant medallion for the North Dakota State University's "Bisons" football team (plate 65), the Indian-head for the University of North Dakota's "Sioux" (plate 64), other medallions for homecoming, women's clubs, 4H and home economics groups, together with curtain pulls (plate 66), trays and tiles, both plain and with surface patterns, were press-molded in large numbers. Animal figurines, (plates 42; 55), intended to serve as paperweights were also popular features.

Tiles for architectural use, for home decorating and for tabletops seem not to have been so important a feature at the University as they were at Rookwood, Grueby, Marblehead and other potteries. However, Cable did furnish tiles for at least one fireplace at Davis Hall on the University of North Dakota campus, in 1935, as well as others for the living rooms of her vacation home at Lake Bemidji and the house in Grand Forks, at 419 Princeton St. (plates 56; 57) she shared with her sister, Mrs. Huckfield, and their nephew Charles Cable.

This last installation features plain tiles in somber, greenish amber tones, that were highlighted by hand-decorated tiles bearing landscape scenes or embellished with personal reminders of the family's happy home life. All tiles are 6" square; thirty-eight tiles form the surround and eighteen the hearth. Immediately above the fireplace opening a row of five plain tiles is surmounted by a row of five decorated tiles forming a landscape frieze in greens, browns, ochre,

Plate 56: The tiled fireplace at 419 Princeton Street, Grand Forks.

Plate 57: Another view of the tiled fireplace.

red, blue and white. The scene is of a lake view with mountains in the background, and amongst the pine trees in the fore- and mid-ground can be seen a house on the lakeshore, with a smoking chimney, and a steepled building. Over the mountains and between the tall trees on both sides of the frieze are five lines of verse reading:

> *"Stay, stay at home my heart and rest*
> *Home-keeping hearts are happiest,*
> *For those that wander they know not where*
> *Are full of trouble and full of care;*
> *To stay at home is best."*

Two tiles on each side of the outer row of the surround, arranged vertically and descending from the top, are also scenic with tall pine trees and mountains against a late-afternoon sky; the left panel of two tiles incorporates, in addition, a human figure sitting by a campfire, while the right panel shows a campfire beside two teepees. Below these two panels, on each side of the surround, in the outer row, the second tile from the hearth also shows an illustration; on the left a fisherman and his dog, in shades of brown, labeled "Charles and Tex," and on the right a pair of caged lovebirds in dark greenish brown labeled "Trudy and Trix." The "Charles" reference is to the Cable sisters' nephew, and the other names are those of household pets. All the decoration

Plate 58: Hand-made and hand-decorated roundels by (left) Martha Ann Barr, and (right) H. Johnson.

Plate 59: Roundels: (left) "Thunder Bird", 1934, by Mattson; (right) Spencer-list item # 58, 1940, by Mattson.

of these scenic and illustrative tiles, and the dark brown colored wording are achieved by slip-trailing and slip-painting. One tile is marked "M. Cable", a second "M.K.C. 1925" and a third "M. Cable. 1925". All tiles on the hearth are dark brown. The fireplace tiles were designed and made before the house on Princeton Street was built and almost two years before the Cable sisters, mother and nephew took occupancy.

That tiles for furniture were in fact produced in the Ceramics Department, though infrequently, is attested to by two items in the catalog of the Bismarck, November 22, 1997, auction of the Ruth Schnell collection: a table-top (lot #215), 14½ inches x 18½ inches, of a Thunderbird design in a bentonite glaze, possibly by Julia Mattson, and another (lot #220), 18 x 30 inches, in a floral design by Schnell.

Plate 60: Test tiles; various marks, most with clay/glaze details; (middle left): marked "FLH".

Tea tiles, or roundels, similar to those of Paul Revere and California Faience, were popular items with both instructors and students, and are endowed with the same range of motifs, colors and glazes as plaques, souvenir items and hollow vessels. While most of these were press-molded, many were hand-pressed and some even totally hand-formed, without the aid of molds, and individually decorated (plate 58). Still others were built and decorated using bentonite slips and glazes (plate 59, left). Occasionally, hanging wall plaques were produced to commemorate University or other local events and as awards to sports and games champions (plate 177), while others might depict well-known scenes, activities and even figures in variations of Scandinavian national dress.

Small tiles and small, thin, flat slabs of clay (some of irregular shape), in a greenware state, were frequently used by students to practice and improve their expertise in various decorating and glazing techniques, then later fired; many of these are unmarked. Even smaller tiles (usually not more than 2 inches square) were very often used as test pieces for different clays and glazes, and are usually marked with appropriate formulations (plate 60). However, decorative tiles for building installation or for framing as wall decoration seem to have been produced infrequently. Of those in the University collection and private collections, most are illustrative of galleons and landscapes, etc. (plate 62), in the Marblehead and Grueby manner, produced by the slip-trailing technique, and others with designs of Oriental origin (plate 171) executed in a manner similar to that of Rhead's Jap Birdimal/Weller Faience patterns for Weller, and some of his designs from the Santa Barbara period. Two unusual, large tiles by Hildegarde Fried (plate 61) and another tile, or plaque, by her, of the same period (plate 188) are not only representative of the refined taste and craftsmanship evident in her conception and treatment of highly decorative schemes, but also unique, in terms of visual appeal and quality of execution, in the output of the School of Mines.

Plate 61: Two tiles, each 8"x 4", marked "HFD No. 655 May, 1926". Nelson Coll.

Plate 62: Tiles, 5¾" sq., framed, with slip-trailed decoration; all with impressed large, rectangular mark (for tiles), and painted marks (left to right) T.233, T.234, T.235. UND Coll. # C-MSC 205 797(-799).

Endnotes

110 *Fired by Ideals*, by Suzanne Baizerman, Lynn Downey and John Toki, Part IV: "The Pottery and Tile from the Arequipa Sanatorium," by Suzanne Baizerman.

111 Cable letter dated January 23, 1926, to President Thomas F. Kane.

112 At that time (and up to 1918) at the Mechanics Institute in Rochester, New York.

113 *Keramic Studio*, I, 1899. "Newcomb Pottery."

114 Sales brochure, 1919: *Marblehead Pottery: An American Industrial Art of Distinction.*

115 *Journal of the Decorative and Propaganda Arts*, Volume 20, 1994: "Myths of Style and Nationalism: American Art Pottery at the Turn of the Century," by Martin Eidelberg.

116 As explained by Cable in her letter dated March 14, 1927, to the Memorial Art Gallery, in Rochester, New York, regarding its exhibit, among other UND pieces, of the "North Dakota Products Vase."

117 Cable letter dated March 5, 1930.

118 Paul Cox letter of late-November, 1926, to Adelaide Ehrich.

119 Cable letter dated December 8, 1932.

On moving to Grand Forks in 1910, Margaret Cable first roomed at Macnie Hall (spelled incorrectly on postcard).

PART VII

Sales and Pricing

In contrast to the policies effective at Newcomb College and Iowa State College, the School of Mines, from the inception of the Ceramics Department, did not envisage the sale of its pottery. In a letter to Marblehead dated November 25, 1911, Cable wrote: "It is understood, of course, that these little tea sets which the students are making are not for sale. Each student is aiming to finish up a set or two for Christmas gifts, but none of the work is anywhere for sale."[120] Very soon, however, Cable came to realize that there might be a demand for the Department's pottery, and decided that pieces made by her, or other staff, might be made available for sale through "direct personal contact." The Board of Administration agreed to permit such sales at the University, and items were kept "in our laboratory" on the "pottery sales shelf."[121] By 1920, the Department had opened an account (known as the "Pottery Sales Fund") into which proceeds from these sales could be deposited (fig. 38).

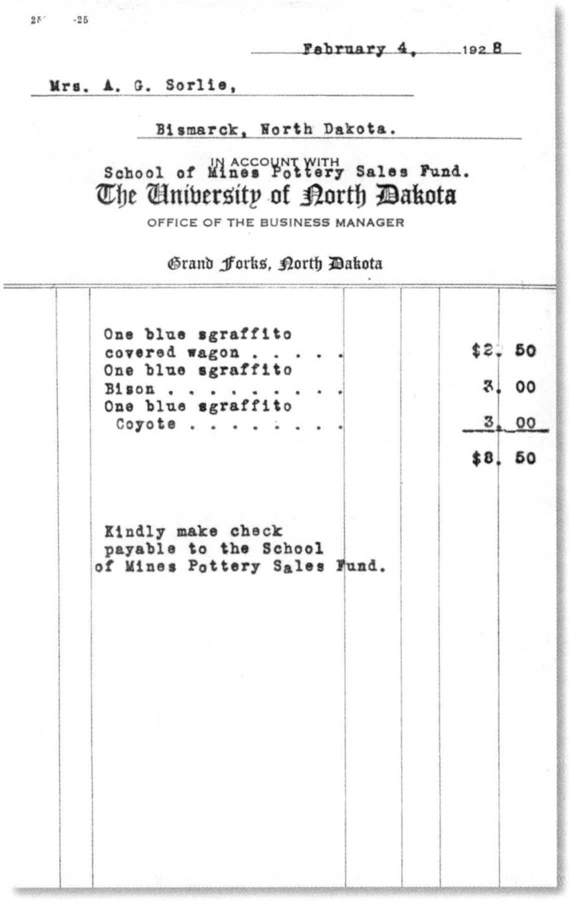

February 4, 1928

Mrs. A. G. Sorlie,

Bismarck, North Dakota.

IN ACCOUNT WITH
School of Mines Pottery Sales Fund.
The University of North Dakota
OFFICE OF THE BUSINESS MANAGER
Grand Forks, North Dakota

One blue sgraffito covered wagon	$2. 50
One blue sgraffito Bison	3. 00
One blue sgraffito Coyote	3. 00
	$8. 50

Kindly make check payable to the School of Mines Pottery Sales Fund.

Fig. 38: Invoice dated February 4, 1928, to the wife of Gov. Sorlie, requesting payment to the Pottery Sales Fund.

Even so, at that time, sales were not encouraged: "The Department does not make a business of selling pottery but occasionally does so at special requests."[122] The aggravations of commerce were not to Cable's liking and she resented the time taken away from her research and teaching duties. In answer to a customer questioning the pricing of her purchases, Cable replied: "I am sorry to have had this occur but it was no doubt due to the fact that your original letter reached me at a very busy time and the amounts which you suggested spending for the pieces were so meager that it made a selection very difficult."[123]

The Department's view of sales began to change gradually during the early 1920s, and, in 1925, when the Department was short of funds, "such sales added quite materially to our depleted income."[124]

The following year, in a budget proposal to Prof E. F. Chandler, Cable suggested that a pay increase for Huckfield, as supervisor of wares made for sale, could "be taken care of from the Pottery Sales Fund."[125] Also, in 1926, Cable indicated to Dr. A. W. Gauger that since "the Administration is in favor of encouraging the sale of pottery," this could be accomplished by "placing it on display" and offering it for sale in selected shops "in a few of the larger cities in the state such as Bismarck, Fargo, Valley City, Dickinson, Minot and the like."[126] Prices could be regulated by having the shop owners handle sales on a commission basis, and there would be no question of competition with any similar product. Cable's proposal was adopted, and, in 1927, she wrote to Professor

Parmelee of the University of Illinois: "Next year...we are going in for the commercial sale of our art pottery," [127] such sale at that time to be of the "limited amount of ware...made by the regular staff of the Ceramic Department." [128] The first shop to offer the University's pottery for sale, in 1927, was the Specialty Shop at the Hotel Prince, in Bismarck.

Most of the wares available for sale were at first undecorated, and were priced "from $1.00 to $2.00 for the smaller pieces, up to $3.00 to $4.00 for medium size vessels;" [129] the price of the occasional decorated pot being "generally double that of an undecorated one." [130] In the period 1927-1928, a total number of one thousand seven hundred and eighty-five glazed pots was fired, as sales had slowly grown, but more importantly during this time an auspicious turning point in the fortunes of the Ceramics Department occurred.

Fig. 39: Display of pottery (possibly for sale) in the Ceramics Department. UAP # 2348.

With reliable, trained staff on salary, with the Department's reputation and its product highly respected throughout the area, and with the Administration's backing for an expanded sales system, Cable was able to accept, with the University's authorization, a large special commission from Ralph Budd, President of the Great Northern Railroad Company, to supply souvenir items for sale at hotel-shops in Glacier National Park. It is believed that a small number of possibly unique vases was also produced and made available for sale, presumably at Ralph Budd's suggestion. These were decorated (principally by incising or low-relief carving) with local imagery -- particularly animal representation. Sales, however, due to the necessarily higher costs must have been unsuccessful, in contrast with those of the souvenir items.

Many special orders were received and filled from that time on, and through the remaining years of Cable's tenure. Most notably, during the Depression, the commercial production of medallions, other commemorative items, and souvenirs (plate 63) boosted sales at a time when income was necessary for the continuation of the ceramics program.

Prior to 1929, all information required for the production of each specific pottery model was detailed on a "Glaze Record Sheet," and in that year a new type of pricing document was instituted, taking into account the costs of materials used and time allocated, and also allowing for the discount to be applied by the selling dealer. A review of these later "Cost Data Sheets" (figs. 41; 45; 51), [131] is useful in gauging the extent of the economies applied during the years of the Depression. For instance, in the academic year 1928-1929 the price of Mattson's pieces averaged $3.26, and in 1934-1935 the average price was 92 cents per piece.

Fig. 40: Display of pottery (possibly for sale) in the Ceramics Department. UAP # 2350.

At first the dealer's discount, or more accurately, the commission granted to the dealer by the University on sales was 25%, then raised to 33¹/₃% by the beginning of 1930. But with the effect of the Depression already being felt by the end of 1931, and increasing during the next couple of years, the commission rate reverted to 20%.

Cable attempted to explain the difficult situation in which both the Department and its customers found themselves: "About price, of course, you must realize we just can't compete with ware made on a quantity production basis, such as Roseville, Weller, etc., or the cheap Italian, German, Jap (sic) and other foreign goods which now flood our markets. Stacked up against Newcomb, Cowan, Paul Revere or even Rookwood, our prices are lower and our quality comparable. But irrespective of other wares and their prices, we find that our margin is generally less than the 20% commission the dealer is allowed for handling. For example on a $3.00 pot the dealer gets 60 cents; our margin of profit runs around 30 cents to 45 cents. We have all the trouble of making; we pack, pay express and allow the dealer to return pieces that do not move within a reasonable time… We only carry on because this is a testing laboratory of North Dakota clays and by making pottery in a small way we are proving out their worth and quality in the hope of laying the foundation for and encouraging the future development of a ceramic industry in North Dakota." [132]

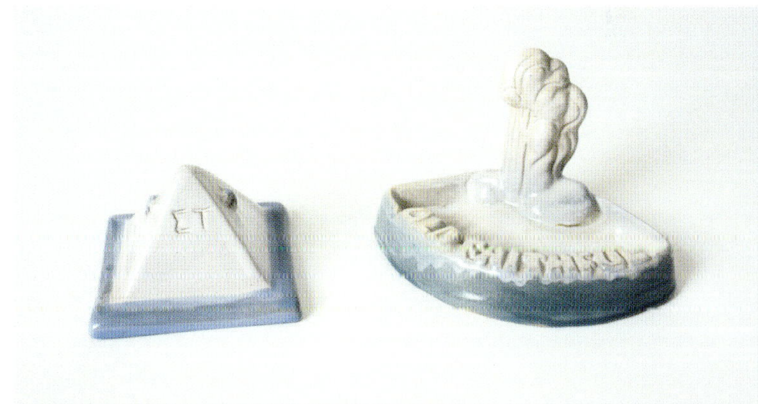

Plate 63: (Left) Sigma Tau paperweight; (right) Old Faithful pin-tray/ashtray.

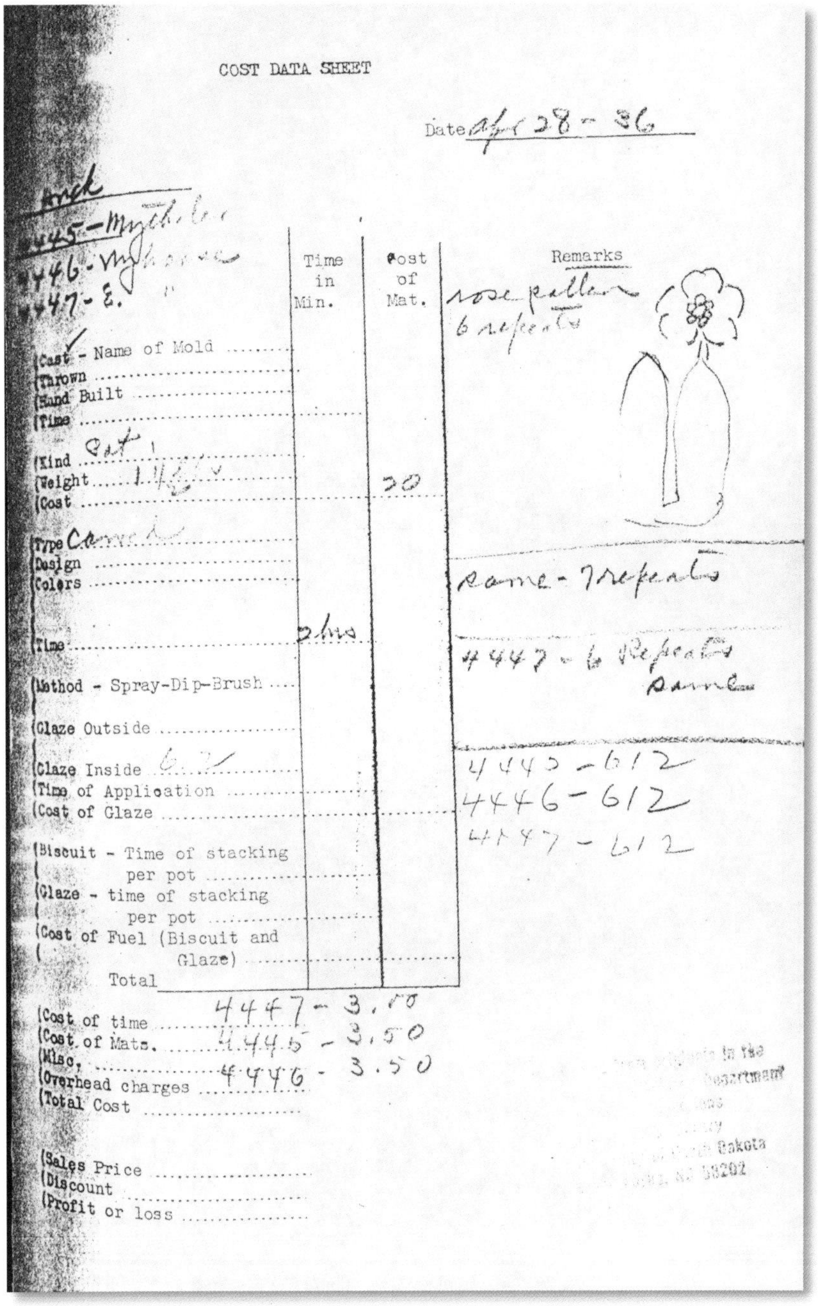
COST DATA SHEET

Date Apr 28 - 36

4445 - Mych...
4446 - ...
4447 - ...

	Time in Min.	Cost of Mat.	Remarks
Cast - Name of Mold			rose pattern 6 repeats
Thrown			
Hand Built			
Time			
Kind			
Weight		20	
Cost			
Type			
Design			same - 7 repeats
Colors			
Time	2 hrs		4447 - 6 Repeats same
Method - Spray-Dip-Brush			
Glaze Outside			
Glaze Inside			4445 - 612
Time of Application			4446 - 612
Cost of Glaze			4447 - 612
Biscuit - Time of stacking per pot			
Glaze - time of stacking per pot			
Cost of Fuel (Biscuit and Glaze)			
Total			

Cost of time ... 4447 - 3.50
Cost of Mats. ... 4445 - 3.50
Misc. ...
Overhead charges ... 4446 - 3.50
Total Cost ...

Sales Price ...
Discount ...
Profit or loss ...

Fig. 41: Cost Data Sheet for Huckfield vases # 4445-4447, dated April 28, 1936. (See also Plate 25.)

Despite Cable's explanation, protests concerning the reduction in the commission rate to 20% continued, and by the fall of 1933, the rate was raised to 30%, and the retail prices charged by the shops were reduced to encourage sales. The What-Not-Shop, in Valley City, received twelve shipments from the University between December 2, 1929, and December 1, 1932; these consisted of one hundred and sixty-seven items at a retail price of $446.75. Checks received from the What-Not-Shop between January 6, 1930 and March 1, 1933 totaled $512.17; and between October 26, 1931 and January 2, 1933, seventy-six pieces, calculated at a retail price of $368.00 were returned unsold to Grand Forks. The shops were experiencing great difficulty in selling the more expensive items at prices between $4.00 and $6.00 per piece, and the commission on items priced below that range was not substantial. Cable continued to point out that: "As things work out the commission of the dealer is frequently double the margin which we get on the pieces and this without counting the express on out-going shipments." [133] Nevertheless, by 1936-1937, invoices were showing discounts of 40%.

Sales were vital to the survival of the program, as funding was already limited by the fall of 1933, and the Department needed to compensate for this through greater partial self-financing. In January, 1935, Cable noted, "in the last session our funds were cut out entirely." To create revenue in the Pottery Sales Fund sales efforts had to be strengthened even further, if not through the shops, then through personal contacts (figs. 42; 43) at exhibitions, shows, etc.

At the Chicago World's Fair in 1933, which Cable said "was no snap," [134] she was able, in intervals between lectures and demonstrations, to sell sixty items at a total price of $118.25 between June 20 and August 20, and a small number of pieces were sold by other people, making a grand total of $141.75 by October 16; during the last two weeks before the Exposition closed on November 12, 1933, the prices of the remaining items were reduced to 50%, without much success. As the

Fig. 42: Pottery exhibit with Cable throwing at the wheel. UAP # 2352.

Fig. 43: Huckfield, Mattson and Cable (left to right) in attendance at an exhibit. UAP # 2465.

Feb. 8, 1938

List of Sample Pottery

A. E. Spencer
1612 Rebecca
Sioux City, Iowa

Sample No.	Maker	Shape	Design	Color	Price
1	JM	Tall Vase	Cowboys - carved	Green Matt	$5.00
2	JM	Large Bowl	Buffalo - carved	Green Matt	4.00
3	JM	Medium Bowl	Buffalo - sgraffito	Blue or cream on red	3.00
4	JM	Small Bowl	Coyote - sgraffito	" "	2.00
5	JM	Medium Bowl	Cowboys - sgraffito	" "	2.50
6	JM	Small Bowl	Wild Goose - sgraffito	" " "	1.50
7	JM	Small Bowl	Conventional - carved	Blue - green	1.00
8	JM	Medium Bowl	Conventional - incised	Blue	1.25
9	JM	Medium Bowl	Conventional - incised	Ivory	1.25
10	JM	Small Vase	Plain	Ivory or Blue	.75
11	JM	Small Bowl	Conventional - incised	Lavendar	.75
12	JM	Bird	Pelican	Blue-green or Ivory	.50
13 AandB	JM	Figure	Cowboy	Bentonite Ivory	1.00 .75
14	Huck	Plate	Conventional Rose - sgraffito	Blue on red	1.50
15	Huck	Tile	Rose - Glaze Painted	Blue and gray	1.00
16	Huck	Ash tray	Indian - carved	Blue - Ivory Blue green Lavendar Matt Brown Matt Green	.50
17	Huck	Paperweight	4 H Club	Green	.25
18	Cable	Large Fruit-Bowl	Waves - thrown on wheel and - carved	Ivory or Blue green	6.00
19	Cable	Medium Fruit-Bowl	Conventional - Thrown on wheel	Ivory	4.00
20		Small Fruit Bowl	Conventional Rose - thrown on - wheel and incised	Blue green	3.00
21 AandB	Cable	Large Bowl and-Wild Goose	Plain	Blue green	5.00
22	Cable	Medium Vase	Deer - carved	Brown or green	4.00
23	Cable	Small Vase	Plain	Blue - Ivory Blue green Lavendar Matt Brown Matt Green	.25
24	Cable	Small Vase	Plain	Blue - Ivory Blue green Lavendar Matt Brown Matt Green	.25
25	Cable	Seal	University	6 colors as in Nos. 16, 23, 24.	.25

Fig. 44: Sample-pottery list attached to Dean Harrington's letter dated February 8, 1938, to Mr. Austin E. Spencer.

Depression deepened, and delinquent accounts continued, Cable redoubled her efforts to solicit commissions for the production of souvenir items and medallions. The monthly sales reports of the period 1935-1937 principally concerned such items as ashtrays, custard cups, paperweights, nut dishes, Park souvenirs and Parents' Day medallions in the ten to twenty-five cent range – inclusive of the applicable dealer's discount. Almost all sales of other, non-commissioned pottery in the mid- to late-1930's were under $3.00 per item, though exceptions such as the sale of "#355 Cable buffalo pot Bentonite" at $20.00 through the Luger Furniture Co., in Fargo, in the spring of 1936, did occasionally raise spirits.

Economies imposed on the Ceramics Department by the University even resulted in the Administration's 1936 reminder to the staff members of the Department that they could retain for personal purposes not more than four pieces per year without cost. Though course fees presumably covered the cost of materials used by students, their work, too, in a very limited quantity and only if considered by Cable to have commercial potential and to be suitably representative of the Department's output, had for several years been offered for sale. According to Marie Fiedler, a student in the early 1930's, "each student had to learn at least one basic pottery making operation thoroughly each semester...(was) also required to contribute...one piece of pottery for sale." [135]

By the fall of 1937, despite the Department's best efforts to sustain itself through its tireless negotiation with the dealerships, steady acceptance of special commissions, and encouragement of increased enrollment by the faculty community and townspeople, revenue was barely sufficient for the continuation of the program. A new approach to expanding sales without increasing the already heavy burden on Cable, Mattson and Huckfield, was initiated with the appointment of Austin E. Spencer of Sioux City, Iowa, as "traveling representative" for sales in the territory of North and South Dakota, Nebraska, Iowa and Minnesota. Spencer would be paid a commission of 10% on all sales in this territory – with the exception of the city of Grand Forks – "we to ship directly to customer who pays transportation charges," and "we to bill customer direct, allowing a 40% discount, cash 30 days, and an additional 2% discount, cash 10 days." [136] Enclosed with Spencer's letter of appointment was a list (fig. 44) of the first shipment of samples sent to him, comprising 27 pieces (items #1-25, with #13A and #21A) by Mattson, Huckfield and Cable, and ranging in price from 25 cents to $6.00.

Form letters were dispatched to the shops introducing Spencer and announcing the change in sales policy from "commission basis to a direct sales basis." Spencer was quickly able to capitalize on his many years of experience in selling china and pottery in the region, [137] and within the first two months submitted fourteen orders for a total of $478.55. The What-Not-Shop, in Valley City, which in the preceding ten years had received thirty-five shipments totaling one thousand one hundred and twenty-nine pieces, continued to be the Department's best customer during the Spencer years; many other accounts were reinvigorated and many new ones initiated, especially during the war years and the mid-1940s.

At the time of Spencer's appointment, Cable introduced a new inventory numbering system, building on the February 8, 1938, list of sample pottery sent to him, and beginning with "#1: Mattson Cowboy Vase" on February 23, 1938. In the next eleven years a total of not less than three hundred and seven items, mainly molded but including some handmade forms, was listed up to #248 – including at least fifty-nine items with suffixed numbers ("A", "B", "C" and "D") indicating a difference in size, a related shape, or a change from plain to decorated form. For

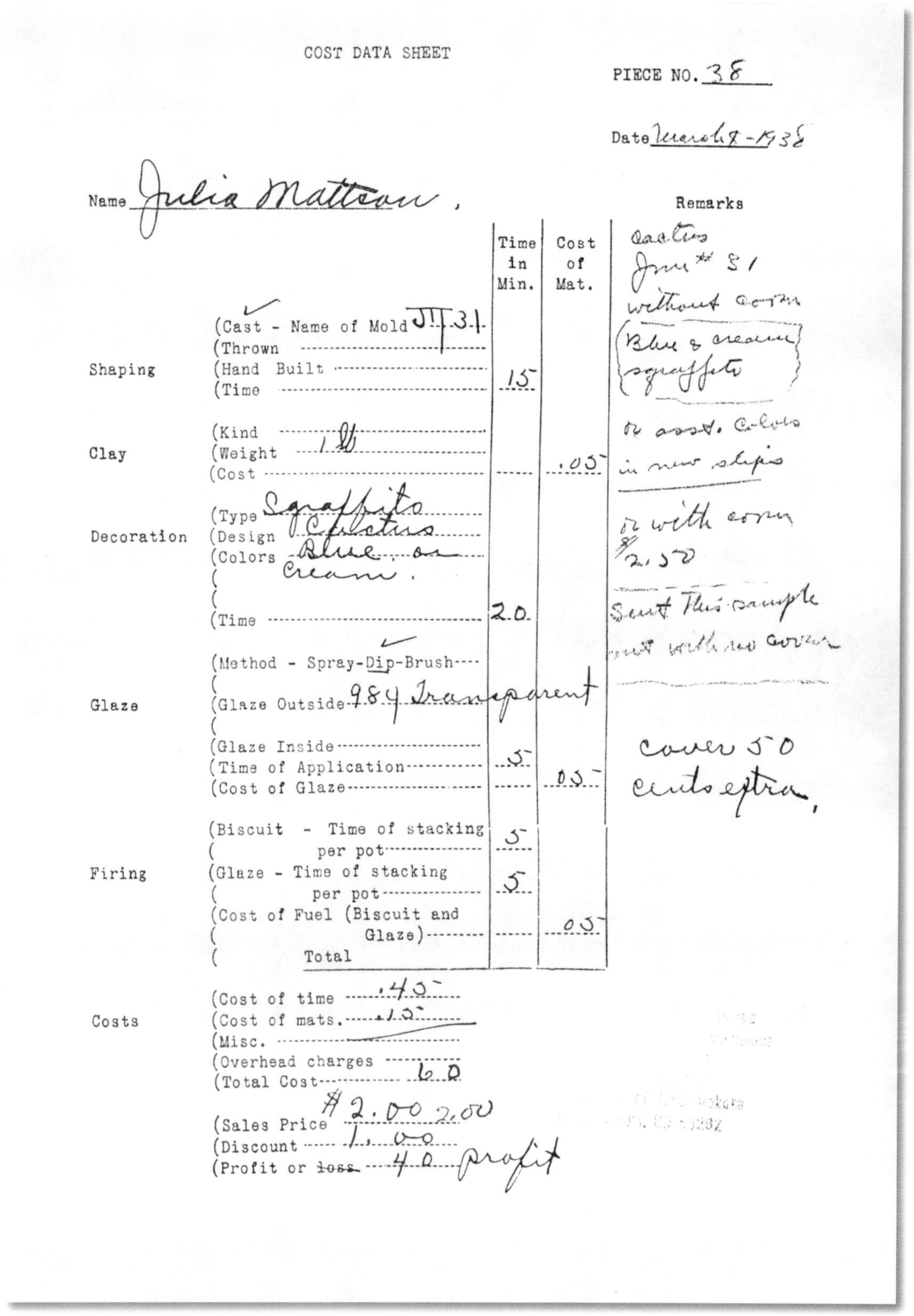

COST DATA SHEET

PIECE NO. 38

Date March 8 - 1938

Name Julia Mattson.

		Time in Min.	Cost of Mat.	Remarks
Shaping	(Cast - Name of Mold JT 31 ✓			Cactus Jar # 31 without cover
	(Thrown			(Blue & cream sgraffito)
	(Hand Built	15		
	(Time			
Clay	(Kind			or asst. colors in new slips
	(Weight 1 lb			
	(Cost		.05	
Decoration	(Type Sgraffito			or with cover $2.50
	(Design Cactus			
	(Colors Blue on cream.			
	(Time	20		Sent this sample out with no cover
Glaze	(Method - Spray-Dip-Brush ✓			
	(Glaze Outside 984 Transparent			
	(Glaze Inside			cover 50 cents extra.
	(Time of Application	5		
	(Cost of Glaze		.05	
Firing	(Biscuit - Time of stacking per pot	5		
	(Glaze - Time of stacking per pot	5		
	(Cost of Fuel (Biscuit and Glaze)		.05	
	Total			

Costs	
(Cost of time	.45
(Cost of mats.	.15
(Misc.	
(Overhead charges	
(Total Cost	.60
(Sales Price	$2.00 2.00
(Discount	1.00
(Profit or ~~loss~~	.40 profit

Fig. 45: Cost Data Sheet for Spencer-list item # 38. (See also plate 97, left.)

example, Huckfield's molds #47 and #47A, are, respectively, for a plain vase and for the same shape with wheat design. The molded items on the list were designed and selected with an eye, particularly, towards merging mass production with handcraftsmanship. Of the total number of models listed, eighty-two items were by Cable, sixty-one by Mattson, forty-three by Huckfield and one hundred twenty-one listed as being by not less than eighty-two other names. Other information on items in the Spencer sample list can be gleaned from the appropriate Cost Data Sheets (fig. 45) of that period, such as the indication on that dated October 10, 1943, for #175, "Why Not Minot" design, that this "new mold with pattern in it" was based on an earlier mold of Mattson's.

Plate 64: Medallions/pendants for UND Sioux.

Sales resulting from special orders also increased in the late 1930s. Between 1938 and 1940, the Department produced, among other such items, 865 Parents' Day plaques (valued at $147.05), 500 P.E.O. paperweights ($75.00), 2,300 football plaques ($186.31), 200 goat medallions (plate 65) for the Non-Partisan League Convention ($25.12), 1,000 Daughters of Norway plaques ($150.00) and 5,000 Sakakawea [138] medallions (plate 66) for the North Dakota Federation of Women's Clubs ($750.00); an additional 1,000 medallions for the G.O.P. were produced and delivered, though the invoice was still unpaid two years later. Similar commissions for emblem trays, paperweights, trophies, awards and medallions, from many other organizations including the Association of Rebekah Assemblies, University of North Dakota football "Sioux" (plate 64) and the North Dakota State University football "Bisons" (plate 65), the Minot Art Club, KEM Temple, and various fraternities, continued through the early and mid-1940s, as did pottery sales from exhibits in Grand Forks such as the Ceramic Open House held annually, on Engineers' Day, in the basement of Babcock Hall.

Furthermore, opportunities for sales beyond the Upper Midwest also occurred at the end of the 1930s: firstly, when a shipment of thirty-three items, at a price of $56.75 less 40%, was sent to Altman & Co., in New York City, in March of 1939 (the first University of North Dakota pottery shown in New York City since an exhibition at W. & J. Sloane in 1931); and secondly, with an approach from America Designs, Inc., also of New York City, in the spring of 1940. This latter company, under the leadership of Russel Wright, was planning an "American Way" craft collection for sale at such major department stores throughout the eastern United States as Macy's, Higbee's, Filene's and Strawbridge and Clothier. The promotion, which was nationally advertised in such magazines as *House Beautiful* (October, 1940), and launched that year by Eleanor

Plate 65: Medallions/pendants for NDSU Bisons, Non-Partisan League, Home Economics Class; curtain pulls/pendants.

Roosevelt in New York City, represented a collaboration between American designers, craftspeople, industry and retailers in an attempt "to create contemporary home furnishings for the American way of life" according to promotional material of 1940, and to uncover "a middle way between the ultra-sophisticated and the truly rural." [139] It had three aims: "the mass production of original designs by both well-known and unknown craftspeople and designers, the creation of a national distribution network for the merchandise, and a co-ordinated promotional campaign." [140] Sixteen samples of Prairie Pottery (fig. 46), along with descriptive literature, were submitted for consideration by America Designs, Inc., and, of these, three pieces, all bentonite, were selected – a plate and a bowl by Mattson, and a bowl by Cable signed "Maggie Mud". The undertaking, however, proved to be fraught with disappointing and time-taking contractual and delivery problems, and was ultimately unsuccessful from the University's point of view. Cable asked Russel Wright to discontinue the sale of the University's three models and to return the samples.

The war years brought new difficulties for Cable and problems for the Ceramics Department. No replacement was hired to fill Hammers' position -- Hammers had been absent due to illness for well over a year before her retirement in 1941 -- so Cable, Mattson and Huckfield had to assume additional duties. Labor shortages were severe, to the extent that, in 1941-1942, Cable found herself digging and bagging clay and transporting it back to Grand Forks in her old car "Polly," -- perhaps not for the first time, but at this time she was fifty-seven years old. Availability of fuel for the kilns, and gas for deliveries, was limited, as were equipment supplies and spare parts. Enrollment in Departmental courses was down -- in spite of encouragement to townswomen -- and Cable herself suffered several bouts of illness. In 1945-1946, delivery and installation of the new kiln was delayed by over eighteen months due to steel shortages, coal strikes and unavailability of manpower. New customers were often referred by Cable to other sources such as Rosemeade, as the University of North Dakota was unable to keep up with demand.

Nevertheless, Cable led her Department through the usual rounds of pottery making and teaching, as conditions allowed, and also participated in outside exhibitions and demonstrations. Efforts were still made by the Department to promote the economic opportunities offered by its research and development. Spencer, through these years, made regular visits to established and potential dealerships, showing samples of each available model number, writing up orders, transferring items from one shop to another, or returning them to Grand Forks for credit. His relationship with the University of North Dakota ended with Cable's retirement, effective July

1, 1949. The invoice-copy dated May 27, 1949, covering his last sale to A. W. Lucas, Bismarck, bears the notation "Spencer paid up to date June 1949."

Plate GG. Sakakawea pendant; curtain pulls/pendants (bottom right: Business and Professional Women Convention, Grand Forks, 1939).

In preparation for Cable's departure from the University of North Dakota, an administrative decision had been made to discontinue the emphasis on what Dean Harrington considered, in his letter of May 25, 1949, to be the large-scale production of pottery for sale. Nevertheless, Mattson was still pouring molds, including many by Cable, through November, 1956, and making shipments of pottery to dealers and other purchasers through at least August, 1960. And already by the time of Mattson's retirement in 1963, the era of pottery sales at the University had effectively ended. In the previously cited letter of April 4, 1972, to Mrs. Darlene Dommel, Mrs. Koth, Administrative Assistant, wrote: "...while some pottery is still being produced in the Ceramics Department, there is very little being made for sale."

Fig. 46: Margaret Cable, on front steps of Babcock Hall, showing examples of Prairie Pottery submitted to America Designs, Inc., c. 1940. UAP # 2460.

TO MARGARET CABLE DR.

Expenses in connection with N. D. A. E. Meeting at Bismarck, No. Dak. October 25 to 30, 1927.

Oct. 25	Railroad fare Grand Forks to Fargo and return - - - - - - - - - - - -	$ 4.23
	Bus in Fargo - - - - - - - - - - - - - - - - -	.35
	Dinner -	.90
	Railroad fare Fargo to Bismarck and return-	10.50
	Bus to hotelat Bismarck - - - - - - - - - - -	.35
Oct. 26	Meal -	.40
	Meal -	.65
Oct. 27	Meal -	.50
	Meal -	.65
	Meal -	.75
Oct. 28	Meal -	.50
	Meal -	.60
	Meal -	.80
	Taxi to Capitol - - - - - - - - - - - - - - - -	.35
	Taxi Capitol to town - - - - - - - - - - - -	.35
Oct. 29	Breakfast - - - - - - - - - - - - - - - - - - -	.50
	Taxi to Capitol - - - - - - - - - - - - - - - -	.35
	Drayage Oct. 25, 26, 27, - - - - - - - - - -	2.00
	Prince Hotel, 4 nights at $3.00 and one meal	12.50
	Hotel at Fargo - - - - - - - - - - - - - - - -	1.50
	Taxi Fargo station to hotel - - - - - - - -	.35
Oct. 30	Fargo taxi hotel to station - - - - - - - -	.35
	Express Grand Forks to Bismarck - - - - -	9.93
	Express Bismarck to Grand Forks - - - - -	8.36
	Total - - - - - - - - -	$57.72

Cable's reimbursement claim for expenses (travel, lodging and meals -- October 25-30, 1927).

Pottery sent to American Ceramic Society Meeting
Chicago, Illinois. January 30, 1929

Student pieces

1. Mary Stephens plain vase, black and yellow, gloss- - - 4.00
2. Lila Argue decorated vase, bees and clover, yellow matt - - 6.00
3. Mrs. Coon decorated vase, harvest scenes, brown matt - 8.00
4. Cora Spriggs incised jar 7 symbols - - - - - - - - - - 2.50
5. Eunice Gronvold decorated jar, four seasons,green matt 6.00
6. Sylvia Adams, incised tile - - - - - - - - - - - - - - 2.00

Staff

7. Mrs. Huckfield carved jar, sea horses, alkaline blue - 10.00
8. Freida Hammers decorated jar, conventional design, alkaline blue - - - - - - - - - - - - - - -- 2.50
9. Julia Mattson decorated bowl, alkaline glazes - - - - 3.00
10. Julia Mattson, decorated bowl, matt grey, - - - - - -- 3.00
11. Julia Mattson, sgraffito coyote - - - - - - - - - - - - 3.00
12. Julia Mattson, sgraffito cowboy - - - - - - - - - - - 5.00
13. Julia Mattson, sgraffito conventional - - - - - - - - 3.00
14. M. Cable decorated jar, Egyptian blue - - - - - - - - 2.50
15. M. Cable carved jar, prairie dogs, matt green - - - - 10.00

Returned ok C

Listing of pottery items (by staff and students) exhibited at the meeting of the American Ceramic Society in Chicago, January 1929; safe return of items to Grand Forks acknowledged by Cable. For an indication of the cost of living during the period 1927-1929, compare these values with expenses of travel, lodging and meals listed on Cable's reimbursement claim on opposite page.

Endnotes

120 Cable letter dated November 25, 1911.
121 Cable letter dated October 28, 1926, to Dr. A. W. Gauger.
122 Cable letter dated December 15, 1920.
123 Cable letter dated January 6, 1921.
124 Cable letter dated October 28, 1926, to Dr. A. W. Gauger.
125 Cable letter dated April 21, 1926, to Prof. E. F. Chandler.
126 Cable letter dated October 28, 1926, to Dr. A. W. Gauger.
127 Cable letter dated May 10, 1927.
128 Cable letter dated February 1, 1927.
129 Cable letter dated January 29, 1927, to Mrs. Adele Zimmerman.
130 Cable letter dated January 29, 1927, to Mrs. Lewis H. Paige.
131 Presently located at the Elwyn B. Robinson Department of Special Collections at the Chester Fritz Library, in Grand Forks.
132 Cable letter dated February 1, 1933, to Mrs. Stella Roseland of the Luger Furniture Co., in Fargo.
133 Cable letter dated March 22, 1934, to the What-Not-Shop.
134 Cable letter dated June 1, 1934.
135 *Journal of the American Art Pottery Association*, Volume 8, No. 1, 1993: "Two UND Artists," by Scott H. Nelson.
136 Dean L. C. Harrington's letter dated February 8, 1938, to Austin Spencer.
137 Cable letter dated December 18, 1939, to John Frank of Frankoma Potteries, regarding a reference for Spencer, and adding: "You will find Mr. Spencer a very delightful gentleman and absolutely reliable in every way. He must be around 50 or 55 and has sold china and pottery in this region for many years."
138 Sakakawea was a Shoshone, adopted as a child by the Hidatsa, who identified herself as Hidatsa, and who was recognized as such by Hidatsa custom; the "Bird Woman" is celebrated for the significant role she played in the success of the Lewis and Clark Expedition in 1804-1806.
139 *Guide to Easier Living*, by Russel and Mary Wright.
140 *Russel Wright creating American Lifestyle*, by Donald Albrecht, Robert Schonfeld, Lindsay Stamm Shapiro.

PART VIII

Beneficiaries of the Ceramics Program at the University of North Dakota

A. The Brick Industry

The *Grand Forks Daily Herald* in its February 12, 1923, edition featured an article entitled "Valuable Clay Deposits in ND; Second Only to Deposits of Lignite Coal," in which attention was drawn to the "easily mined locations within the state" for different kinds and grades of clay. Paving brick and fire brick clays were widespread, as were also brick clay for brick, terra cotta and other construction material, fine white clays for pressed brick, clay for pottery and semi-porous ware such as drain tile, flower pots, redware, etc., and stoneware clays for sewer pipe, white earthenware, etc.

Plate 67: (Left) promotional bricklet; (right) small test jar for glaze # 1034A with color additives # 9-16, marked "JMattson 1935".

By 1892, twenty-four brick plants had been established in North Dakota due to the plentiful supplies of local clays available for processing. By the end of the century, and for the next ten to twenty years, a thriving brick industry was in position to support the building boom in Grand Forks and some other cities. One of the more prominent companies at that time – growing out of the 1892 Dakota Land and Colonization Co. brick plant – was the Dickinson Fire and Processed Brick Co., founded in 1898, and which later became the Dickinson Clay Products Co.

The development of the industry was greatly assisted by research and experimentation on the selection and refinement of native minerals and improved methods of production, conducted by Earle Babcock when he was State Geologist and Dean of the School of Mines. After the establishment of the Ceramics Department, Babcock continued this work, aided by Margaret Cable and later by Hildegarde Fried. In her "Post-War Ceramic Opportunities in North Dakota," Cable wrote: "...clay is indispensable to man...Bricks, as in the days of old, are unexcelled for building purposes...He relies upon it for the tiles on his roof and the porous tile to drain his land, for the dishes on his table, the crockery in his kitchen, the bricks and flue tile of his chimney, the lining of his furnace, the sanitary fixtures in his bathroom, and the sewer pipe to drain the plumbing system...porcelain spark plugs...insulators...vats...crucibles..."

Cable explained how the work of her Department was divided: "We have also felt that if we could prove, in our research work with our high grade clays, their fitness for the more exacting and more beautiful types of products, we could, with comparative ease, work downward in

Plate 68: WPA vases. SHSND Coll. # 8846 & 8842.

our research into these types of clays fitted for the more common products."[141] But by the 1930s the emphasis on the production of ceramics had increased within the Department, and research and testing of brick, building block, sewer tile, etc., had become more properly the concern of the more technical/industrial sections of the Engineering Department. The brick industry in North Dakota gradually declined as the twentieth century progressed, and today the only survivor is the Hebron Brick Co., founded in 1904.

B. **WPA (Works Progress Administration) Ceramics Project**

During the Depression, as part of President Franklin D. Roosevelt's New Deal to assist artists in need and train craftsmen for employment, Federal Arts Projects were established in various areas of the United States by the Works Progress Administration. In 1936, Professor William Budge, director of the Ceramic Engineering Department at the University of North Dakota, who had been appointed to organize the WPA's ceramic project in North Dakota, named Laura Taylor State Supervisor of the WPA/FAP in Dickinson, and later in Mandan.

Taylor had earlier studied at the State Teachers College in Valley City and had taken classes -- "in pottery built up with coils and finished on the potter's wheel" -- under Glen Lukens, [142] before enrolling to study art and ceramics, in 1931, at the University of North Dakota. In 1933, she was a student assistant. At Dickinson (for the first six months) and then at Mandan, she gave instruction in the design and making of pottery to a group of previously untrained craftspeople in the hope that their experience, so gained, would assist them in earning a livelihood. Assistance was rendered, as early as 1936, by Cable and Hammers, who prepared Instructions for "Summer Work in Ceramics Department -WPA," and for "Kiln Stacking" and "Kiln Firing," and who also provided information on materials for Taylor's benefit. At first all items had to be sent to the University or to the Dickinson Clay Products Co., for bisque and glaze firing, and the finished products – nursery rhyme figural groups (Old King Cole, Humpty Dumpty, Little Jack Horner, Peter the Pumpkin Eater, etc.), animal figures, vases, bowls, pitchers, coffee sets and custard cups (plates 68 through 72) – could be dispersed to such designated destinations as schools, libraries and other public buildings and put on display, or used in hot lunch programs. By the end of 1936, as reported in the *Mandan Daily Pioneer* of January 13, 1937, nine regularly employed WPA workers were enrolled as members of Taylor's pottery class; and a second lot of approximately 150 pieces was being prepared for shipment to the University. Some WPA items were both made and fired at the University, including some of the thirteen pieces sent, in 1936, and also some of the forty-eight pieces sent later, in 1939, for exhibit in Washington, DC. In spite of the frequent production delays at the time, caused by the shortages of the Depression era, supplies of WPA products were finished and twenty-two such items, for example, were sent in April 1939, as part of the NYA (National Youth Administration) Work Project pottery exhibition, to Public School

#61 in Woodhaven, Queens, Long Island, New York.

Plate 69: WPA vases.

In 1939, when Taylor was requested, by the WPA to go to New York to demonstrate throwing at the wheel at the opening of the World's Fair, she was replaced in Mandan by another of Margaret Cable's former students, Charles Grantier. At this time, the WPA greenware was still being sent for firing at the University or in the kiln at Standing Rock Indian School in Fort Yates. This involved long-distance transportation, often over dirt and gravel roads. Losses due to breakage were extremely high; Cable added a note on Dean Harrington's letter of June 9, 1939, to the WPA at Bismarck: "At least half of the pottery received lately has been broken due to faulty packing." Under Grantier's direction, a complete studio, where the total process of pottery-making could be completed, was established by mid-1940, and the Mandan project "complete in its own right and under one roof" -- began firing "in the portable kiln recently purchased." [143] In 1941, in an article in the Bismarck *Tribune* of May 31, entitled "From Ugly Native Clay -- Ceramic Artisans Fashion Works of Beauty in Mandan WPA Project," it was reported that twelve craftsmen and women were working under Charles Grantier in the WPA ceramics project described as the "only one of its kind in the state and one of the few operating in the country." The article went on to explain how, on average per day, 75 finished products were made of clay, dug from a location nine miles west of Mandan. The process consisted of mixing the clay with water until thoroughly saturated and then filtering it through several screens to produce clay slip for casting; alternatively, the screened clay could be allowed to dry, until assuming a solid form, though still moist and pliable, that could be used to produce a workable plastic clay. Shapes could then be formed of the plastic clay, jiggered (for close trimming), smoothed, rounded and sponged, before being bisque-fired, to be glazed later (often in two colors, sometimes more), glaze-fired for 8 hours in a kiln pre-heated to a high temperature, and allowed to cool for a further 8 hours. What resulted were high-glazed, softly colored products. By May, 1941, nine of the WPA workers, who had developed ceramic skills since the beginning of the program five years previously, had found employment in private industry.

Plate 70: Unique, sgraffito-decorated WPA plaque, 10½" dia. SHSND Coll. # 1981.75.7.

Plate 71: WPA assembled coffee service; creamer and sugar used at Wing Public School, Wing, ND -- SHSND Coll. # 1994.79.8 and .9; coffee pot – SHSND Coll. # 1981.75.3.

That same year, Grantier shipped twenty of the Mandan figurines to the University of North Dakota "for use as illustrative material in your department." [144] In doing this he acknowledged the great support and practical assistance offered him by Cable and earlier by Hammers, particularly the loan of equipment -- including a "foot-power potter's wheel... made out of a part of a sewing machine" [145] -- and the formulation of compatible glazes for use with the local Mandan clay. Also, for a brief period, some WPA workers received additional training at the University in all aspects of ceramic work.

Clear colorless glazes were applied to the Mandan WPA pottery to give a natural clay-colored appearance, either alone or in combination with a range of muted, soft and dark colors, contrasting strongly with similar pieces in bright, high-gloss enamel glazes produced by Edris Eckhardt and her WPA co-workers in Cleveland (plate 73). The production of figurines and utilitarian ware continued at Mandan through the beginning of 1943, when the entire WPA program was closed on President Roosevelt's executive order of December 4, 1942. By this time, the United States government had expended $90 million on such WPA projects in North Dakota

Plate 72: WPA figurines. UND Coll. # not assigned.

as the construction of 800 public buildings, airports in four cities, new dams and reservoirs and the completion of road improvements, which, during the peak period of 1937-8, employed 43,000 workers (including 30,000 farm workers) and an administrative staff of approximately 300. No estimate is available of the total number of ceramic workers in the state.

Plate 73: Figurines designed by Edris Eckhardt for the Federal Art Project in Cleveland, Ohio.

C. **Dickota and Rosemeade**

Two other operations in North Dakota, which benefited directly from the work of the University of North Dakota Ceramics Department, were the Dickinson Clay Products Co. and the Wahpeton Pottery Co. In 1935, Charles Grantier was hired by Dickinson Clay Products Co. to work alongside Howard Lewis, recently recruited from the Niloak Pottery Co. in Benton, Arkansas, to oversee a program of researching and producing "Dickota" pottery from local clays. Together Grantier and Lewis brought with them a wealth of knowledge and experience: Lewis was a graduate of Iowa State College's ceramic engineering department and had studied with Paul Cox, while Grantier was a former student of Margaret Cable's and had been a student assistant in the Ceramics Department at Grand Forks. As a native North Dakotan, Grantier delighted in using local motifs and themes in his distinctive designs for such souvenir items as his "Sundogs" ashtrays and "Teepee" incense burners, as well as the more usual vases and bowls. Lewis introduced the technique of swirl pottery, with which he had made himself familiar at Niloak, and the resulting "Badlands Pottery" proved to be popular.

On occasion both Margaret Cable and Laura Taylor spent time at the Dickinson plant, and a line of dinnerware, called "Cableware" (plate 74) -- some pieces in 1936 bearing her signature -- was produced from Cable's design. In her Cableware design Margaret Cable paid homage to Frederick Rhead, who had by that time inaugurated his Fiesta line at the Homer Laughlin China Company, in Newell, West Virginia; it is also reminiscent of a similar dinnerware pattern produced by the Bauer Potteries of California.

The Dickota Pottery closed at the end of 1937.

The Wahpeton Pottery Co., whose pottery was marketed under the trade name "Rosemeade," was founded, in 1940, by Robert Hughes and Laura Taylor, later Mrs. Robert Hughes. For the next twenty-one years, the company produced Taylor's bright, colorful designs for figurines, souvenir items, lamps, pitchers, plaques, bookends, vases, spoon rests, salt and pepper shakers, etc., based on birds, animals and flowers, many native to North Dakota. Taylor was twice honored by the selection committees of the Ceramic National Exhibitions in Syracuse, in 1934 and 1951, and her career, along with that of Grantier at Dickota, represented to some extent the achievement of the goal, which was the reason for the founding of the University of North

Plate 74: "Cableware" plates, marked "Dickota".

Dakota's Ceramics Department – the establishment of a regional ceramics industry. Notice of Laura Taylor Hughes' death, on August 2, 1959, appeared in the *Alumni Review* in the September issue of that year.

D. **Pine Ridge Pottery**

Cable's fascination with Indian art and tradition was expressed in her correspondence, in the 1930s, with administrators of Indian schools at Turtle Mountain, Pine Ridge and Wahpeton. In 1937, she was appointed Traveling Educational Expert in Ceramics by the Indian Service at Large for the United States Field Services. She came to the Pine Ridge Reservation of the Lakota Indians in South Dakota for three months in 1936 and for six months in 1937. There she taught in the Indian school and in summer classes, where she also trained teachers in modern methods of producing utilitarian tableware decorated with Sioux motifs, while at the same time researching the local clay; the bases of a few early Pine Ridge Pottery pieces are inscribed with her name. One of Cable's students there, Bruce Doyle, who had previous experience in ceramics and chemistry, was named Director of the Pine Ridge Pottery program at the school, where he shortly after inaugurated classes for adult Native Americans, and where the pottery soon became a commercial undertaking. Three such students, sisters Olive, Ella and Bernice Irving, took over the pottery in 1942 when Doyle left, and pottery continued to be made until the destruction of Ella Irving's premises in the early 1980s. The techniques taught by Cable at Pine Ridge were the basis of the pottery's sgraffito and incised designs using Sioux symbols and imagery and also its plain, utilitarian ware. Although very familiar with and admiring of the Southwestern Indian pottery traditions, Cable encouraged at Pine Ridge the free employment of the Lakota Sioux imagination, aesthetic sense and handcrafting skill adapted from their quill and bead work.

Endnotes

141 Cable's letter of 1923/4 to Bertha R. Palmer.
142 Taylor letter dated October 23, 1931.
143 Grantier letter dated June 28, 1940.
144 Grantier letter dated May 7, 1941.
145 WPA letter dated May 23, 1942.

PART IX

Identification, Dating and Items of Special Interest

On the subject of pottery coming from the kiln unmarked, Margaret Cable wrote: "we do not care to send it into the world unmarked and unnamed." [146] Such was her concern for the creations of her Department, that she assured herself that all pieces would be plainly and indelibly marked/stamped to identify them as having been produced in the Ceramics Department of the University of North Dakota.

Plate 75: Stamp for circular seal; underside of bowl by Josephine Clark, c. 1927, bearing stamped seal-mark incorporating the name "M. CABLE" and the date "1927". UND Coll. # C-MSC Gift 146-739.`

Early pieces were usually marked by a stamped or hand-printed "UND", or "U.N.D." -- and small pieces, after 1913, continued to be marked in this way – sometimes, if space allowed, with the addition of "Grand Forks" or "Grand Forks, N.D." Some other early pieces were marked "University of North Dakota" with or without the addition of "Grand Forks." Very infrequently a paper label can be found attached to the base of a vessel bearing the notation "U.N.D. GRAND FORKS ND." By 1913, a round seal (plate 75) was designed incorporating the words "University of North Dakota Grand Forks N.D. Made at School of Mines N.D. Clay", with a later variant including the name "M Cable" (referencing her position as head of the Ceramics Department) and sometimes a year (usually 1927 or 1930, though not necessarily or specifically alluding to the date of production of the appropriate item). On structural wares such as sewer pipe and utilitarian wares such as crockery, the seal was, most often, stamped in brown stain (plates 76; 77).

Plate 76: Crock, with stamp in brown stain. UND Coll. # C-CBL Gift 112-714.

Plate 77: Sewer pipe section, 5¾" long, with stamp in brown stain. UND Coll. # C-MSC 327-923.

Margaret Cable insisted: "Each piece of pottery that comes from the kiln proudly bears the stamp of the University on its base, applied under the glaze in cobalt blue, the

Plate 78: Modernistic vase, marked with a black seal-stamp and incised signature "Dorothy Olson", c. 1954.

most indestructible color of the potter."[147] And in her "Preparation of Color used for Stamp or Marking," she gives the following instructions for the application of the stain: "Pour about a tablespoonful of color on a ground glass slab and grind thoroughly with a large spatula...When free from lumps or grit, add a little water, then gum Arabic, then a little glycerin to prevent the mixture from drying out from day to day. Add more gum solution and grind in thoroughly to the proper consistency. The stamp does not print plainly if there is insufficient gum. The underglaze colors used are Best Black or Kings Blue." The blue stamp, with variations, was used almost uniformly for fifty years; however, pieces appropriately marked in black are rarely encountered (plate 78). The use of the seal was discontinued in 1963 with the retirement of Julia Mattson, and after that time only the name "Pachl" or students' names are to be found.

Plaques, tea tiles, emblem trays, medallions and figurines were also, where space permitted, marked with the stamped seal, though several unique examples of plaques, and ornamental tiles of high quality, are known to bear only the designer's mark or signature, possibly with the addition of a date or title. Several tiles, medallions, pendants and some small emblem trays do not show any University identification, as is also the case for some vases and bowls used as trial pieces. Other ornamental tiles, mostly in the 6"-square format (plates 79; 80), originally destined for architectural purposes or for framing, and other plain architectural tiles are impressed on the reverse with the large rectangular four-line mark "MADE AT THE / COLLEGE OF MINING ENGINEERING / STATE UNIVERSITY / GRAND FORKS, N.D."

Base and underside markings – both including some form of University of North Dakota identification and without any such designation of origin – refer, especially on trial pieces, to clay- or glaze-types and to the proportions of their formulations (plates 81 through 84). Most often, for instance, on Hammers' pieces, and sometimes also on Mattson's pieces, a number – in a circle or square or unframed – identifies the clay used. Often the entire base of a bowl, vase or tile will be occupied, solely, by information comprehensible only to a ceramic chemist.

Plate 79: Marking on reverse of plain tile (plate 80).

Plate 80: Matt-glazed, plain tile, 5½" sq.

Plate 81: Test pieces.

Plate 82: Undersides of test pieces in plate 81.

Plate 83: Test bowls.

Plate 84: Undersides of test bowls in plate 83.

Plate 85: Deeply carved vase, marked "PFP 1928". SHSND Coll. # 1988.148.22.

Instructors' marks are as follows:

for **Margaret Kelly Cable**: Cable, M. Cable, MKC, MC, Maggie, Maggie Mud;

for **Hildegarde Fried**: Fried, HF, HUF, HFD, Dreps;

for **Flora Cable Huckfield**: Huck, Huck (circled), Huckie, H, H (circled), FCH, Flossie;

for **Julia Edna Mattson**: Mattson, JEM, JM monogram;

for **Freida Louise Hammers**: Hammers, FLH, FH (with reversed F).

These signatures appear incised or painted on the base of the piece.

Plate 86: Vase or planter, 6"h., with deeply incised linear decoration, by Richard Woodward (c. 1949 – c. 1954).

Original work by students – thrown/hand-built forms, plain or decorated, and molded forms with hand-applied decoration – is usually marked, in addition to the stamped seal, with painted or incised names, initials or monograms, and also sometimes with a date (plate 85). The student names encountered -- certainly in the years up to c. 1950 -- are mostly those of women; less than 5% are of male students (plate 86).

Often the base marking will indicate, by name, initials or monogram, the possibility of two originators in collaboration. This can point, occasionally, to an instructor and a student working together – to create an item, to decorate a plain shape made by their own hands, or to improve an already decorated form made by them. Alternatively, and more commonly, the presence of two signatures can signify a decorator's embellishment of a plain shape designed by another hand, or the application of enhanced or sharpened detail to a pot where the original designer's mold already incorporated the design. On the bases of pieces made during the 1920s and into the 1930s, a notation prefixing a name – the letter "S" in parentheses, in a circle or unframed – indicates that the named instructor/student was responsible for the earlier design of – and possibly the mold-making in respect of – that form; the decorator's name usually, though not always, follows that of the shape-originator. When the names of two staff members appear on the base of a piece, for example Huckfield-Mattson (plate 26) and Hammers-Huckfield (plates 50; 96, right), they are to be interpreted as indicating that the decoration is by Huckfield using forms by Mattson or Hammers, and possibly with clay bodies and/or with glazes made and formulated by that colleague.

It is thought that Huckfield, without a background in ceramics or science, and as a non-faculty member, had little, if any, experience in throwing or building, so, as a decorator, worked necessarily only on forms made by others; there is no evidence of her throwing pottery shapes or hand-building them at the University of North Dakota. Consequently, most of her work – though by no means all – is marked, with or without the "S" prefix, with the name of the shape-designer.

Plates 87 – 94: Student work

Plate 87: Vase, marked with "HS" or "SH" monogram. UND Coll. # C-MSC Gift 65-588.

Plate 88: Vase, by Mrs. James Conners, marked "CONNERS 1944".

Plate 89: Vase, c. 1922, marked "BBB" (possibly by a member of the Berg, Brown or Budge families).

In addition, in those instances where the markings indicate the participation of two staff members, the signatures are usually accompanied by a number and possibly a letter (other than "S") or letters, sometimes in a square, circle, or parentheses, that refer to a clay type, and infrequently glaze designations (plate 96, right).

In the case of those pieces, that do not have names marked on their bases, then it is virtually impossible to identify, definitively, their makers. Here, even more so than in other instances, the collector is faced with the question of the relative importance of artist-identification versus the aesthetic quality, alone, of the pot. In Rookwood, Newcomb College and a few other potteries an identification of the artist/craftsman and an acquaintance with his/her work adds to one's appreciation of a specific item by him/her, as well as to the collectibility and value in many cases. Whereas, in these categories, a collector might be principally interested, for example, in the works of Sara Sax and Kataro Shirayamadani at Rookwood, or Marie De Hoa LeBlanc and Sadie Irvine at Newcomb, it is highly unlikely that a collector – unless a relative of the student in question – would be interested in acquiring any sizeable collection of works by particular, named students/decorators at the University of North Dakota. There, almost all of the decorators must remain, if not anonymous, then at best identifiable with only a brief notation as to name, sex and years of enrollment in the Ceramics Department. The careers of Cable, Fried, Mattson, Huckfield, Hammers and several assistants/students such as Taylor (LAT), Grantier (CGG), Seymour Anderson and Ruth Schnell (RRS), are at least adequately documented, but, to audiences other than well-informed family members, the work histories and personal circumstances of the vast majority of the students, from 1910 through 1963, will probably never become a matter of record. Furthermore, in many instances, it is difficult to know which generation of a family of students/decorators was responsible for any pot bearing only family names such as Berg, Thompson, Smith, Peterson, Olson, Johnson, Hanson and Erickson, especially when only one name, without initials, is indicated. Other complicating factors are the knowledge that members of some families attended the "special classes" over a period of many years, and the fact that, in the case of women students, both maiden names and married surnames, and personal and husbands' initials or first names might have been used almost indiscriminately (plates 87 through 94). Of course, unidentified pots can be evaluated in comparison with others with respect to aesthetic appeal, complexity of technique, successful execution and size; and such comparisons may, in some instances, yield clues about the identities of the makers. Ultimately, however, the quality of a pot should be assessed without reference to the name (known or otherwise) of its maker.

Occasionally, base markings include an incised or painted date. Others bear numbers, which, by reference to Departmental records, are found to be either -- pre-1938 -- the designer's model number, or -- in the case of pieces made for sale during the Spencer years -- the inventory item number. In the former case, between 1918 and 1937, numbers were assigned by each individual staff member to her own models.

Plate 90: Vase, marked with "MML", "LMM" or "MLM" monogram and "1931". UND Coll. # C-MSC 24-411.

Plate 91: Vase, marked "A1".

Plate 92: Vase, marked "M. NORTH 1935".

Plate 93: Vase, 9"h., marked "ADR" or "AGR". UND Coll. # C-MSC 18-405.

Plate 94: Vase, marked "Midkiff".

Plate 95: (Left) vase, by Huckfield, c. 1927, marked "13–HUCK–Pasque Flower". (Right) unsigned, unnumbered, miniature sgraffito bowl, c. 1927, by Huckfield; later, Spencer-list item # 32: "bowl, small, incised - wheat," (to be overall-glazed in a single color), 1938.

Fried's production up to the time of her resignation in 1924 was numbered from #1 through #348; the first 49 were probably test pieces of one kind or another, while #50-250 identified tiles, and #251-348 pots. Pieces made by her, at the University of North Dakota, after her resignation, do not appear to have been included in any numbering system.

Regarding Huckfield's, output the situation is somewhat confusing. The records reveal her use of the numbers #450 through #729 for the models decorated by her during her first four years in the Ceramics Department. They do not, however, make clear whether, or not, her later list of models, #1 through # 5056, for the period 1927-1937 (plate 95, left), includes a duplication of that earlier numbered series. Her vase #557 – "Flickertails and Wheat" (plate 24) – was probably decorated in 1925, though it might well date from 1929; also, her vase #654 of 1926 – "Mad March Hares" (plate 121) – might similarly have been decorated in 1929. It is possible that the numbers #450 through #729 were not re-assigned (between 1927 and 1929), just as eleven numbers from #2000 through #2010 (in 1930) were not ever allocated. Furthermore, as is also the problem with the numbering systems of other staff members, the records do not prove that all models were, in fact, numbered (and/or signed by the maker) when marked with the seal-mark of the School of Mines (plate 95, right).

Of the more than 4400 designs by Mattson, it is thought that 350 were made in her first four years in the Department, and that, between 1928 and 1937, her models are numbered #1 through at least #4045. Hammers' numbers, mostly test pieces, are #1 through #1370 for the

Plate 96: (Left) Mattson vase, c. 1927, marked "MC-JM"; (right) vase, c. 1930, with Huckfield decoration on Hammers form (using a trial clay formula), marked "S FLH 3 HUCK 999".

Plate 97: (Left) vase by Mattson, 1938, Spencer-list item # 38. (See also fig. 45.) (Right) vase thrown and decorated by Cable, with pattern motifs hand-incised on underside.

years 1927-1937. In 1932, Laura Taylor produced forms of her own design and also adapted forms by Cable, Mattson, Hammers and a few students for her models #1 through #49; the following year she made a further 152 models, #50 through #201, of her own design. Many of Cable's pieces produced up to 1938 were also numbered, but it is not possible to deduce from available records any kind of systematic identification. Cable further confused the situation, apparently, by sometimes linking her signature with that of one of her associates (plate 96, left; also plates 28; 29) and with one of that designer's special model numbers; it is possible that such markings are to be found on items decorated by Mattson, Huckfield or Hammers under the supervision, or otherwise with the assistance, of the head of the Ceramics Department.

Plate 98: Thrown vase, high-glaze blue on red clay, marked with seal incorporating date "1930". SHSND Coll. # 1988.148.3.

In this earlier period, therefore, through the beginning of 1938, it is often possible, in the case of an undated pot, through the identification of the marks indicating the designer and the model number, to assign at least an approximate design date to the piece. Since multiple copies could be made from each mold produced, it is very much more difficult to attribute a definite date of manufacture in addition to the date of design. For instance, Taylor's first five designs – all ashtrays, #1 Buffalo, #2 Wheat Sheaf, #3 Indian Head, etc. – produced a total of 398 copies in various glazes over the span of several years.

From 1938 on, when base-marked numbers, #1 through 248, identified inventory items used to fill Spencer's orders for his dealerships through 1948, there remains little, if any, information regarding the number of pieces made from each sample item or the specific dates of the manufacture of such pieces, though item-list dates and, frequently, designer attributions, are indeed indicated in the list. The Spencer "sample" list proceeds numerically with each number representing a molded or, infrequently, handmade item by a named designer (or designers), and with a description given on the relevant Cost Data Sheet (plate 97, left; fig. 45). For example, sample #3 is a cast bowl, by Mattson, decorated with a buffalo motif in sgraffito technique, with the item number assigned in early 1938; and sample #28, by Huckfield, of the same year, is a molded pot decorated with wheat shocks on an original shape by Bridgeman. Samples #59 and #59A, in 1940, are, respectively, Cable designs for a footed bowl and a bowl with grooved decoration, both adapted from an original shape by Gruenfelder; #59B and #59C are, respectively, a tall bowl and low bowl, both unfooted, and both adapted from an original shape by Whitney. Other useful information can also be gleaned from the Cost Data sheets. For example, a sheet from 1942 describes Cable item #120 -- a vase with jonquil decoration -- as the "first pattern carved in relief with mold made over it" -- and notes that it was an adaptation of an earlier mold #82 for a plain vase by French of 1940. On the base of each of these items, it is most probable that in addition to the model number (with or without suffix), the name of one designer (Mattson for #3, Huckfield for #28, French for #82) or the names of two designers (Cable-Gruenfelder for #59 and #59A, Cable-Whitney for #59B and #59C, and Cable-French for #120) would be marked, where appropriate, and where space permitted. A number of Cost Data Sheets from this period are annotated "Worn Out," and it is possible, if not probable, that new replacement molds were constructed to continue the supply of popular designs, such as one of the "Why Not Minot" vases (plate 22).

Plate 99: Bentonite vases with black decoration; (left) c. 1933, by Mattson; (right) c. 1932, by Huckfield, on shape by Mrs. V. S. Dahl.

Though some confusion might result from errors and inaccuracies in the Ceramic Department's record-keeping with regard to the Spencer list items, the great majority of those pieces produced for sale under the Cable-Spencer system are immediately recognizable by the model-number marking in the series #1-248. On consultation of the extant list the number is identified and the model itself described – except when the records are incomplete. More complicated is the problem of those esoteric, marked designations, letters and/or numbers and pattern outlines, etc., occasionally encountered, and for which no explanation has as yet been discovered.

The dating of pieces, which are marked with the signatures of students but not a date, is problematic. However, if the years of a student's enrollment are known, it is possible to assign an approximate date. In the case of adult students who would often resume studies after years of interruption due to family exigencies, illness or need, dating can often be only inexact. In such instances, where a date is not included in the marks, the only other helpful consideration in the assignment of a period of manufacture of a University pot is the color of the clay body – ivory-tinted white or cream-colored in the years 1918-1926, and buff-colored after the introduction of the "New Body Mix" in 1938. In the intervening years, 1927-1937, during which Hammers experimented with different clay bodies (plate 98), the justification for date assignment of a pot by this method of clay-color indication becomes untenable, however. Bentonite production, of course, cannot date before the 1930s, and the simpler black decoration on the red ground (plate 99) usually predominated earlier than the more complex color combinations (plates 35 thru 37).

In summary, of assistance in developing approximate date attributions for University of North Dakota pottery are such factors as: the determination of clay color, instructors' tenures, students' enrollment years and a knowledge of the various numbering systems assigned over the years in the Department. It might be thought that considerations of style could be helpful also in designating the period of design or manufacture of a particular vessel, but this is not always so since such decorative methods and devices as those associated with Arts and Crafts, Art Nouveau and Art Deco decoration continued to be employed later at the University of North Dakota (plates 88; 125; 155; 165) than at most of the American potteries that influenced the staff of the Ceramics Department. In addition, stylistic trends in the work of the Department's artists/craftspeople are not consistently tied to one of their specific periods of activity; for instance, a student returning to class after, say, a ten year absence, might have continued to work in the same earlier style.

The names of some designs are sometimes to be found on the bases of pieces, where space permitted. For example, design names, such as "Pasque Flower" (plate 95, left), "Viking Ship" (plate 212, far right), "Covered Wagon" (plate 50) or "Meadowlark" (plate 213, right), were often included in the markings on pieces made by staff members and students.

Fig. 47: The "North Dakota Products Vase." UAP # 2641. (See also plate 1.)

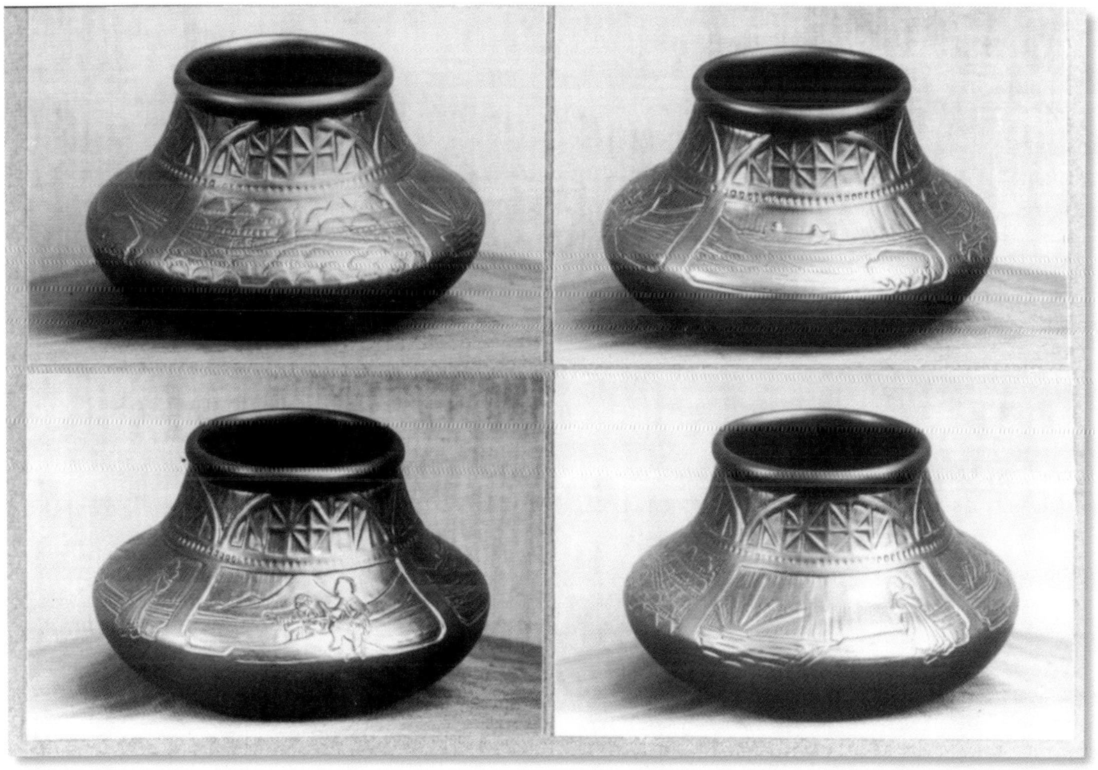

Fig. 48: The "Lewis and Clark Bowl." UAP # 2640.

Plate 100: "Astor Medal."

Also, items of special interest were usually referred to by title. In addition to the "North Dakota Products Vase" (made originally for Gov. Sorlie in 1926 – plate 1, fig. 47 -- with three others made later for President Budd of the Great Northern Railroad Company, Professor Thomas Kane of the university, and Executive Secretary James Milloy of the Greater North Dakota Association), the "Queen Marie of Romania Vase and Bowl" and the "President John F. Kennedy Vase," already mentioned, other presentation pieces included the "Lewis and Clark Bowl" (fig. 48), the "Scott Vase" and the "Crown Princess Martha Vase." The "Lewis and Clark Bowl" was made by Cable, in 1927, to commemorate the dedication of the Missouri River bridge in Williston, North Dakota, named to honor the famous explorers. Its decoration represents both the landscapes traversed by the expedition leaders accompanied by Sakakawea and the design of the bridge itself with its arches and piers. In the decoration of the "Scott Vase," made in 1939 for presentation to Charles E. Scott on his appointment as President of the State Teachers College in Dickinson, North Dakota, Cable included such motifs as a buffalo, a cowboy on horseback, Teddy Roosevelt's cabin and the State seal, all in panels divided by torches of learning. Again in 1939, when the Crown Prince and Princess of Norway visited Grand Forks, Cable created a vase with Indian imagery, a buffalo design and a bentonite glaze.

In 1926, a train, carrying President Budd of the Great Northern Railroad Company and his invited guests, traveled from Chicago westwards through Grand Forks to Astoria, Oregon, to commemorate the early history of the Northwest fur trade. For this occasion Cable replicated in North Dakota clay the original silver "Astor Peace Medal" of 1832, using one of the original medals in the collection of the railroad company as the basis for her design. The pottery "Astor Medals," pierced for wearing as pendants on cords strung with beads of colored glass (plate 100), bear a portrait of John Jacob Astor, the words "Peace and Friendship", and tomahawk and peace-pipe motifs, and the inscriptions "The Columbia River Historical Expedition 1926" and "University of North Dakota, North Dakota Clay".

In contrast to these complex and sophisticated designs, a simpler line of handmade and decorated forms was developed, in the mid-1930s, under the name of "Prairie Pottery." Professor W. E. Budge of the Engineering Department wrote in an article on "Ceramics in North Dakota"[148] "The Department has developed what is named 'Prairie Pottery,' made entirely of N.D. materials of a type which may be found in numerous localities in the state and can be made by simple equipment of low cost." The experimentation, which led to the introduction of this new and distinctive ware, was conducted simultaneously with Cable's research into methods of pottery making which could be employed by schoolchildren and other students of young age at the Indian schools in rural areas of the state. "Prairie Pottery" (plates 101 through 103) which incorporated very basic, straightforward shapes, decorated in a simple manner, reminiscent of vernacular ceramics, using Indian and other regional motifs, was marked: "PRAIRIE POTTERY / U.N.D. / GRAND FORKS", and Cable's examples are usually signed "Maggie Mud".

Plate 101: Plate, Prairie Pottery item # 13, by Huckfield, later Spencer-list item # 66.

Plate 102: Plate, probably Prairie Pottery item # 16, 6" dia., marked "Maggie Mud"; later, possibly, Spencer-list item # 68. UND Coll. # C-CBL 80-250.

Plate 103: Plate, Prairie Pottery, marked "Maggie Mud". UND Coll. # C-CBL 81-251.

The same markings were used in 1940 for pieces submitted to America Designs, Inc., for the American Way campaign to introduce American crafts by American designers for American homes (fig. 46).

Endnotes

146 Cable letter dated October 31, 1929.

147 "Post-War Ceramic Opportunities in North Dakota," by Margaret Cable.

148 Published in the *North Dakota Engineer*, May, 1936.

PART X

Ultimate Outcome

In her "Post-war Ceramic Opportunities in North Dakota," Margaret Cable spoke of the "vast quantities" and "great abundance" of the clay deposits in the state. Julia Mattson, in her instruction sheet for the course "Building and Modeling –Bentonite," wrote of the "large deposit…about thirty-two sections contain bentonite and the deposits range from a few feet to thirty in thickness." Virtually every promotion and brochure presented by the School of Mines, and much of the correspondence conducted in the first half of the twentieth century stressed the extent of these resources. Commissioner W. C. Gilbreath of the Department of Agriculture and Labor, State of North Dakota, emphasized in a letter to Dean Babcock that "the clay beds of North Dakota are too valuable and the prospective manufacturing industry is of too great importance." [149] For her part, Cable never resisted the opportunity to explain to her audiences that the University was "endeavoring to lay the foundations for a great future ceramic industry in the state," as she wrote in "Possibilities of Pottery Making from North Dakota Clays." But as Babcock informed Maude Pollock of Ferock Studios in 1910: "there is no one contemplating the immediate starting of a pottery in the state," [150] and so the situation was to remain for the next twenty-five years. There were great expectations in 1935 with the founding of Dickota, and in 1940 with Rosemeade; however, in spite of the exhortative climax to Charles Grantier's 1936 brochure: "The industry is now in its infancy – but, *Watch* "DICKOTA" *grow*!" Dickota was in fact closed by the end of 1937. Rosemeade, which never employed as many as thirty workers in Wahpeton, only survived Laura Taylor's death, in 1959, by two years.

Today, commercially prepared potter's clay from North Dakota is not available in the state, as processed clay, ready for use, can be purchased more advantageously elsewhere. Local clays are now prepared, if at all, and used by only a very few artist-potters. [151]

The vision of industrial development and utilization, which had been the guiding force in Babcock's mandate to Cable in 1910, and toward which goal she and her associates had striven, was not in fact realized. The principal legacy of the Ceramics Department, therefore, lies in the quantity, variety and quality of its art pottery production, which is admiringly recognized and exhibited and ardently collected today by scholars, museums and individual enthusiasts.

Endnotes

149 Gilbreath letter dated January 8, 1908, to Babcock.

150 Babcock letter dated May 7, 1910.

151 *North Dakota History, Journal of the Northern Plains*, Volume 65, No. 2 & 3, Spring/Summer, 1998: "A Century of North Dakota Pottery," by Claudia Berg and Mark J. Halvorson.

The President's House, otherwise known as Oxford House, now called the Stone Alumni Association Building, was designed by Joseph Bell DeRemer. A collection of University of North Dakota pottery, including "The North Dakota Products Vase" (the Sorlie Vase), is on display at the Alumni Association Building.

PART XI

Conclusion

Long before 1910, when the Ceramics Department was established at the University of North Dakota, Mary Louise McLaughlin had discovered her method of underglaze slip-decoration, Laura Fry had introduced the use of the airbrush and Hugh C. Robertson at Chelsea Keramic Art Works (later Dedham Pottery) in Massachusetts, had conducted and completed his experimentation to produce sang-de-boeuf, volcanic and crackle glazes. Several years before founding Pewabic in 1903, Mary Chase Perry had initiated her studies in ceramic decoration and glaze. In the period 1900-1904 alone, Rookwood and Grueby between them had received three Grand Prizes, seven Gold Medals and two Highest Awards at International Expositions in Buffalo, St. Louis, Paris, St. Petersburg and Turin. In its first decade, Newcomb Pottery was awarded five medals (one bronze, three silver and one gold) at international exhibitions in Paris, Buffalo and St. Louis and national exhibitions in Charleston, South Carolina, and Norfolk, Virginia. Rookwood and Grueby were collected by American and European museums, were represented in Paris by S. Bing and in New York City by Tiffany & Co., and were also sold in England and Germany; Newcomb pottery would later be available for purchase at Tiffany & Co. By 1900, the Roblin Art Pottery and the Stockton Art Pottery had been established in California, and the Roseville, Weller and Owens pottery companies were in operation in Zanesville, Ohio. Ten years later, George Ohr had already made his last pot; Artus Van Briggle, who had won five medals – two gold, one silver and two bronze – at the St. Louis Exposition, died while the exposition was in progress; Grueby was in decline; and Teco ware, introduced to the public in 1901, had already reached its apogee. The first school of ceramics was opened, in the period 1894-1896, at Ohio State University, and the second, the New York State School of Clayworking (later, from 1932, the New York State College of Ceramics) under Binns, at Alfred, in 1900.

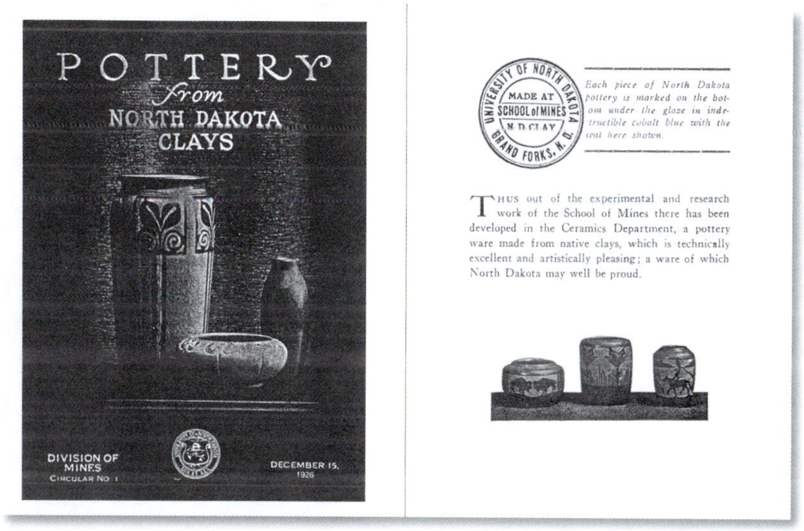
POTTERY from NORTH DAKOTA CLAYS

DIVISION OF MINES CIRCULAR NO 1

DECEMBER 15, 1926

Each piece of North Dakota pottery is marked on the bottom under the glaze in indestructible cobalt blue with the seal here shown.

THUS out of the experimental and research work of the School of Mines there has been developed in the Ceramics Department, a pottery ware made from native clays, which is technically excellent and artistically pleasing; a ware of which North Dakota may well be proud.

Fig. 49: Cover-page and last page of a promotional brochure, dated December 15, 1926 – "Prepared by Margaret Kelly Cable / Assistant Professor of Ceramics / College of Engineering / University of North Dakota."

Thus, thirty-four years after the 1876 Centennial Exposition in Philadelphia, which had provided the initial impetus for the American art pottery movement, Margaret Cable arrived in Grand Forks, a very small town in a state that had been in existence for barely twenty years. Not only a late arrival, in strictly chronological terms, on the American art pottery scene, the University of North Dakota, from a geographical standpoint, was also disadvantaged in a way in which other pottery producers in most areas of the United States could not be. Chicago was

Plates 104 – 107: Designs by Cable

Plate 104: Vase, 9¼"h., marked "MKC T.324". UND Coll. # C-CBL 15-185.

at that time exulting in an innovative atmosphere which influenced its art, architecture, and crafts; Ohio and the Northeast could look back on a history of industrial and cultural development; and even New Orleans and California had a head start over an Upper Midwest struggling to evolve from a frontier economy. What Ellsworth Woodward, thinking of Newcomb College, wrote of the immense difficulties experienced by schools and colleges in areas "remote from manufacturing and publishing centers,"[152] was of even greater concern to the instructors of the University of North Dakota. And Susan Frackelton's description of Newcomb Pottery as "...a charming building... large airy rooms with their beautiful fenestration, the cleanliness, the complete individual work tables..."[153] has nothing in common with Margaret Cable's "basement in an old building"[154] where the potters' wheels were powered by "sewing machine treadles attached to a reverse gear."[155]

Unlike the situation at Newcomb Pottery, where the craftswomen had all graduated from a course of study at the College's art school before becoming full-time decorators with a small salary and a commission on sales, at the University of North Dakota product quality was determined not only by the artistry, craftsmanship and technical knowledge of the staff members, but also by a classroom of students, who, in many cases, had little previous artistic training or craft experience. Consequently, many University of North Dakota pieces, as a commentator has kindly observed of Arequipa, were "not refined masterpieces, but rather exhibited the naiveté of a less experienced hand."[156]

The underlying basis of Cable's original commission – research and experimentation – and her teaching duties were the focus of the early years of the existence of the Ceramics Department, but nonetheless, by the early 1920s, the University's pottery was already a proud and desirable commodity. As early as June of 1922, in a review of an annual exhibition of ceramic works by Cable, Fried and students, arranged at the University, the *Grand Forks Herald* noted: "Rookwood has long held the standard mark for pottery making in this country, and authorities on the subject concede that the pieces being turned out by the ceramics workers here equal in every way the Rookwood products." Grandiose comment or wishful thinking, perhaps, at this early date, but the University of North Dakota was certainly considered to be a contender in the national ranks of art pottery manufacturers by the mid-1920s, when, at an exhibition presented under the auspices of the General Federation of Women's Clubs, the School of Mines was represented alongside Rookwood, Marblehead, Pewabic, Newcomb College, Van Briggle, Fulper, Paul Revere, Overbeck and Dedham. Cable admired and studied the attainments of these contemporaries and filtered their techniques and styles through her own imagination to build on her technical knowledge and craftsmanship.

Plate 105: Stain-painted vase, marked "MKC 1920 - T.000". UND Coll. # C-CDL 29-189.

The Arts and Crafts Movement's spatial and dimensional emphases, as displayed by Marblehead and Walrath, the borders and banded decoration, framed and unframed, of Dedham, the Saturday Evening Girls and Paul Revere Pottery, the conventionalized motifs and design techniques of Rhead in Ohio and California, the blended glazes and atmospheric effects of Rookwood, and the Art Nouveau associations of Newcomb's low-relief decoration were all characteristics of Cable's style during the first twenty years at the School of Mines. If there is little, if any, innovation in her work at this time, it is due to the mandate given her by Dean Babcock in 1910, but even so, out of an inborn interest in and search for artistic creativity in pottery making, Cable, in her comparative isolation in the Upper Midwest, first adopted and then adapted the techniques and styles of prevailing trends of the past ten to twenty years. Her early training in Minneapolis under Ernest Batchelder provided the initial stimulus, and her capacity for study and hard work were vital to her facility in all aspects of ceramic work. Doubtlessly not as consummate a craftsman at the wheel as Joseph Meyer or George Ohr, Cable nevertheless accomplished tasks scarcely envisioned by the women of Newcomb Pottery. Sadie Irvine may have spent fifty-two years at Newcomb, but that longevity barely overshadows Cable's thirty-nine years at the University of North Dakota, both throwing and decorating pots, researching clays and glazes, teaching well-attended classes, supervising sales to finance the program, traveling extensively to lecture and demonstrate, and carrying out the promotional mandate of her original appointment.

The *Potter's Craft*, *The Potter* and *Keramic Studio* were her bibles. Binns was her mentor, Rhead her teacher, and Baggs, Cox and Sheerer her advisors. Carrying out the legacies of Binns' teachings and Rhead's design principles, the Ceramics Department under Cable's leadership produced economically viable pottery, both turned and cast, which was well-finished and endowed with glaze treatments that enhanced shapes of simple strength and elegance. The substitution of molded relief with applied color for slip-painted decoration, initiated by Rhead at Weller and Roseville in the first decade of the twentieth century, was continued at the University of North Dakota along with all principal decorating techniques. Conventionalized motifs from nature, regional imagery, excised and textured grounds leaving design in low, flat relief, and the use of decoration to articulate form were supported by an extensive color palette and a wide range of glazes with varying degrees of transparency.

On this foundation, developed by Cable and her colleagues in the first two decades of the Department's existence, were constructed the innovations of the late 1920s and the 1930s. Rigorous analysis of clay and glaze led to such technical achievements as the bentonite pottery and the further refinement of outstanding glaze/color combinations and effects. Intensive study of, and a natural empathy for, the geography and history of their Northwestern homeland contributed to the creation of a wealth of original imagery incorporating prairie themes and Indian symbolism.

Margaret Cable's career at the University of North Dakota was sustained by her belief that "science, industry and art are coordinated in the work of the potter which attains its highest expression only when scientific knowledge coupled with skillful technique is guided by artistic design." [157] To sustain the program of the Ceramics Department she was prepared to explore all avenues of generating publicity, through lectures, exhibitions and sales, no matter what

Plate 106: Vase, 5¼"h., marked "T.302 MKC". UND Coll. # C-CBL 34-627.

problems, inconveniences or annoyances were involved. In 1926, the promotional brochure *Pottery from North Dakota Clays*, which she prepared for distribution to audiences, correspondents, retail shops and visitors to her Department, explained the history of pottery making and the methods of production and decoration used at the School of Mines (fig. 49). In addition, research and experimentation were of premier importance to her, and though the School of Mines focus on them may have lessened during the years of the Depression and World War II, when the continued existence of Cable's program depended so heavily on income from sales and teaching, she remained committed to the Department's mission as "symbolic, not only of the great Dakota of today but prophetic of the greater Dakota of tomorrow, when the industrial development made possible by the utilization of her coals and clays shall have become not a vision but a realization." [158]

Plate 107: Plate, 8" dia., slip-painted, marked "M. Cable 1948". UND Coll. # C-CBL 70-240.

The young state of North Dakota continued to grow during the twentieth century, as did the city of Grand Forks, whose population was estimated at 12,500 in 1910, the year Cable arrived there from Minneapolis. At the end of the century the city's population was slightly less than 50,000 (Grand Forks metropolitan area: approx. 97,500) and the University of North Dakota student enrollment was about twelve and a half thousand.

In letters, dated January 14 and 23, 1932, endorsing Cable's application for fellowship in the American Ceramic Society, Paul Cox wrote that, while admiring her as "one of the outstanding ceramists in her particular field," with "high professional standards," and deserving of recognition for having worked "under the limitations and with the success that this woman has shown," he opined that "from the standpoint of the very, very scientific I presume she is still an amateur in every sense." He added that "her papers have not been exceptional" though "helpful to studio workers" and "her pottery is good, honest, and intelligently made" from a commercial point of view. In this Cox may have damned Cable with faint praise, but that is probably more a reflection on Cox's personality and an indication of the prevailing male attitude towards women in professional life. It was Cox, after all, whose patronizing appraisal of Mary Given Sheerer at Newcomb Pottery amounted to little more than "a china painter of great skill" [159] and who, along with Joseph Meyer at Newcomb, resented Sheerer's aspiring intrusion into their field and took pleasure in "bedeviling" her. [160]

What is undeniably and unarguably true is this: not the tribulations of distance and climate, nor the deprivations of limited funding and inadequate equipment during the Depression and war years, nor yet the discomforts and inconveniences of long distance travel and hours of tireless labor, nor yet again the meager esteem accorded members of their sex in professional occupations, could deter the women of the Ceramics Department at the University of North Dakota, during the first half of the twentieth century, in the fulfillment of their service to their University and, in most cases, their adopted state. Because they allowed themselves no deviation from their devotion to art, science and vocation as craftswomen, researchers and instructors, they merit their inclusion in the upper echelons of those outstanding women, like Adelaide Alsop Robineau, Susan Frackelton, Louise McLaughlin, Maria Longworth Nichols Storer and Mary Chase Perry Stratton, who were of immense importance to the development and history of the art pottery movement in America.

Endnotes

152 *Art Education,* 6, May, 1898: "An Experiment in Applied Art in Newcomb College."

153 *The Sketch Book*, 5, July, 1906: "Our American Potteries – Newcomb College."

154 Cable letter dated January 19, 1931.

155 Letter dated October 26, 1977, from John E. Howard.

156 *Fired by Ideals*, by Suzanne Baizerman, Lynn Downey and John Toki, Part IV: "The Pottery and Tile from the Arequipa Sanatorium," by Suzanne Baizerman.

157 Undated announcement by Cable of the annual Ceramics Department Open House on Engineers' Day.

158 Cable letter dated December 7, 1928.

159 *Bulletin of the American Ceramic Society*, 13, May, 1934: "Newcomb Pottery Active," by Paul Cox.

160 *Newcomb Pottery*, by Jessie Poesch.

Plates 108 – 109: Designs by Fried

Plate 108: Tile, 6 3/8" sq., marked "H. Fried" -- (without stamped seal mark). UND Coll. # C-HLD 30-658.

Plate 109: Pitcher, marked "H. Fried 19-- Apr. 1–24". UND Coll. # C-HLD 36-664.

Plates 110 –111: Designs by Mattson

Plate 110: Two Spencer-list items with Indian decoration, (left) 1945, marked "JMATTSON 199 SIOUX CALENDAR" (shape by Elaine Odegard) – see also Fig. 17; and (right) 1940, marked "JMATTSON 78".

Plate 111: Sgraffito vase, 1937, marked "JM 4135". SHSND Coll. # 1993.179.3.

Plates 112 – 113: Designs by Huckfield

Plate 112: Vase, c. 1932, marked "Wilkins – No. Dakota Turkeys – HUCKFIELD – 1656 Turkey" (shape by Wilkins). UND Coll. # C-HCK 53-360.

Plate 113: Three vases, marked (left to right) "FELT - HUCKFIELD - SEA HORSES" (shape by Felt); "HUCKFIELD - 2562", bentonite, c. 1933; "HUCK" with indecipherable name of shape-designer. UND Coll. # C-HCK 8-316/11-319/48-352.

Plates 114 – 115: Designs by Hammers

Plate 114: Bowl, c. 1927, marked "FLH 4". Nelson Coll.

Plate 115: Sgraffito bowl, c. 1927, marked "WILD ROSE FLH – 64 S (shape) ERICKSON".

Plates 116 – 119: Student designs

Plate 116: (Left) vase, marked "M. MOE"; (middle) vase, marked "JHC" or "JHL" or "JHD"; (right) vase, no artist-mark; possible Zanesville mold. (Left to right) UND Coll. # C-MSC Gift 59-582, C-MSC 35-422, C-MSC 22-409.

Plate 117: (Left) rabbit vase, by Elizabeth Bready, c. 1934; (right) swan bowl, by Jane Irwin, c. 1952.

Plate 118: (Left) vase, by Florence Gregoire, c. 1951; (right) vase, by Hazel Klug, c. 1954.

Plate 119: (Left) vase by Minnie Serum; (middle) unidentified vase from a model with original carved decoration in the manner of Laura Taylor; (right) vase, marked "JOAN IVERSON 3/20/42".

Plates 120 – 123: Some decorative schemes/techniques representative of design trends in the period 1918-1938.

Plate 120: Coffee service by Cable, marked "MKC 1922 T.262"; probably from Knowles, Taylor & Knowles Co. molds. UND Coll. # C-CBL 40-220(-222).

Plate 121: Vase, c. 1926, marked "S (shape) Bryson-Huckfield - MAD - MARCH - HARES - 654". UND Coll. # C-HCK 45-333.

Plate 122: Vase, marked "H. Fried". UND Coll. # C-HLD 13-64.

Plate 123: Slab-built vase by Mattson, marked "Julia 1931". UND Coll. # C-MTT 97-284.

Plates 124 – 127: Sgraffito designs

Plate 124: Vase, marked "The Bronco Rider I. NELON 1944 Mar 16". Rustand Coll.

Plate 125: Vase, marked "MJ 3-48", possibly by Mabelle Jacobson, 1948.

Plate 127: Vase, marked "1937 E. Robinson". Nelson Coll.

Plate 126: Two vases by Mattson, c. 1937, marked "JM" and (left to right) "3911" and "17 3897".

APPENDIX I

Cable Family History

George A. Cable (born November, 1845, in Ohio), physician, and his wife Josephine B. (born March, 1848, in Ohio) were married in 1868, and resided in Cleveland, Ohio, at least in the years 1875-1876. In Ohio, two daughters were born – Cora C., who was to become a teacher and who left the Minneapolis family home in 1897, and Flora M. Two other children, a son Charles R., and a daughter Margaret, were born in 1883 and 1884 respectively, in Crookston, Minnesota. By 1897, the Cable family was occupying an apartment at 616 8th Street South, in Minneapolis, where they were listed in the 1900 U.S. Census as follows:

George A.	white	male	b. Ohio	11/45	age 54	married 32 yrs.	physician
Josephine B.–wife	white	female	b. Ohio	3/48	age 52	married 32 yrs.	saleslady, cloaks
Flora M.–daughter	white	female	b. Ohio	12/76	age 23	single	reader, clipping bureau
Charles R.–son	white	male	b. Minn.	4/83	age 17	single	
Marguerite–daughter	white	female	b. Minn.	4/84	age 16	single	

Mrs. Cable and daughter Flora M., clerk, continued to live at this address even after the death of Dr. Cable, and by 1909, Margaret B., who had previously been listed, in the Minneapolis City directories, as a student boarding at other addresses, joined them there; her occupation was noted as "pottery maker, Handicraft Guild," and her last previous address, as student artist, had been at 89 10th Street, (together with 91, the site of the Handicraft Guild building). After Margaret left Minneapolis, Mrs. Cable and daughter Flora M., designer, moved to 4116½ Queen Avenue, South, from which address Flora was married to Benjamin E. L. Huckfield, landscape gardener, sometime before 1919. Mrs. Cable remained at that address through at least 1925, presumably to be near her son, Charles R., chauffeur, who lived on Eastman Avenue, in Minneapolis.

Fig. 50: Postcard, c.1910, showing Macnie Hall and the School of Mines building.

On moving to Grand Forks in 1910, Margaret first roomed at Macnie Hall (fig. 50) for a short time before taking up residence at Davis Hall, and by 1925, had rented an apartment at 309½ Hamline Street. That same year she purchased a lot and began to build a home at 419 Princeton Street, a few blocks from the School of Mines building, later Babcock Hall (fig. 50), where the Ceramics Department was located. She took occupancy in November, 1927, and lived there with her mother Josephine B., who died, aged 81, on January 2, 1929, and her widowed elder sister Flora (Mrs. Benjamin E.) Huckfield.

By 1930, her nephew Charles, son of her elder brother Charles R. Cable, was living with Margaret and Flora, and the U.S. Census for that year lists the house occupants as follows:

Owner/householder	Margaret Cable	white	female	age 46	b. Minn.	single	teacher at university
Sister	Flora Huckfield	white	female	age 53	b. Ohio	widow	teacher at university
Nephew	Charles Cable	white	male	age 10	b. Minn.	single	
Lodger	Jerome Hall	white	male	age 29	b. Ill.	single	teacher at university
Lodger	Myrtle Foresberg	white	female	age 32	b. Minn.	single	teacher at university
Lodger	Clara Rom	white	female	age 22	b. ND	single	asst. registrar at university

Plate 128: The Cable-Huckfield home at 419 Princeton Street, Grand Forks (1999 photo).

(Coincidentally, Freida Hammers, who had previously boarded at Davis Hall, was registered as living, in the years 1936 through 1939, at 421 Princeton Street.)

In 1933, the 419 Princeton Street home was sold, and the Cable-Huckfield family moved to an apartment at 1523 5th Avenue North, for two years, before moving back to the apartment at 309½ Hamline Street, where Margaret had lived prior to Thanksgiving, 1927. The Cable sisters remained at this last address until their retirement from the university in 1949.

APPENDIX II

Associations, Comparisons and Parallels

A. **Period of Development 1900 – c. 1918**

J. B. OWENS COMPANY – CLAY TESTING / FEROCK STUDIOS ASSOCIATION

Owens' Utopian line was introduced in 1896-1897 as a late competitor to Rookwood's Standard line and William Long's Lonhuda ware – and the other Zanesville copyists' products, including Weller's Louwelsa and Aurelian and Roseville's Rozane wares. Within a short time this line was available also in a matt finish, which was given the name Matt Utopian (plate 129) to describe a light-colored floral decoration against a brown to light tan background with a soft, non-gloss effect. For his exhibit at the St. Louis Exposition in 1904, Dean Babcock ordered, from Owens, examples of both high-gloss and matt lines (plate 130) made up from North Dakota clay. Through his association with Owens from that time Babcock was able to establish a relationship with Ferock Studios, which was to be instrumental in the success of his exhibit at the National Corn Exposition in Omaha some five years later.

Plate 129: Owens Matt Utopian vase, marked "Owens 1010", (Owens regular production).

Plate 130: Owens Matt Utopian vase, marked "OWENS UTOPIAN" with 3-digit number (160?) and "ND". UND Coll. NC-MSC 3-926.

Plate 131: Owens Matt Green vase, marked "OWENS 26", also "Pollock" on side of vase, possibly by Maude Sibyl Pollock (see also fig. 4).

FEROCK STUDIOS – CLAY TESTING AND STYLE

Prior to the inauguration of this partnership between Frank Ferrell and Maude Pollock (plate 131) in 1909, their most recent employment had been with the J. B. Owens Company, where Ferrell was apparently engaged in designing, modeling and decorating, and whose latest lines included several in an Arts and Crafts manner. Owens' last line, Aqua Verdi, introduced at the Jamestown Exposition in 1907, was a matt-glazed artware, with embossed decoration, mainly in a deep, rich green shade, and it is, therefore, not surprising that the character of some of the Ferock designs, and even, in some instances, the color, are reminiscent of that Owens style (plate 132, left). Again, some of the Indian-esque patterns (plates 6; 132, right) may have been inspired by Ferrell's familiarity with Owens' Aborigine line, made to compete with William A. Long's Indian Ware at Clifton in 1906, and decorated in imitation of Indian pottery. There is, however, little precedent at Owens for the rectilinear emphasis or use of reticulation so strikingly employed in the making of some other Ferock designs (plates 5; 133); only a very small number of matt green models with reticulated decoration were produced at Owens (plate 134), as also at Weller, during the time Ferrell spent at these potteries. Strangely, his technique of piercing does not reappear for another twenty years until his introduction of cut-out design in the trim of the body, at the top and base of the vessel, in the 1930 Roseville line, Ferella, which was named for him (plate 135).

Plate 132: Ferock vases.

Plate 133: Ferock vases.

Plate 134: Owens Matt Green vase, marked "Owens 52".

Plate 135: Roseville Ferella vase.

HANDICRAFT GUILD, MINNEAPOLIS – TECHNIQUE AND STYLE

Ernest Batchelder's design principles and Margaret Cable's practical training at the Handicraft Guild (plate 136) are strongly evidenced in her early work at the School of Mines. She continued to produce utilitarian pottery of simple design in plain, functional forms, thick-walled and heavy, and invested with dark, somber and subdued coloring in a matt finish. Most of the pieces made at this time in Grand Forks show a rustic and – in many ways – charmingly straightforward quality which would not be suited to further ornamentation (plate 137).

Plate 136: Vase, marked "HANDICRAFT GUILD MINNEAPOLIS". UND Coll. # NC-MSC 1-924.

Plate 137: Vase, by Hena Parizek, 1911-1912, marked with "HP" monogram, "UND", (without stamped seal mark). UND Coll. # C-MSC Gift 89-683.

Plate 138: (Left) coffee pot, by Fried, marked "HFD". (Right) Rosenthal, Bavaria, porcelain coffee pot in the Donatello pattern.

ZANESVILLE COMPANIES / EAST LIVERPOOL-AREA COMPANIES -- EARLY SHAPES

In the first ten years of the Ceramics Department, pottery items were often cast from molds acquired from other sources. Babcock had purchased molds and other materials during the time that he was examining and evaluating the commercial potential of the native clays, and Cable continued to search for suitable forms after she took over responsibility for the day-to-day running of the Department.

Some of the pieces included in the Panama-Pacific Exposition exhibit were cast from molds which had originated in Zanesville (plate 116, right) -- principally at Roseville and Owens -- whilst other items, such as tea services and some tableware (figs. 12; 13), were produced from molds acquired, not only from Zanesville, but also from such other sources as Knowles, Taylor & Knowles of East Liverpool, Ohio (plate 120). Many of these shapes may themselves have been adapted as variations of older American, even foreign, designs -- some even strongly reminiscent of the circa 1905 Bavarian forms for the Rosenthal Company's Donatello, Empire and Botticelli services (plate 138, right), as were also Roseville's pre-1916 Donatella tea sets in the Landscape and Persian-type Ceramic Design patterns. Several forms popular at the School of Mines (plates 138, left; 139, right) were also used by, amongst others, the Edwin M. Knowles China Co. of Chester and Newell, West Virginia (plate 139, left).

Plate 139: (Left) "Semi Vitreous" pitcher, by Edwin M. Knowles China Co. (Right) UND pitcher, marked "T.259".

The greater part of the tableware produced at the School of Mines was decorated on these shapes, as at Roseville, using decal patterns obtained by Cable from commercial sources. Alternatively, and to a lesser degree -- except in early gift- or souvenir-work by students -- stencil designs were applied; occasionally tea and coffee services were completed that had freehand-painted patterns of original composition by Cable (plate 120), Fried and more advanced students.

B. **Period of Major Production c. 1919 – c. 1963**

The use of the principal decorating techniques employed at the University of North Dakota was foreshadowed by artists and potteries in other areas of the United States. Several of these techniques, introduced elsewhere ten to thirty years earlier, had been developed and improved in the intervening years with more up-to-date adaptations benefiting from the advantages of modern materials and equipment, and were adopted in Grand Forks. Some of the interesting and instructive relationships between the Ceramics Department and precursors – both potteries and individuals – reflect significant comparisons, influences and associated theories and practices, particularly in matters of technique and style. Those relationships are as follows:

ROOKWOOD

Underglaze painting was a major feature of Rookwood's earliest output in the 1880s, and slip-painting afterwards provided the enhanced two-dimensional effect in the representational decoration of its Standard, Sea Green and Iris lines, all of which had been embellished by the use of the spray gun. Considerable advances had been made in the use of the spray gun, or airbrush, since Laura Fry first discovered the possibilities of the atomizer in 1883, in Cincinnati. The airbrush could be utilized to apply underglaze grounds and the glaze itself, achieving an evenly colored surface capable of being shaded and blended. Beyond the production of delicate gradations of one color, from light to dark and from top to base -- as in Rookwood's Standard Glaze ware of the 1880s and 1890s -- the technique was extended to allow the soft transition from one color to another. This resulted in controlled, subtle blending in both high-gloss and matt finishes, as, for instance, in Rookwood's Iris/Sea Green (plates 140; 142) and Vellum (plate 193) glazes, respectively. The decorators of the two University of North Dakota vases pictured here (plates 141; 143) seem to have been well acquainted with the techniques and objectives of their Cincinnati counterparts, as well as cognizant of the standards set by them.

Plate 140: Rookwood Iris vase, 9½" h., c. 1898, by Sara Sax.

Other competing companies in Ohio followed Rookwood's lead, as did many Midwestern potteries. Van Briggle, too, in Colorado, starting in 1900, initiated a program of shaded and blended glazes. The airbrush technique was "the method used in the School of Mines for the production of the soft blending and shaded effects that characterize the pottery." [161] Using the lyrical, poetical language, which her artistry inspired, Cable described these color studies (plates 44; 105; 109) as, for example, "a delicate rose shading into lavender suggestive of a dove's breast; or a celadon green which loses itself in a hyacinth blue." [162]

Plate 141: Fried vase, 10" h., marked "HFD April 1926". UND Coll. # C-HLD 20-648.

Plate 142: Rookwood Sea Green vase, 6¾" h., 1900, by Sara Sax.

Plate 143: UND vase, 10" h., marked "D Kane". Nelson Coll.

WELLER / ROSEVILLE

Incising/carving and sgraffito, so prevalent in designs produced by both staff and students at the University of North Dakota Ceramics Department (figs. 32; 35; 37), were popularized in Zanesville at the turn of the twentieth century. The former technique was used by Charles Upjohn, in 1900, to produce his Dickensware II line at Weller (plate 144). Prior to 1948, all three instructors, working under Margaret Cable, including Cable herself (plate 13) and fellow staff member Flora Huckfield (plate 145), practiced the incising/carving technique.

Plate 144: Weller Dickensware II vase, incised decoration by, and signed, "Sites" – possibly from a design by Charles Upjohn.

Plate 145: UND vase, incised decoration by Huckfield, c. 1936, marked "APPLE BLOSSOMS SHOGREN HUCK 1395" (shape by Dorothy Shogren).

Plate 146: Roseville Della Robbia vase. Barbara Gerr Coll.

Plate 147: Hammers sgraffito vase, c. 1931; shape by Cooley. UND Coll. # C-MSC Gift 211-944.

Plate 148: Roseville experimental vase. Barbara Gerr Coll.

Plate 149: Hammers sgraffito vase, c. 1928. Risser / Dilley Coll.

Six years later at Roseville, Frederick Rhead introduced the Della Robbia line (plate 146), which possessed a unique form of sgraffito, whereby he cast two layers of different colored slips -- one after the other -- to form the vessel's wall, from which, through which and into which his design could be cut. Other experiments in incised/ sgraffito design (plate 148) conducted at Roseville in the first decade of the twentieth century prefigured much of the work produced, in that manner, at the School of Mines twenty to thirty years later (plates 147; 149).

Plate 150: (Left) Rookwood vase, 1945; (middle) Weller Etna mug; (right) Weller Floretta vase.

In Zanesville, for reasons of economy, techniques were developed, principally by Frederick Rhead at both Weller and Roseville, that made it possible to produce wares with a handcrafted appearance without the involvement of professional decorators. Workers with little training or expertise could achieve an effect similar to slip-painting by applying color, by brush, sponge, etc., to cast pieces in which relief decoration had been incorporated into the molded form (plate 150, middle and right). This method of manufacture became predominant in Zanesville from 1904 on. It was utilized also at Rookwood (plate 150, left) and became prevalent at the University of North Dakota, particularly in the late 1930s and 1940s (plate 151).

Plate 151: (Left) vase by Huckfield, Spencer-list item #226, 1945 (shape by Patten); (right) rabbit figure "Billy", Spencer-list item # 105, 1942 (shape by Cable).

FREDERICK RHEAD

Plate 152: Slip-decorated jardinière (part of a jardinière/pedestal set) designed by Frederick Rhead for Vance/Avon Faience; upper decorative band with stylized landscape design above script "The Glorious Summers Symphony of Love Laughter and Life".

At Weller, in 1904, Rhead continued his use of slip-trailing (plate 164, right) -- so well employed the year before at Vance/Avon Faience -- in the Jap Birdimal (Weller Rhead Faience) designs, and then later at Arequipa, which, in turn, led to Cable's own tile decoration (plates 62; 170). Rhead was acquainted with the slip-trailed, beaded/textured patterns of Heinrich (Henry) Schmidt for the porcelain line, Lotusware, of Knowles, Taylor and Knowles, and incorporated some of Schmidt's technique into the process he had studied and first used in his native England. Included in his designs at Vance Avon (plate 152), and also for the Weller Faience line (plate 153), were aphorisms, inscriptions, quotations and lines of verse in slip-trailed script. This followed in the tradition of earlier English Staffordshire pottery and is also reminiscent of the incised/painted motto-ware of the southwestern area of England. An aspect similar to this last feature of Rhead's early work is later encountered in Cable's design for such trophy vases as "The All-American Turkey Show" pots (plate 154), as well as the tile-work for her own fireplace (plates 56; 57).

Plate 153: Jap Birdimal (Weller Rhead Faience) milk pitcher; slip-decorated "Frae the Coo" (From the Cow); signed "VMH". UND Coll. # C-MSC 126-720.

Rhead also employed incised decoration, in the form of a simply drawn line, or a line with rounded edges, with the appearance of shallow modeling, on damp ware or bisque with mineral oxide pigments, at University City, Arequipa and at Rhead Pottery. His technique [163] greatly influenced Newcomb Pottery in its creation of underglaze-painted, incised designs with soft-edged effects, and was to find reverberations later at the University of North Dakota. The texturing of backgrounds, promoted by Rhead as an effective artistic device and used extensively by him, particularly in conjunction with sgraffito and other low-relief carving, was carried over simultaneously to Frank Ferrell's designs for Roseville after 1919, and Margaret Cable's teaching and design principles at Grand Forks (plates 49; 121; 155).

Plate 154: Cable vase, 8" h., marked "M. Cable 1933 #856"; bentonite; "Awarded by The 1933 All-American Turkey Show Grand (misspelled 'Grad') Forks N.D. For Excellence". UND Coll. # C-CBL 106-708.

Plate 155: UND covered jar, 7¼" h., by L. T. Staley, 1937. UND Coll. # C-MSC Gift 284-865.

NEWCOMB COLLEGE / IOWA STATE COLLEGE

Similarities between the pottery outputs of the University of North Dakota and Newcomb College relate back to the influence of Rhead's example and Robineau's theories as published in *Keramic Studio*. This association extends also to Iowa State College through the agency of Paul Cox. Whereas all three producers adopted incising and excising as two of the principal techniques employed, and were concerned with the placement and directional dimension of the decoration applied, differences occur in the range, depth and brightness of colors and the transparency of glazes used, and also in the degree of precision and severity of design outlines and contours. Newcomb Pottery (plate 156) and Iowa State College (plate 157) shared technique and, in many instances, a rhythmic treatment of motifs, which was sometimes echoed at the School of Mines. Both the University of North Dakota and Iowa State College emulated Newcomb Pottery's choice of local imagery and reserved conventionalization of ornament. Though Cable was greatly impressed with Mary Yancey's color combinations/contrasts as with Cox's use of enamel glazes at Ames, the University of North Dakota's design vocabulary and color palette greatly exceeded those of both Iowa State College and Newcomb College. Newcomb College's subdued color schemes and soft contours were replaced very largely, at Iowa State College, by vibrant hues, and, at the University of North Dakota, by a vast selection of colors, shades and tints, in matt, high-gloss, shaded and blended glazes (plate 158), and by more precise outlining of design (plate 159) in both Midwestern locations.

Plate 156: Newcomb College vase, by Mary Sheerer, 1904. Stewart Coll.

Plate 157: Iowa State College vase, 9" h., by Mary Yancey.

Plate 159: UND vase, possibly by Doris Brown, marked "DEB 1934".

Plate 158: UND vase, marked "Gertrude Galbraith Feb. 9, 1931". Nelson Coll.

MARBLEHEAD

Plate 160: UND tobacco jar; seal-mark only. UND Coll. # C-MSC 37-431.

Even prior to her visit to Marblehead, Massachusetts, in 1918, Margaret Cable had recognized that Arthur Baggs' two-dimensional schematized designs, in matt glazes, with subtle and harmonious color contrasts, were the basis of his pottery's appeal. Though sometimes incised or lightly modeled, Marblehead's decoration consisted mainly of flat, abstract patterns of conventionalized motifs against matt-glazed backgrounds (plate 161). It consequently presented Cable with a pleasing alternative (plate 160) to the Newcomb College style, which she also emulated. The simplification of nature and the restraint so evident in many of Cable's and Fried's stylized designs of the late teens and early 1920s (plates 11 through 13; 16 through 18; 122) – usually in matt glazes, though sometimes glossy – unarguably evidence the two women's admiration for what Marblehead had taught them: that ornament is just as effective as an abstraction from nature as it is as a literal representation of nature.

Plate 161: Marblehead: (Left) vase and (middle) tobacco jar, both with incised/modeled decoration; (right) vase, flat-painted by Hannah Tutt.

Plate 162: (Left) vase, by Walrath, at NYSS, Alfred, 1902. (Right) mug, by Walrath, at the Mechanics Institute.

Plate 163: UND sugar and creamer, by Fried (as student), marked "U.N.D. 1912 HF". Nelson Coll.

WALRATH POTTERY

Though he did not complete his course of study under Professor Binns, Frederick Walrath left Alfred as an accomplished practical potter, glaze chemist, technician and designer. His early student work at Alfred in all techniques of decoration, especially carving (plate 162, left), was exceptional, and his later work at the Mechanics Institute, in Rochester, New York, in many ways rivaled that of his contemporary Arthur Baggs at Marblehead. His use of sparse, abstracted floral and sometimes almost geometrical ornament in flat patterns (plate 162, right) reveals a vertical, rectilinear emphasis in accord with Marblehead design and in contrast to the rhythmic swirls of some later work by Newcomb decorators. Some designs at the School of Mines, from the period c. 1912-1920, by Cable and Fried (plate 163) are reminiscent of some of Walrath's decorative schemes at the Mechanics Institute between 1908 and 1918.

JERVIS POTTERY / UNIVERSITY CITY / AREQUIPA / RHEAD POTTERY

At Jervis Pottery (plate 164, left and middle), conventionalized ornament was often further schematized into geometric devices reminiscent of both Scottish and Viennese design and some Prairie School architectural phenomena. This was sometimes the case at Marblehead as well. Frederick Rhead, who had previously worked at Vance/Avon Faience with his compatriot William Jervis, joined him in this venture at Oyster Bay, New York, for a short time before becoming active at University City. Rhead and Jervis shared an enthusiasm for slip-trailing, sgraffito and matt glazes. Sgraffito employed at Oyster Bay was based on Rhead's conception of that technique as he had used it at Roseville. [164] Shapes were designed, molded, and decorated by Rhead for a short time, and Jervis also provided designs.

At the University of North Dakota, vessels were decorated, using an incising/carving technique and incorporating a textured background with underglaze stain (plate 165), in a style approved by Rhead and Jervis.

While Professor of Pottery at University City, Rhead insisted, as he had at Roseville, on the complementary relationship of shape and decoration, whereby the structure of the form itself enhances the surface pattern (plate 166, left) or where the design treatment accentuates the

Plate 164: (Left and middle) two pitchers, with Jervis, Oyster Bay, mark; one with a matt-glazed iris design against a textured background with underglaze stain. (Right) Weller Faience mug, marked "Rhead", artist-initialed (on body) "CMM".

Plate 165: UND vase, marked "E. JELLIFF 1950", with a matt-glazed iris design on a background with underglaze stain.

Plate 166: University City vases: (left) with crystalline glaze; (right) with incised landscape design.

Plate 167: Two Arequipa vases with incised/carved decoration.

sculptural quality of the shape (plate 166, right). This aspect of Rhead's design, together with his use of textured grounds and an insistence on rhythmic verticality in scenic decoration, is at the very core of much of the work produced at Grand Forks.

At Arequipa, Rhead developed clays, shapes, glazes and designs while hired male assistants threw or built the vessel forms, which were to be finished and decorated by hand, under his careful supervision, by the female patients of the sanatorium. Later, casting became prevalent there. Polychrome, incising/carving (plate 167), slip-trailed decoration -- for instance, of a band of leaves and berries applied at the top of the vessel (plate 169) -- also overall patterning, in matt and high glazes, as well as interesting glaze effects, were all introduced there by Rhead. Later, these techniques and effects were gradually superceded by excised designs invented by him and by his successor (in 1913) Albert L. Solon, emphasizing vertical schemes of sparse, abstracted decoration. The progress of work at Arequipa was avidly followed by

Plate 168: UND vase, 1925, with incised decoration; marked "EMH 2-25". UND Coll. # C-HMM Gift 21-390.

Plate 169: Arequipa vase, with slip-trailed decoration.

Plate 170: UND tile, 3 5/8" sq., with slip-trailed decoration, attributed to Margaret Cable; unmarked.

Margaret Cable (plate 170), whose own students' output occasionally pursued the same aspect of appeal (plate 168), and regularly reflected the same range of competence (in design and execution), from highly accomplished to amateurish.

At Rhead Pottery, the designs, glaze formulae and almost all decorating was accomplished by Frederick Rhead. An incising technique in conjunction with the inlaying of color characterized much of his work in Santa Barbara. Decoration was painted in outline, background slip applied and designs filled in with various colored slips, all on greenware. When completely dry and hard, the applied slip was cut back to the outline color or to the clay body. Most of the familiar techniques, preferred earlier by him at other locations, were also employed here, and greatly influenced Margaret Cable's work in Grand Forks. A tile panel with a motif of fish, completed by Rhead -- echoing an earlier Jap Birdimal fish design at Weller -- was the inspiration for one of a set of tiles (plate 171) made at the University of North Dakota, probably by Hildegarde Fried though possibly by Cable. "The densely textured scales of the fish are organized in a diagonal, diamond-shaped pattern that balances the strict rectilinearity of the tile,"[165] while a rhythmic conventionalization of the motif affords vitality and harmony and avoids any possible static quality.

Plate 171: Three UND slip-decorated tiles, 5¾" sq., with large, impressed, rectangular mark (for tiles). UND Coll. # not assigned.

Plate 172: Dedham plate in the horse chestnut pattern.

DEDHAM / SATURDAY EVENING GIRLS / PAUL REVERE POTTERY

Another signal characteristic of the Arts and Crafts style, so evident particularly at Marblehead and Newcomb Pottery, is to be seen in the constrained border decorations, consisting of simple repeat designs with dark outlines and confined by bands of flat color, in the products of Dedham Pottery (plate 172) and Saturday Evening Girls -- later Paul Revere Pottery (plate 174). The staff members and students alike, in the Ceramics Department at the University of North Dakota, frequently availed themselves of designs incorporating such borders or bands of horizontal decoration (plates 173; 175) and exhibiting the "naiveté of design... rusticity of material... and a kind of vertical rigidity"[166] seen in the Massachusetts pottery.

Plate 173: UND vase, by Cable, 1935, marked "The Big Ones That Got Away". UND Coll. # C-CBL 30-200.

Plate 174: SEG (left) covered jar; and (right) pitcher, 1909, marked "FR (in a rectangle) 12.6.09".

Plate 175: UND vase, by Huckfield, marked "Huck". UND Coll. # C-HCK 14-322.

Plate 176: Overbeck plaque or tile, 8" dia., by Elizabeth and Hannah Overbeck.

OVERBECK POTTERY

This same appearance of naiveté is to be found in the work of the Overbeck sisters (plate 176), whose thrown and built pottery, with carved two-dimensional decoration of stylized imagery by Mary Frances (from her own designs and also from designs by Hannah) and glaze inlays invented by Elizabeth, in many ways matched the progress made by Cable and her colleagues between 1915 and the late 1930s (plate 177). For the Overbecks, subdued color tones in matt glazes were later joined by bright, vibrant glazes through 1937. Also, figurines (plate 178), often molded and prevalent particularly after 1936, were humorously conceived, sometimes grotesquely so, in the same manner as those at the University of North Dakota and also apparent in some of the depictions of Scandinavian dancers and cowboys in figurative design on vessels (plates 118; 209, left; 212, second from right) and tiles at Grand Forks.

Plate 177: UND tennis-award plaque, 1933, by Mattson; reverse inscribed "Irene McCaffrey Runner Up 1934".

Plate 178: Overbeck figurines. Dommel Coll.

Plate 179: Two UND tea tiles/trivets/roundels; (right) c. 1936, marked "Huck 4786".

Plate 180: Rookwood trivet, 1925.

CALIFORNIA FAIENCE

Decorative tea tiles, trivets, roundels and small plaques were produced frequently, during the period 1910-1950, by many potteries, including the School of Mines, employing methods of press-molding, hand-pressing and hand-forming; some were individually decorated (plates 20; 58). The University of North Dakota (plate 179, right) and Rookwood (plate 180) used the technique of painting on carved, sometimes textured grounds (particularly on press-molded items). Along with the New York State School at Alfred (plate 181, left), both of these potteries also used the technique of applying color within excised background areas; and along with Saturday Evening Girls/Paul Revere Pottery (plate 181, right), that of color-painting within incised outlines. At California Faience (plate 182), principally, another treatment in the design of these objects – one favored also at Grand Forks (plate 179, left) – was to contain the design within raised ridges. Specifically, an incised design was cut into a plaster mold into which clay was then hand-pressed. Later, if a monochrome effect was not intended, the ridge-outlined fields would be filled in with polychrome glazes in order to enrich the design.

Plate 181: (Left) roundel made at Alfred, marked "Stacey 1917"; (right) SEG tea tile/trivet, 1915, marked "7-15".

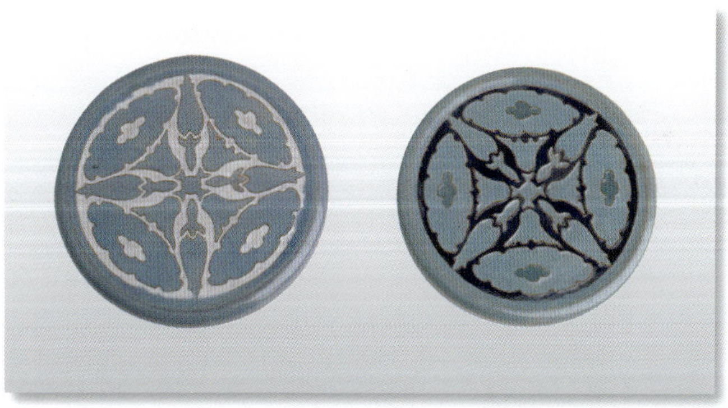

Plate 182: Two California Faience roundels.

MARIA MARTINEZ

Margaret Cable, who visited the San Ildefonso Pueblo, near Santa Fe, New Mexico, in 1935, was fascinated and highly admiring of the accomplishments of potter Maria Martinez, who, at that time, was working with her husband Julian. Maria and Julian had demonstrated their technique at the St. Louis Exposition in 1904. After her husband's death in 1943, Maria continued to work, assisted by family members, until shortly before her death in 1980. Her pots were hand-built, layer by layer, then sun-dried, sanded, burnished with a stone or piece of bone, decorated and fired in an open fire; her polychrome wares incorporated indigenous and geometric designs in red, cream and black. From c. 1919, Maria and Julian began to produce black-on-black pottery by an innovative method that produced opposing matt black designs on a shiny black body (plate 183). These results, together with their redware designs, which were unique at that time, were inspiring to both Cable and Julia Mattson, since Maria's technique and designs conformed so authentically with the native tradition and aesthetic, and were a welcome alternative to the Indian-esque products of such makers as Clifton, Owens and Weller (plate 184). The Southwestern Indian techniques also led Cable, working with Hammers, to develop a system of pottery making, using available, local materials and simple methods. This system could be taught in rural schools and recreational projects by, amongst others, University of North Dakota students who had completed teacher training classes in the Ceramics Department. Indian schools and adult education programs at such reservations as Pine Ridge and Turtle Mountain were early beneficiaries of this School of Mines research and instruction.

Plate 183: Low bowl, 12¼" dia., by Maria and Julian Martinez, and given by them, in the early 1930s, to Wolf Robe Hunt, Tulsa, Oklahoma; script signature: "Marie & Julian". Kearns Coll.

Plate 184: (Left) Weller Souevo vase; (middle) Owens Aborigine vase; (right) Clifton Indian vase.

Fig. 51: Indian decoration at the School of Mines.

Plate 185: Weller vase with relief scenic decoration, signed "R.L." for Rudolph Lorber.

Plate 186: Newcomb College vase, by Aurelia Arbo, 1936. Stewart Coll.

C. "Trees" and Other Imagery / Commissions and Commemoratives

The poet Joyce Kilmer – a contemporary and favorite of both Cable and Hildegarde Fried – and Frederick Rhead shared a reverence for trees which was inherited by Margaret Cable, particularly, in the sparsely wooded, flat country of eastern North Dakota. An "anthology" of Rhead's arboreal designs, from the time of his first studies and employment in England, through his work at Vance/Avon Faience and other locations, to his appointment as designer, later Director of Research, at the American Encaustic Tiling Co., in Zanesville, reveals an interesting evolution in his approach to decoration. In his Vance/ Avon Faience designs, tree trunks and branches are frequently depicted through slip-trailing, and the surmounting or encircling foliage either through this same technique or by slip-painting. At the same time, he emphasized the dynamic tension between the curvature of the vessel's form and the verticality of the design (plate 152). At Roseville, his sgraffito stylizations are striking (plate 146), and often in these, as later in designs at Jervis Pottery (plate 164, left and middle), trees were not merely the lateral framework or decorative border for other pictorial motifs -- as seen in several of his Jap Birdimal designs at Weller -- but rather the central image. This concept of an abstracted, wooded landscape as the design itself was continued at University City, where Rhead, as Professor of Pottery, introduced a decorative scheme based on a conventionalized forest scene with stylized trunks, limbs and branches, now delineated within incised outlines (plate 166, right), emphasizing a rhythmic verticality, which was to reach fruition during his time in California.

Rhead's tree designs – and also the Rhead-inspired tree designs of Newcomb College (plate 186), and even the forested elaborations of Rudolph Lorber at Weller (plate 185) – are reflected in the work of Cable and Fried and some of the more gifted students in the Ceramics Department at Grand Forks. In her address "Pots and Pines, a Decorative Problem for the Artist Potter," presented at the Annual Meeting of the American Ceramic Society in February, 1925, Cable introduced her topic with the words: "My vacations are spent among the pines of northern Minnesota. I drink them in all summer, I long for them all winter, and being a potter they naturally have formed the 'theme' of many a pot." Her inspiration for the tiled fireplace surround at her home (plates 56; 57) and for her other landscape tiles (plates 61, left and middle; 170) was given practical realization through her close study of Rhead's slip-trailing technique. In addition, much of Cable's pottery (plate 194) and many examples of work by Hildegarde Fried (plates 188; 191)

Plate 187: UND vase, 1924, marked "3/24 WW", probably by Wanda Wells.

Plate 188: UND plaque, 7¼"x 6¾", by Fried, marked "H.U.F." and "H. Dreps May 1926".

-- and by some students (plates 143; 187) -- exhibit these two instructors' wish to emulate both Marblehead's conventionalized "arboretum" and Rookwood's pictorial representation of forest scenes in its Vellum (plate 193) and Iris lines. Specifically, Hannah Tutt's vase for Marblehead

Plate 189: Marblehead vase, 7" h., flat-painted by Hannah Tutt.

Plate 190: UND slip-painted vase, by Cable, marked "MKC". UND Coll. # C-CBL 86-256.

(plate 189) not only has the stylistic appeal of Cable's vase (plate 190) with its vertical emphasis, but also provides an interesting and striking parallel with the high-glazed orange tree design (plate 87) by an unidentified artist at Grand Forks.

Along with technique, other imagery was "borrowed" (consciously, inadvertently or coincidentally) and adapted by instructors and students alike in Grand Forks. For instance, they introduced galleons from Grueby (plate 61, right); trellised arrangements and seagulls from Marblehead (plate 195); cattails, undulating fern fronds and swirling leaves from Arequipa (plate 168) and, together with other flora and botanical studies, from Newcomb Pottery (plates 158; 159); mountain and lake views and various fauna from Rookwood (plates 141; 143; 192); Persian motifs examined by Rhead at Santa Barbara (plate 196); and abstract, modernistic idiom from American studio potters of the 1950s and 1960s. Such decoration continues to compete today, in collectors' preferences, with the innovative Indian design, bentonite effects, prairie themes, indigenous features and other Western compositions popularized by the Ceramics Department at the School of Mines. The variety of technique, design and decoration in the University of North Dakota pottery, available now for consideration by scholars, collectors and admirers, surpasses that of most other American potteries of the period.

Plate 191: UND vase, 12" h., by Fried, marked "HUF". UND Coll. # C-HLD 17-645.

Plate 192: UND vase, 6"x 7", c. 1927, by Huckfield, marked "H (in a circle) 74". Nelson Coll.

Plate 193: Rookwood scenic Vellum vase, 8½" h., 1908, by E. T. Hurley. McCormack Coll.

Plate 194: Early UND vase, 8" h., by Cable, marked "MKC 1916"; decorative band of landscape scene with slip-painted trees and hills, under a semi-gloss glaze.

Grand Forks was by no means the only source of ceramic items specially commissioned by customers for promotional purposes, or designed, and made, to commemorate an anniversary, jubilee, convention or other event. During its almost ninety years of existence, the Rookwood Pottery Co. from 1880 on -- beginning with the manufacture of three annual tankard designs for the Cincinnati Cooperage Company -- produced jugs, mugs, ashtrays, pin-trays, vases and paperweights, some cast and some hand-decorated, for clubs, public organizations, medical associations, the Post Office Department, Elks conventions and various business firms in Cincinnati; for the National Association for the Deaf, the Association of Catholic Charities and the Shrine of the Immaculate Conception in Washington, DC; and, in the mid-1960s, a range of commemorative ashtrays for various colleges and universities. In 1935, Rookwood introduced its own "Potter" souvenir medallion for sale to visitors to its Mount Adams property. Twenty years earlier it had made beer steins for the Delta Kappa Epsilon Fraternity, just as S. A. Weller, in 1928, produced fundraising items commissioned by the Indianapolis Alumnae Association for the Kappa Kappa Gamma Sorority. In 1904, Weller celebrated its participation in the St. Louis World's Fair with a small range of commemorative objects. California Faience, later, produced a striking plaque, in blue and white high-glaze, celebrating the 1933 Century of Progress Chicago World's Fair (plate 197). Mary Chase Perry Stratton, at Pewabic Pottery, designed several plaques/roundels, in her spectacular luster glazes, for such universities as Ohio State and Wayne State (plate 198), while Cowan, in 1925, made not less than 156 candle-lamps in the shape of a groundhog, designed by Frank Wilcox of the Cleveland School of Art, for presentation to the membership of the Rowfant Club, in Cleveland, Ohio (plate 199). The New York State College of Ceramics, with a small transfer-printed dish, and the Georgia Institute of Technology, with its glaze-inlaid tile of 1940, were each eager to promote their ceramics programs in ceramic form (plate 200).

Plate 195: UND covered jar, 10" h., marked "Marie". Nelson Coll.

Plate 196: UND footed low compote, 9 7/8" dia., marked "M. Cable 1932 #810". UND Coll. # C-CBL 53-223.

Plate 197: Plaque by California Faience.

Plate 198: Plaque by Pewabic for Wayne State University.

Plate 199: Cowan candle lamp, 1925, for the Rowfant Club, Cleveland.

Plate 200: (Left) promotional item for the New York State College of Ceramics at Alfred University, Alfred, NY; (right) commemorative tile, 1940, by and for the Georgia Institute of Technology.

D. **Glaze Effects**

The basic tenets of Binns' teaching suffused Cable's theory and practice throughout her career, and not least of what she gained from him was the importance of glaze chemistry. Prior to 1880, and in some areas even well after that date, glazes were learned and applied empirically, and were zealously guarded, as vital secrets, from potential competitors. Though this secretive and protective attitude was to continue for several decades into the twentieth century, a change was afoot to move from tradition and chance towards scientific study and knowledge in the formulation of glazes.

Plate 201: Vase with a vibrant red glaze, probably formulated by Binns and produced by a copper oxide reduction technique, with an exuberant crystalline effect on an overall iridescent background; marked "N.Y.S.C. ALFRED 1912".

Binns researched, developed, announced and published his own basc recipes of matt and other glazes together with information concerning additive agents to effect and modify color and visual texture, as explained in his "Matt Glazes at High Temperatures." [167] In *The Potter's Craft* he also listed many of these materials including such oxides as cobalt, copper, iron, chrome, nickel and zinc, together with molybdenum, titanium, tungsten and rutile. Much of Binns' own ceramic work was produced by techniques of oxidation or reduction in firing, requiring both time and patience, when he was not otherwise occupied with teaching or extensively documented experimentation. Several of his more advanced students assisted him eagerly in his research (plate 201). Formerly in the author's collection was a set of 18 test-glaze miniature vases, slip-cast and fired, c. 1905, in various high-fired glazes, marked with Roman numerals and tagged with small labels describing glaze formulae, -- accompanied by a note reading "Test pieces made in laboratory Alfred University School of Ceramics under Prof. C. F. Binns." [168]

An intense program of glaze research and formulation -- to which even senior decorators were not privy -- was conducted at Rookwood, first by superintendent Joseph Bailey, Sr. (plate 202, right), Karl Langenbeck in 1885, and later by Stanley G. Burt, who was sent to Germany in 1894 to study ceramic chemistry for two years. By that time, with Burt working under Bailey and possibly with assistance from William P. McDonald, the Iris, Sea Green and Aerial Blue glazes had been developed. In the twentieth century, under superintendent and chemist Burt, glaze experiments were conducted continually at Rookwood, especially with glaze colors in red, blue and green categories, identified, for instance, as Ox Blood, Egyptian Turquoise and Antique Olive Green.

Plate 202: Red glaze vases: (left) two by Newcomb College, 1907 and 1932 (the second possibly by Aurelia Arbo); (second from right) by Hammers at UND, c. 1928, using glaze # 538B; (right) by Rookwood, 1895, (so-called Bailey's red).

A red-glazed vase with redroot motif by Newcomb Pottery was exhibited at the Pan-American Exposition, in 1901, at Buffalo, New York. By 1903, forms in metallic and luster glazes were produced, many undecorated though some with deeply incised designs, with some regularity before 1910, in New Orleans.[169] In 1904, at St. Louis, a silver medal, amongst others, was awarded to Joseph Meyer for experimental glazes. At the 1907 Jamestown Ter-Centennial Exhibition, at Norfolk, Virginia, Newcomb College received a gold medal for an exhibit including a number of pieces in reduction red glaze, alone or with underglaze, and some with luster or iridescence on different colored – white, cream, buff and red – clay bodies (plate 202, left). This appears to have been a short-lived experiment at the College, possibly because the special reduction firing was unpredictable or because the results lacked variety in color and design. Nevertheless, experimental red glazes were occasionally used in later years, particularly in the 1930s (plate 202, second from left).

Plate 203: Candleholder by Cowan Pottery; Persian blue glaze.

Oxblood glaze, and such other monochrome glazes as Persian blue and Chinese rose, white and various green tones, occupied the attentions of Hugh Robertson, in the 1880s, at the Chelsea Keramic Art Works, and Fred H. Robertson, in the early twentieth century, at the Robertson Pottery in Los Angeles.

Plate 204: UND vase, 3¼" h., with crystalline glaze. UND Coll. # C-MSC 184-777.

Other experiments, though on a lesser scale, into red glazes were conducted at Roseville (resulting in the Mongol line of 1904, developed by John Herrold), Weller (the Chengtu line of 1925), Pewabic (with gold lustres and other iridescence) and Fulper, whose Chinese-type glazes, including the Famille Rose line, so intrigued Dean Babcock at the time of his "museum" purchases. Experiments into Persian or Egyptian blue glaze were conducted by Albert Solon at Arequipa, Leon Volkmar at Durant Kilns, Arthur Baggs at Cowan Pottery Studio (plate 203) and later (with his work in copper red glaze and salt glazing) at Ohio State University, and by Mrs. Stratton at Pewabic. As well, Frederick Rhead produced work in Chinese black in Santa Barbara, and, previously, metallic effects and copper lusters at Jervis, and flowing/drip glazes at Arequipa (plate 205, left). Frederick Walrath, in Rochester, New York, also experimented with flowing/drip glazes.

Plate 205: Vases with flowing/drip glazes, by (left) Arequipa; and (right) by Mattson at UND, c. 1932.

Plate 206: UND vase, c. 1929, by Mattson; with metallic black glaze bands and dripping against high-glaze turquoise ground; on buff-colored clay. SHSND Coll. # 1988.148.20.

At University City, the few more gifted students in attendance in the ceramics department – as opposed to the greater number enrolled in the correspondence course – were ensured a very high level of instruction, indeed, by Taxile Doat and his foreign assistants, and by Adelaide Alsop Robineau. There, high-fired porcelain bodies were invested with crystalline glazes of the highest order (plate 166, left). As Instructor of Pottery at University City, Frederick Rhead, who, in his earlier days at Roseville, had developed a crystalline glaze for the Crystalis line, was not only responsible for instruction in glaze science in his specialty, but also refined his interest in the more advanced formulae through his association with Doat and Robineau. Later, at the American Encaustic Tiling Co., he continued his research into crystalline and "pate changeant" glazes.

Other potteries experimented, with differing degrees of success, with crystalline and metallic glazes, and they included Rookwood, Fulper, Teco, Norweta and Roseville.

Very infrequently a University of North Dakota vessel might be found, which is marked to indicate the experimental use of identified, mixed clays with a trial glaze, possibly with a surface treatment formulated to produce a particular effect; for instance, a bowl of striking appeal -- in red clay with a mirror-like, lustered finish on a glaze of blended colors -- marked "B" for Beulah clay, "RR" for Red Ross and the word "Treated." Again, some unusual vessels (for example, plate 206) though bearing only the usual UND markings -- can be considered to be experiments in the use and combination of clay and glaze.

Research into North Dakota mineral deposits suitable for the formulation of glazes, as well as for clay bodies, was of course the major purpose, at least in the period 1910-1938, of the Ceramics Department at the School of Mines (plate 207). This research was first pursued by Cable and Fried, and later by Mattson and, most importantly, Freida Hammers. The Glaze Records completed and filed by Hammers since the first days of her analysis and research in the

Plate 207: Three UND bowls by Hammers, c. 1928, with Persian/Egyptian blue glaze; (left) marked "682-B", (middle) marked "G682-D D.F.C." and (right) marked "574 H Egyptian Blue – Middle 1. Hebron 2. Dickinson". UND Coll. # (left to right) C-HMM 16-385, C-HMM 7-376, C-HMM 18-387.

Ceramics Department show many experiments, particularly in 1926, to produce a suitable blue glaze, simulating the color of Persian (or Egyptian) faience (plate 33). The most notable of these experiments involved raw alkaline glazes number 574A-H and number G682A-D (plate 207) on various clay bodies.

During the previous year, she had begun research into such red glazes (fig. 52) as number 538 (plate 202, second from right; see also plate 34).

The search for these two effects, particularly, had been conducted by generations of potters/chemists in Europe and the United States in the latter half of the nineteenth century and into the twentieth. Cable's correspondence, in 1931, with Glen Lukens (then teaching in the pottery department of Fullerton Junior College, in California) also gives insight into American ceramists' extensive interest in glaze chemistry at this time. Lukens had read Cable's "Colored Glazes and Indian Design on North Dakota Pottery," as published in the *Journal of the American Ceramic Society* in 1924, and requested information on sources for the glaze colorants she had discussed. As well, he suggested that she consider several other glazes and underglaze stains available from such suppliers as the Drakenfeld Company and the R & H Company.

Also, at Grand Forks, some test pieces were produced, and marked "SD" possibly to indicate the experimental use of clays from South Dakota, quite often in combination with trial glazes of green (G939-B, G944-A, G951, G958) or brown (G935) hue -- the colors used most effectively in the decoration of Pine Ridge pottery.

GLAZES Red gloss glaze

Glaze Body No. 85 Date April 28, 1925

Test No. Glaze No. 538.

Chemical Formula: Regular 119c formula with barium substituted for zinc to give better color quality.

PbO--.2836

CaO--.2917 Al_2O_3--.4352 SiO_2--2.2978

BaO--.2160

K_2O--.2093

Batch Formula:

(For formula 7x see G-542)

White lead	73.19 x 3 =	219.57
Whiting	29.17	87.51
Barium Carbonate	42.55	127.65
Feldspar	116.31	348.93
Body Clay	58.56	175.68
Flint	35.40	106.20
	355 .18	1065.54
Pink Oxide	36. x 3	108

Fineness

Develops at Cone No. 2 down--3 tipping

Color Ver nice, rich, dark red.

Surface and Texture Fine and smooth.

Imperfections and Causes

Remarks: Oct. 1925 This looks like a good glaze, and is a lovely red color. Am not sure as yet as to whether it will stand without crazing on Potter's clay. The test cup is O.K. after summer standing while the test a little underfired and perhaps a bit heavy in glaze is crazed--make up-- and try out and watch for crazing.

Fig. 52: Glaze Record Sheet, dated April 28, 1925, for "Red gloss glaze" No. 538, with "Remarks" added in October, 1925, -- see also plate 202, second from right.

E. **Intramural Comparisons / Contrasts**

Margaret Cable, her three assistants on the faculty of the Ceramics Department and fellow staff member Flora Huckfield, were all capable of producing brilliant designs in a variety of styles and techniques. The similarities in their output -- if not appropriately marked -- in a particular manner are such as to confuse, if not prohibit, occasionally, one's ability to distinguish between them. Fried, Mattson and Hammers took instruction in pottery making and decoration from Cable, and, initially at least, used her techniques and her suggested design schemes, to produce their own pottery, while Huckfield, also in her early years in the Department, decorated pots under Cable's guidance. Cable, herself, though lacking the formal training and academic qualifications of Fried, Mattson and Hammers, was an accomplished all-rounder, eager to capitalize on her knowledge, exercise her talents and extend her artistic and technical horizons. She and Fried especially, but also Mattson and, though with little opportunity, Hammers, were adept at the wheel. Mattson was preeminent in hand-building. Fried had considerable knowledge of chemistry; and Hammers, with similar training, was able to contribute greatly from her scientific knowledge and research to the continuation and expansion of the ceramics program. Mattson, with a Bachelor's degree in art and education, a Master's degree in educational psychology and ceramics and a Master's thesis on the subject of Indian art and symbolism, was well qualified to fulfill the requirements of her position in the Department and to enlarge its portfolio of ceramic design.

Fried's aesthetic sensibility, evident in the delicacy and refinement of her Arts and Crafts and Art Nouveau-type design schemes, and her craftsmanship and respect for materials, nurtured by her studies under Binns, are in contrast to those manifested in Mattson's more robust treatment of her innovative themes of Indian and other Western inspiration (plates 208, left; 209, left). Hammers' considerable artistic abilities are overshadowed by her technical achievements in clay and glaze research for the Ceramics Department, but, as Cable wrote of her, she was a scientist "endowed with artistic talent" with "a splendid technique as a potter and decorator."[170] Huckfield – as decorator only – employed, in the main, the techniques of painting, sgraffito

Plate 208: (Left) vase, c. 1929, by Mattson; incised rose decoration; (right) covered jar, 1954, marked "Veronica Bird Arnold 4/21/54".

and carving, emulating the designs of both her sister and Mattson, to develop a large body of work utilizing the molded forms produced by the other staff members and by students (plate 209, right); her facility in the glazing booth was beneficial to all.

Plate 209: (Left) vase, by Mattson (shape by Holton); (right) vase, c. 1936, by Huckfield, marked "BUSTIN-HUCK (in a circle) 4315" (shape by Bustin).

Margaret Pachl's training, design ethos and ceramic output stand in stark contrast to those of her predecessors on the faculty of the Department. Her approach was that of the new generation of national and international studio potters and reflected the progression of ceramic instruction in the United States, the changing considerations of style, technique and production, and the dismissal of previous art pottery traditions. As was to be expected, time was an overriding factor contributing to this new age in American ceramics, just as it had been, though to a somewhat lesser degree, in the evolution of style during the past forty to fifty years in the Ceramics Department. This is nowhere more apparent than in the contrasting visions and achievements of students prior to 1925 -- for instance in the work of Rena Parizek, c. 1912 (plate 137) and Marguerite Moe, c. 1917 (plate 116, left) -- and those after 1950 – for instance in the work, c. 1954, of Dorothy Olson, (plate 78) and Veronica Bird Arnold (plate 208, right).

Quality standards, of course, differ widely in the output of the University of North Dakota. On the one hand -- regardless of form, technique, style and period -- there is the best, or even standard, work of the professional staff members, together with the best work of the most accomplished student decorators; on the other, there are the products by students of possibly average talent, not to mention the more unfortunate, if not execrable, "course souvenirs" of the least gifted student amateurs. In addition, handcraftsmanship, in the case of original decoration, can be contrasted with the multiple reproduction of the slip-cast, though well-finished, items on the Spencer list (plate 210).

Plate 210: (Left) small wheat vase; Spencer-list item # 134, 1942, from Hicks shape #112. (Right) handmade vase by Wells, with hand-applied slash-marks under dripped glaze; on buff-colored clay.

F. **Incidental Influence – Anton Lang**

Anton Lang, a Bavarian potter who produced designs in a folk-art manner, many expressing German regional themes or bearing German adages, proverbs, sayings and inscriptions, rendered through slip-painting and slip-trailing, was well known in the United States during the 1920s. He was celebrated internationally for having, on three occasions, portrayed Christ in the productions of the Passion Play at Oberammergau, and in the United States he was also acclaimed in ceramic circles by Arts and Crafts enthusiasts.

Though the mid-teens signaled a decline in interest in the Arts and Crafts Movement as a whole and though the demand for a union of art and industry was received with excitement, particularly in Europe in the post-war years, the Arts and Crafts style, if not its social philosophy, survived, in the United States, for almost two more decades. Even after the time of the 1925 Exposition Internationale des Arts Decoratifs et Industriels Modernes, in Paris, the 1926 Exhibition of French Decorative Arts, and the 1928 International Exhibition of Ceramic Art, both at the Metropolitan Museum of Art in New York, many major American collectors were still focused on the older handcrafted product and continued to add examples of it – such as the work of Marblehead, Paul Revere and Newcomb – to their collections well into the 1930s.

It is not surprising, therefore, that Anton Lang and his brother Andreas, who was also a potter, should be welcomed and feted by ceramics devotees in both Cleveland and Cincinnati during a fund-raising tour, which featured an exhibit of Bavarian crafts, in 1923-1924. [171] "Pilgrimages" to his home and studio in Germany were made by, among other such American pottery "faithful," Hildegarde Fried, whose August 9, 1922, postcard to Margaret Cable is shown here (fig. 53), and later, Julia Mattson.

Fig. 53: Postcard showing Anton Lang in his studio in Oberammergau, Germany.

G. The Charles Fergus Binns Medal for Excellence in Ceramic Art

First awarded, in 1926, to Marion Lawrence Fosdick, professor of modeling and pottery at Alfred through 1953, the medal's later recipients included Arthur Baggs (1927), Stanley G. Burt (1929), Myrtle Merritt French (1930), R. Guy Cowan (1931), Frederick Hurten Rhead (1934), Viktor Schreckengost (1938), Waylande Gregory (1939), Mary Chase Perry Stratton (1947), Glen Lukens (1949), Bernard Leach (1950), Margaret Cable (1951) and Paul Cox (1952).

Endnotes

161 "Possibilities of Pottery Making from North Dakota Clays," by Margaret Cable.

162 *Pottery from North Dakota Clays*, by Margaret Cable, December 15, 1926.

163 As explained in Rhead's articles in the three issues of his magazine *The Potter*, of 1916-7.

164 *The Potter*, issue I, December, 1916/January, 1917.

165 *Frederick Hurten Rhead: An English Potter in America*, by Sharon Dale.

166 *The Arts and Crafts Movement in America, 1876-1916*, edited by Robert Judson Clark: "Art Pottery," by Martin Eidelberg.

167 *Journal of the American Ceramic Society*, 7, 1905.

168 David Rago auction catalog of 11/13/1994, *Arts and Crafts in New York*, lot #29. Also listed as #17 in the "Catalogue Raisonne," included in *Charles Fergus Binns: The Father of American Studio Ceramics*, by Margaret Carney.

169 *Sunset Magazine*, June, 1903.

170 Cable letter dated April 21, 1926, to Prof. E. F. Chandler.

171 During his visit to Rookwood Pottery, Lang exhibited his expertise at the wheel.

250
UNIVERSITY OF NORTH DAKOTA, GRAND FORKS, N. D.
PRESIDENT'S RESIDENCE.
UNIVERSITY COMMONS
HISTORIC PAGEANT, BANKSIDE THEATRE
UNIVERSITY CAMPUS
LAW BUILDING
CHEMISTRY BUILDING
102783

APPENDIX III

Spencer "Sample" Inventory List (February, 1938, through 1948)

This list is derived from the Ceramics Department's Cost Data Sheets, with augmentations from the Spencer correspondence and dealership invoices. It contains a total of not less than 318 Spencer sample items, the greater proportion of which were produced from molds. Many were plain models which were intended solely to be glazed in a single color (with or without shading) or which were to benefit from the easy and quick addition of color as simple painted decoration. Others incorporating in-mold decoration were to receive, possibly, a limited amount of hand-finishing -- particularly, where appropriate, a refinement of incised, intaglio detail or carved/excised background (leaving a motif in relief), and also an enrichment of the design through the application of some surface color-painting or background shading. Even with such enhancement, for commercial reasons, as painted decoration on plain items, or as sharpened contouring for models incorporating incised, carved or sgraffito designs (plates 97, left; 151; 212 through 215), these wares on the Spencer list would have been easily, quickly and cheaply made to order to fill the salesman's requests. On the other hand, not less than twenty-one of the forms on the list, if the Prairie Pottery models, # 62 - # 69, are included, were, in fact, handmade (built or thrown) and possibly, if not plain models, hand-decorated. Since these latter would, therefore, have required more time and skill to produce, they would presumably have been more costly.

Also, the list includes a small sub-group of pottery which should be considered separately as original work. Several of the molded, usually plain forms, if considered suited to the purpose, were available to instructors and students for use as design projects for the application of their own unique decorative schemes, either through painting or incising/

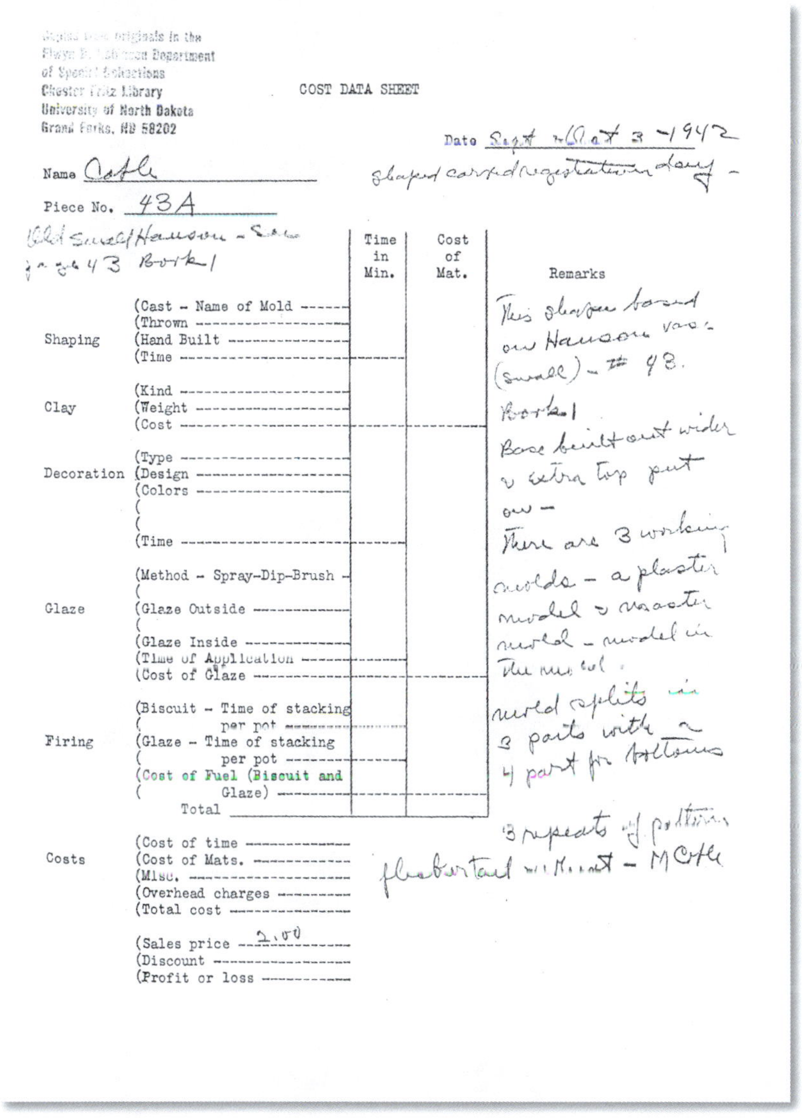
Copied from originals in the Elwyn B. Robinson Department of Special Collections, Chester Fritz Library, University of North Dakota, Grand Forks, ND 58202

COST DATA SHEET

Date Sept [illegible] 3 - 1942

shaped carved [illegible] -

Name Cable

Piece No. 43A

		Time in Min.	Cost of Mat.	Remarks
Shaping	(Cast - Name of Mold (Thrown (Hand Built (Time			This shape based on Hanson vase (small) - # 43. Book 1
Clay	(Kind (Weight (Cost			Base built out wider & extra top put on -
Decoration	(Type (Design (Colors (((Time			There are 3 working molds - a plaster model & master mold - model in the mold.
Glaze	(Method - Spray-Dip-Brush ((Glaze Outside ((Glaze Inside (Time of Application (Cost of Glaze			mold splits in 3 parts with a 4 part for bottoms
Firing	(Biscuit - Time of stacking (per pot (Glaze - Time of stacking (per pot (Cost of Fuel (Biscuit and (Glaze)			
	Total			

3 repeats of pattern

Costs (Cost of time
(Cost of Mats.
(Misc.
(Overhead charges
(Total cost

(Sales price 2.00
(Discount
(Profit or loss

Fig. 54: Cost Data Sheet for Spencer-list item #(43B) erroneously noted here as #43A.

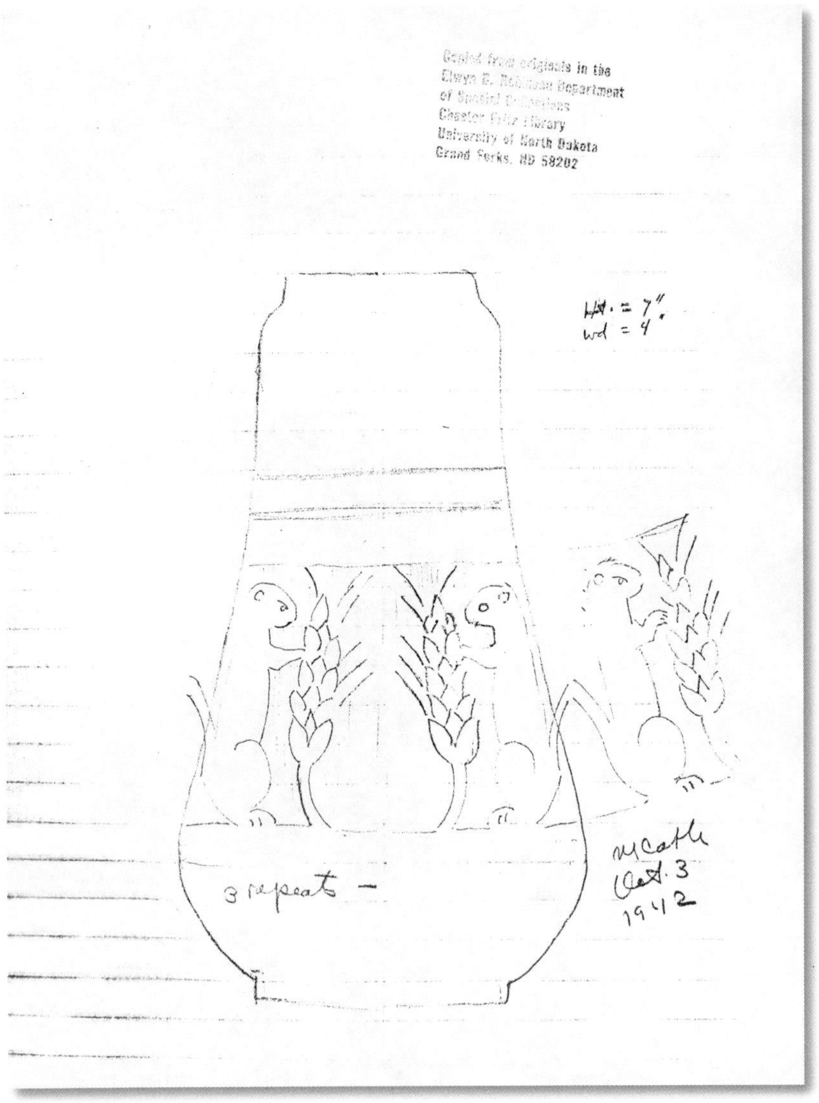

Fig. 55: Reverse of Fig. 54.

excising techniques. For instance, the planter/bookends #177, of 1944, by Cable/Odegard (plain with incised grooves) were further enriched with an incised fish design by Mary Haessle on March 21 and 24, 1944; the plain Chinese ginger jar #191, also of 1944, by Anna Bridston received an original sgraffito design by Nat Miller in January and March of 1948 (plate 211). This last-mentioned student, Miller, using Cable's plain mold #222 of 1945, was also the decorator of a toasting pitcher, painted with an original floral design with blue bands on the body and with the word "SKAAL" (English equivalent: "Cheers") under the lip. And again, Cable's rabbit, plain model #105 "Billy" (probably named for another of nephew Charles's pets) of 1942 (plate 151, right), was decorated, at a later date, with various schemes incorporating caricature eyes and ears and abstract, floral motifs in polychrome, either by Cable herself or by unknown hands – listed here, for convenience, as # (105A-?).

Today's collector can check his acquisitions against the Spencer list and if the piece in question corresponds to the description given, then he can date production of the item to the period 1938-1948. Dating in respect of the original introduction of the shape and the initiation of the decoration of that item, as has been already discussed, would be a totally different matter, as molds, of this time, but incorporating popular and long-used shapes and/or decoration schemes originating from a possibly much earlier period, appear frequently on the Spencer list. For example, Cable's co-maker in respect of items #22-22A of 1938 was Eva Syre, who was active in the Ceramics Department courses probably only in the year 1922.

It should be noted that, in some cases, the invoices in the Departmental files contradict the information contained in this inventory list, assigning a different shape, technique or decoration to a specific item number. This is perhaps due to human error in record-keeping, the omission of, or error in, a suffixed number, inadvertent duplication or even uncertainty as to whether a certain shape should be considered a vase or bowl. For instance, item #6 is decorated, according to the appropriate Cost Data Sheet, with "floating ducks," and, according to the Harrington-Spencer letter of February 8, 1938, with "wild goose" (fig. 44). Also, the 1942 model decorated with "wheat and flickertail," (plate 212, second from left), based on a modified form of the 1938 mold (for plain vase) #43, is found to be marked "43" and should surely be #43B (figs. 54; 55), since #43A already exists as "prairie rose" decoration on plain shape #43 of 1938.

Other contradictions are more seriously confusing. For instance, the description of #20 is questionable; also, the "bison" vase #117A by Cable on a Tallman shape is the Spencer-list version of a late-1920s vase, marked "MC-JM", which is believed to have been designed by Mattson, possibly with Cable's guidance or assistance (plate 96, left). In general, however, it is thought that the details contained in the Cost Data Sheets are ultimately more reliable than those included in the invoices.

The Ceramics Department at the University of North Dakota is currently collecting information to add to this list as numbered examples of shapes/decoration are located, thereby filling in the gaps to be found in the list as it is included here.

Plates 211 – 215: Spencer-list Items

Plate 211: Ginger jar, 8" h.; Spencer-list form #191, with original decoration; marked "Nat Miller, Mar. 1948". Nelson Coll.

Plate 212: (Left to right) # 169, vase by Mattson, 1943; # 43 (should be 43B), vase by Cable, 1942, "Flickertail – Wheat"; # 115 (should be 115A), vase by Mattson, 1942; # 56, vase by Mattson, 1939, "Viking Ship."

Plate 213: (Left to right) # 192, # 111A and # 155, vases/bowls by Cable; (left), 1944, shape by Verona Kumm; (middle), 1941; (right), 1943, "MEADOW LARK."

Plate 214: (Left to right) # 172, # 211 and # 164, vases by Huckfield; (left), 1943; (middle), 1945, "SIOUX," shape by McGregor; (right), 1943, from Cable shape # 37C.

Plate 215: "Aunt Susan" cookie-jar, 10¼" h., by Cable; Spencer-list #118A, 1942. UND Coll. # C-CBL Gift 123-850.

Models represented by parenthesized numbers were not listed in this manner in the files of the Ceramics Department, but are so designated here, principally to elucidate and facilitate identification, and to clarify the difference between two or more shapes and/or designs marked with the same number on the underside of vessels produced during the Spencer period. This organization, by the author, also corrects what were, apparently, omissions by the original record keepers in the Ceramics Department.

Sample #	Year	Item	Motif	Made by
1	1938	vase, tall, carved	cowboy	Mattson
2	1938	bowl, large, carved	bison/buffalo	Mattson
3	1938	bowl, medium, sgraffito	buffalo	Mattson
3A	1938	bowl	snowmen	Mattson
4	1938	vase, small, sgraffito	coyote	Mattson
5	1938	bowl, medium, sgraffito	cowpony/cowboy	Mattson
6	1938	bowl, small, sgraffito	floating ducks/wild goose	Mattson
7	1938	vase, small, carved	leaf and circle	Mattson
8	1938	vase, medium, incised	abstract, letter C	Mattson
9	1938	vase, medium, incised	abstract, letter O	Mattson
10	1938	vase, small	plain, 3 or 4 bands	Mattson
11	1938	bowl, small, carved/incised	geometric design	Mattson
12	1938	figure, pressed	pelican	Mattson
13/13A	1938	figure, pressed	cowboy (one of which: bentonite)	Mattson
14	1938	plate, incised	conventional rose	Huckfield
15	1938	tea tile, glaze painted	prairie rose	Huckfield
16	1938	ashtray, carved	Indian head	Huckfield
17	1938	paperweight, pressed	4-H Club	Huckfield
18	1938	fruit bowl, large, footed, thrown/carved	waves	Cable
19	1938	fruit bowl, medium, footed, thrown/incised	center rose	Cable
20	1938	compote, tall, footed, or fruit bowl, small, thrown/incised	center rose	Cable
21	1938	bowl, large	plain	Cable
21A	1938	flower frog	wild goose	Cable
22	1938	vase, medium	plain	Cable/Syre
22A	1938	vase, medium, incised	deer and pine tree	Cable/Syre
23	1938	vase, small	grooves	Cable
24	1938	vase, small	grooves	Cable/Bushaw
25	1938	seal	UND	Cable
26	1938	bowl, thrown	plain	Cable
27/A/B/C/D	1938	vases, small, thrown		Cable
28	1938		wheat shocks	Huckfield/Bridgeman
28A	1938		wheat shocks	Huckfield
28B	1938		wheat spray	Huckfield
29	1938	bowl	prairie rose	Huckfield/Bridgeman
30	1938	vase	plain	Huckfield/Sorlie
30A	1938	vase, incised	wheat	Huckfield
31	1938	bowl, small, incised	wheat	Huckfield
32	1938	bowl, small, incised	wheat	Huckfield
33	1938	tile	covered wagon	Huckfield

Sample #	Year	Item	Motif	Made by
34	1938	bowl	leaf	Huckfield/Erickson
35	1938	plate, small, sgraffito	goose	Huckfield
36	1938		deer	Huckfield/Davies
37	1938	vase, thrown		Cable
37A	1938	vase, bell-shaped, thrown		Cable
37B	1938	bowl, thrown		Cable/Lindholm
37C	(not known)	vase	plain	Cable
37D	(not known)	vase	plain	Huckfield
38	1938	vase, sgraffito	cactus	Mattson
39	1938	bud	vase	Cable
40	1938	vase, fat, incised	3 grooved rings	Huckfield
41	1938			Cable
42	1938	medallions	Sioux and bison	
43	1938	vase, small	plain	Cable/Hanson
43A	1938	vase	prairie rose	Cable/Hanson
(43B)	1942	vase (modified shape)	wheat and flickertail	Cable/Hanson
44	1938	vase, tall	plain	Cable/LaBrant
44A	1938	vase	rose	Cable
45	1938	vase, medium	plain (WPA)	Cable
(45A)	1938	vase, medium	prairie rose	Cable
46	1938	bowl	plain (WPA)	Huckfield/Cable
46A	1938	bowl	flickertail and wheat	Huckfield
46B	1938	bowl	oxcart	Huckfield
47	1938	vase	plain	Huckfield
47A	1938	vase	wheat	Huckfield
48	1938	figure	horse	Mattson
49	1938	figure, pressed	lion	Mattson
50	1939	figure	camel, plain	Mattson
50A	1939	figure	camel, marked "KEM"	Mattson
51	1941	bowl	prairie rose	Huckfield
51A	1941	bowl	rose	Huckfield
52	1941	creamer/sugar	plain	Cable
52A	1941	pitcher, incised	prairie rose	Cable
52B	1941	creamer	prairie rose	Cable
53	1942	vase, incised	pasque flower	Huckfield
53A	1942	vase, thrown		Cable
54	1940	bowl, incised/painted	grooved rings	Huckfield
54A	1940	bowl	covered wagon	Huckfield
54B	1940	bowl	prairie dogs	Huckfield
54C	1940	bowl	cowboy	Mattson
55	1939	bowl, sgraffito	flower	Cable
56	1939	vase, small, sgraffito	Viking ship	Mattson
56A	1942	vase	Viking ship	Mattson
57	1939	bowl, carved	flower	Mattson/Steen
57A	1942	bowl	snow ladies	Mattson/Steen
58 and (58A-?)	1940	trays	cowboy, Roosevelt cabin, Red River ox cart, covered wagon, floral, thunderbird, prairie rose, rabbits, coyote, buffalo, flickertail, etc.	Mattson

Sample #	Year	Item	Motif	Made by
59	1940	bowl, footed		Cable/Gruenfelder
59A	1940	bowl, incised	grooved rings	Cable/Gruenfelder
59B	1940	bowl, tall, without foot		Cable/Whitney
59C	1940	bowl, low, without foot		Cable/Whitney
60	1940	bowl	plain	Bridgeman
60A	1940	bowl	wheat and leaves	Bridgeman
61	1940	vase, incised	wheat	Huckfield/Howell
62	1940	plate (Prairie Pottery #3)	plowman	Huckfield
63	1940	plate (Prairie Pottery #7)	lamb	Cable
64	1940	vase (Prairie Pottery #8)	deer and pines, bentonite	Mattson
65	1940	bowl (Prairie Pottery #11)	rose	Cable
66	1940	plate (Prairie Pottery #13)	deer	Huckfield
67	1940	bowl (Prairie Pottery #14)	flower	Cable/Burns
68	1940	plate, small (Prairie Pottery #16)	chicken	Cable
69	1940	plate, bentonite (Prairie Pottery)		Mattson
70	1940	vase, large		Hicks
71	1940	vase	plain	Coundit
71A	1940	vase	decorated	Coundit
72	1940	vase	plain	Griffith
73	1940	vase	plain	Berg
73A	1940	vase	decorated	Berg
74	1940	bowl	plain	Ellingson/Spencer
74A	1940	bowl	iris	Ellingson
75	1940	vase	plain	Mattson/Byrne
75A	1943	vase	cowboy roping bronco	Mattson
76	1940	vase	plain	Mythaler
76A	1940	vase	decorated	Mythaler
77	1940	bowl, large	plain	Tucker
77A	1940	bowl	roses	Tucker
78	1940	tobacco jar, incised	OPE	Mattson
79	1940	bowl	plain	Wolff
80	1940	vase	plain	Overn
80A	1940	vase	decorated	Overn
81	1940	bowl	plain	Erickson
82	1940	vase	plain	French
83	1941	honey jar and cover	(probably) plain; bee finial	Cable
84	1941	vase		Shogren
85	1941	bowl	plain	Freeman
85A	1941	bowl	pasque flower	Freeman
86	1941	pitcher or jug	plain	Cable/Lie
86A	1941	pitcher or jug, incised	pasque flower	Cable/Lie
87	1941	bowl	plain	Harris
87A	1941	bowl	pine trees	Harris
88	1941	bookends		Maxwell
89	1941	vase		Taylor
89A	1941	vase	covered wagon	Taylor
90	1941	ashtray	Flossie the fish	Cable
91	1941	lamp/vase		Commons
92	1941			WMG

Sample #	Year	Item	Motif	Made by
93	1941	bowl, small	plain	Wallace
93A	1941	bowl	victory "V"	Wallace
94	1941	vase		Mynster
95	1942	bowl, small, incised	two grooved rings at neck	Lynch
95A	1942	bowl	leaf	Huckfield
96	1942	bowl		Bustin
97	1942	vase, small		Johnston
98	1942	bud vase, incised	yucca	Cable/Anderson
99	1942	vase		Devins
100	1942	bowl, flat	wheat	King
101	1942		wild geese	McGregor
102	1941	vase	"Why Not Minot"	Mattson
103	1941	figure	duck	Cable
104	1941	(probably) figure	"Lightfoot" fawn	Cable
(104A)	1941	candle holder	"Lightfoot" fawn	Cable
105	1942	figure	rabbit, plain	Cable
(105A-?)	1942	figure, painted	rabbit -various decorative schemes by various hands	Cable
106	1942	bowl, small		Hoffman
107	1942	bowl, large		Werner
107A	1942	bowl, large	Red River oxcart	Werner
108	1941	lamp chimney		Mattson
109	1942	bud vase		Mattson
110	1941	vase, small, incised/painted	grooved rings at neck and base	Cochrane
111	1941	bowl, small	(probably) plain	Kumm
111A	1941	bowl	prairie rose	Cable/Kumm
111B	1941	bowl, incised	prairie rose	Cable/Kumm or Huckfield/Cable
112	1941	vase, small	plain	Hicks
113	1942	vase		Bitzen
114	1941	bowl, flat	(probably) plain	Schoenig
114A	1941	bowl, flat, incised	wheat spray	Huckfield/Schoenig
115	1942	vase, small	(probably) plain	Bollinger
115A	1942	vase, incised	cowboy	Mattson/Bollinger
116	1942	vase		Hancock
117	1942	vase	(probably) plain	Tallman
117A	1942	vase, decorated	bison	Cable/Tallman
118	1942	cookie jar, plain	Aunt Susan	Cable/Tallman
118A	1942	cookie jar, painted	Aunt Susan	Cable/Tallman
119	1942	bowl	(probably) plain	Nugent
119A	1942	bowl	plowman	Huckfield/Nugent
120	1942	vase	jonquil	Cable/French #82
121	1942	pitcher, incised	victory eagle	Cable
122	1942	bowl		Mayer
123	1942	vase or lamp, large	(probably) plain	Collins
124	1942	figure	Madonna	Osborn
125	1942	figure	angel	French
126	1942	figure	monk	D. Thompson

Sample #	Year	Item	Motif	Made by
127	1942	figure	bambino	Mattson
128	1942	figure	dog (cocker spaniel)	Mattson/ D. Thompson
129	1942	masks	Negro/lady	Schoenig
130	1942	bowl, small, incised	wheat and grooved rings	Cable
131	(not known)	bowl	(probably) plain	Colton
131A	1942	bowl	prairie rose	Cable/Colton
132	(not known)	vase, tall	(probably) plain	
132A	1942	vase, tall, incised	wheat	Cable
133	1942	vase	(probably) plain	Rudser
133A	1942	vase	bronco rider	Mattson/Rudser
134	1942	vase, small (see #112)	wheat	Cable/Hicks
135	1942	vase		Morrow
136	1942	vase	flower	O'Brien
137	1942	bowl, small		Barnes
138	1942			Ball
139	1942	bowl		Fretz
140	1942	pitcher, incised	oxcart	Cable
141	1942	bowl, small	wheat spray	Patton
142	1942	vase, small	wheat spray	Patton
143	1942			Palmer
144	1942	bowl, small, incised	leaves	Rudser
144A	1942	bowl, large	geese	Huckfield/Rudser
145	1942	bowl		Kirk
146	1942	pitcher		Cable/Morrow
147	1942	honey jar and cover, (see #83) incised	(probably) prairie rose	Cable
148	1943	vase	(probably) plain	Wyand
148A	1943	vase	tulip	Mattson/Wyand
149	1943	vase	(probably) plain	D. Grant
149A	1943	vase	Viking ship	Mattson/Grant
150	1943	vase, carved	prairie rose	Cable/Adams
151	1943	vase or tobacco jar with cover, carved	Sioux	Huckfield
152	1943	bowl, low, incised	prairie rose	Cable/Clarke
153	1943	bowl	North Dakota, panels with Indian, oxcart, buffalo, wheat, rose, cowboy; flickertail, on bottom	Cable/McGregor
154	1943	bowl, incised	pasque flower	Cable/Kirk
155	1943	bowl, incised	meadowlark	Cable/Putman
156	1943	covered bowl	Indian head, dancing couple, Viking ship, cowboy	Cable
157	1943	bowl (from teapot shape)		Barnes
158	1943	vase		McVay
159	1943	vase		Lippet
160	1943	tobacco jar	Indian dancers	Cable/Mattson
161	1943	vase		Cooley
162	1943	covered box, rectangular	cowboy	Cable

Sample #	Year	Item	Motif	Made by
163	1943	bowl (modified #26), carved	wheat spray	Huckfield/Cable
164	1943	vase, incised	wheat bundle	Huckfield/Cable
165	1943	bud vase	wild rose	Mattson
166	1943	vase, small, incised	wheat	Cable
167	1943	vase, small, incised	flower	Cable
168	1943	bookends	university seal	Mattson
169	1943	bowl, small	flickertail	Mattson
170	1943	bowl	turkey	Mattson
171	1943	bookends	wheat sheaf	Cable
172	1943	bowl, small, incised	covered wagon and oxen	Huckfield
173	1943	bowl, small	symbols	Mattson
174	1943	box or ashtray, small, incised	Red River oxcart	Cable
175	1943	vase	"Why Not Minot"	Mattson
176	1943	vase, small, incised	lines	Mattson
177	1944	bookends, incised	grooved rings	Cable/Odegard
(177A)	1944	bookends, incised	ivy	Cable/Odegard
178	1944	cookie jar and cover		Cable
179	1944	vase		Mattson
		or: vase (not complete)		Hammers
180	1944	vase, small	plain	Cable/Morrow
181	1944	vase	duck hunter	Mattson/Devins
182	1944	vase, low	wolf/dog	Thormodsgard/Adams
183	1944	Chinese jar		Cable/Overn
184	1944	vase, carved	Indian travois & Sioux	Huckfield/Lippet
185	1944	bowl, carved	coyote	Mattson/Wallace
186	1944	vase	covered wagon	Cable/Stewart
187	1944	vase	wheat	Hicks
188	1944	bowl, incised	harvesting wheat	Mattson
189	1944	vase	plain	Cable
190	1944	bowl	horse	Svedahl
191	1944	Chinese jar	plain	Bridston
192	1944	bowl	ducks or geese	Cable/Conners
193	1944	bowl	flower and leaf	Person
194	1944		Viking ship	Hauser
195	1944	vase		Berg
196	1944	vase		C.A.S.
197	1944	bowl, incised	prairie rose	Huckfield/O.V.
198	1945	covered candy jar, incised/painted	grooved rings and floral	Huckfield/Nelson
199	1945	water bottle and cover	Sioux calendar	Mattson/Odegard
200	1945	bowl, small	plain	Kumm
(200A)	1945	bowl, small	painted bands	Huckfield/Kumm
201	1945			Gordon
202	1945	vase, small, (collar added to #95), incised	two grooved rings below collar	Lynch
203	1945	bowl, small		Werner
204	1945			White
205	1945	bowl, small		Cable
206	1945	vase	prairie rose	Stallman

Sample #	Year	Item	Motif	Made by
207	1945	vase	flower and leaf	Larson
208	1945	vase	cowboy and rodeo pony	Huckfield
209	1945	vase, incised	prairie rose	Cable/LaBrant
210	1945	vase	cowboy	Mattson/Olson
211	1945	bowl, incised	Sioux geometric design	Huckfield/ McGregor
212	1945	pitcher	Viking ship	Cable/Connors
213	1945	(possibly) figure, painted	Norwegian girl	Mattson/Dahl
214	1945	vase	Devils Lake	Mattson
215	1945	bowl		Humphries
216	1945			Logan
217	1945	lamp		Johnson
218	1945			McCracken
219	1945			Steen
220	1945	lamp		Odegard
221	1945	bowl, low		Bollinger
222	1945	pitcher, medium	plain	Cable
(222A)	1945	pitcher, medium, incised	floral	Cable
223	1945	vase	narcissus	Cable/Howell
224	1945	pitcher		Cable
225	1945	vase/lamp, incised	man and woman on horseback	Mattson
226	1945	vase, small, incised/painted	floral with horizontal bands	Huckfield/ Patten
227	1945			Clark
228	1945	bowl, flat		Johnson
229	1945	bowl, flat		Sallee
230	1945			Stephens
231	1946	tray		Mattson
232	1946	tray	UND seal	Cable
233	1946	vase	Dutch girl	Mattson/Rudser
234	1946	vase	Swedish girl	Mattson/Vold
235	1946	vase	"Ring around a Rosie"	Mattson/Steen
236	1946	vase	Viking ship	Mattson/Dahl
237	1946	bud vase	plain	Cable
(237A)	1946	bud vase, incised	grooved rings	Cable
238	1946	bud vase		Mattson
239	1946	bud vase, small	plain	Cable
240	1946	bud vase, small	plain	Cable
241	1946	bud vase, small		Mattson
242	1946	creamer/sugar, painted	flowers and leaves	Cable
243	1946	flower pot		Cable
244	1947	vase, large		Haesle
245	1947	bowl, small	(American Way)	Haesle
246	1947	fruit bowl, large		Haesle
247	1947	plate bowl, large		Haesle
248	1948	bowl		

Graduates of the Ceramics Program at the University of North Dakota

Hildegarde Fried, Julia Mattson, Freida Hammers, Laura Taylor and Charles Grantier were all graduates of the University of North Dakota, who took courses from Margaret Cable. The first three went on to teach and research in the Ceramics Department there, assisting Cable, as did Laura Taylor before her WPA appointment and her subsequent founding of her own company Rosemeade (plate 216). Charles G. Grantier also directed the WPA ceramics project after first being recruited as ceramic artist with the Dickinson Clay Products Co., where he was responsible for their artistic Dickota pottery production (plate 217).

Both Taylor and Grantier helped put into practice – though on a small scale and for relatively short periods – Babcock's and Cable's ideas regarding the establishment of a viable ceramic industry using native materials within the state. Grantier was also to become the originator of North Dakota's "newest industry, handweaving"; his work was represented at the All States Fair in Washington, DC, in 1950. [172]

Plate 216: Bookends, by Laura Taylor, marked "LAT", also (left) "201 (M)" and (right) "180". UND Coll. # C-MSC Gift 74-597.

Two unrelated University of North Dakota students between 1910 and 1915 were Maxwell Anderson and Seymour Anderson. Maxwell Anderson, the most well known of all alumni of the University of North Dakota, [173] graduated in 1911. Seymour E. Anderson, of the class of 1913, was a student assistant in the Ceramics Department (figs. 24; 56), whose later career in educational work with the United States Government was to last for over 40 years. He headed Indian Schools in Dunseith and Fort Totten, North Dakota, before being appointed, in the mid-1930s, Director of the United States Department of the Interior, Office of Indian Affairs, Field Service, in North Dakota, with responsibility for the Wahpeton Indian School. His correspondence with Margaret Cable, during the period 1933-1935, concerned the teaching of pottery modeling to Indian children. In 1937, he directed the Indian Affairs service in Leupp, Arizona, and by the late 1940s, the same service in Ganado, Arizona, with responsibility for the Klagetoh-area schools. After his death in Ryderwood, Washington, in 1968, his wife wrote: "He served our Indian friends for 26 years in ND, the Chippewas, the Crees and the Sioux; in Santa Fe, NM, the Northern Pueblo and the Navajo; and then 15 years with the Navajo in NM and Arizona." [174]

Plate 217: Vase, by Charles Grantier, marked "Grantier Feb. 1931". UND Coll. # C-MSC Gift 87-681.

Fig. 56: Seymour Anderson at the bisque kiln.

Many graduates went on to teach in public school systems throughout the Upper Midwest. Other former students at the School of Mines (possibly graduates) taught, assisted and worked at schools on Indian reservations in the region, where classes on pottery making were offered. At the Turtle Mountain Indian School and Pottery, in Belcourt, North Dakota, for instance, "the pottery operation started out with elementary school students in the upper grades, many of whom were teenagers, but eventually included adults in an adult education program." [175] At this location pottery was made by the Chippewa in the late-1930s, using methods advocated by Margaret Cable, and under the instruction of Mrs. Carey (or Carrie) Grant and Emma Parisien, both of whom had received training from her at the University of North Dakota.

Endnotes

172 *Alumni Review*, September, 1950.

173 Maxwell Anderson, born 1888, embarked, after graduation, on a brilliant career as a playwright for the next 45 years, winning two Pulitzer Prizes (for *What Price Glory*, in 1924, and *Both Your Houses*, in 1933), two New York Drama Critics Circle Awards (for *Winterset*, in 1935, and *High Tor*, in 1936) and the National Institute for Arts and Letters 1954 Gold Medal for Drama, and also had a string of New York smash hits with some of his more than thirty plays as *Key Largo*, *The Bad Seed*, *Elizabeth the Queen* and *Anne of the Thousand Days*, before his death in 1959.

174 Vera Marshall Anderson letter to Margaret Barr, at the time of the publication of Mrs. Barr's booklet on University of North Dakota pottery.

175 *North Dakota Pottery Collectors Society Newsletter*, Vol. 14, Issue 4, October 2003: "History of Turtle Mountain Indian Pottery" (author not noted), reprinted from *Minot Daily News* (undated).

APPENDIX V

Some Noteworthy Students Enrolled in the Ceramics Department Courses

Since, at the University, the records covering student-enrollment in the Ceramics Department, over the course of more than five decades, are incomplete, it is only possible to estimate, at over two thousand students, the number of those attending classes, taught by Margaret Cable, Hildegarde Fried, Julia Mattson, Freida Hammers and Margaret Pachl, prior to the time of Mattson's retirement. A great proportion of the names to be found in University files and encountered in an inventory of University of North Dakota pottery, appears to be those of special, adult students, who may have undertaken an often-interrupted course of study over several, if not many, years. As mentioned earlier, many of these surnames are familiar as those of presidents, deans, directors, professors and other instructors of the University. From a consideration of the Ceramics Department lists, one can infer that many of the students were members, mainly women, of the Chandler, McVey, Babcock, Budge, Gauger, Kane, Harrington, Barr and other faculty families. Other names, such as Vold, Sorlie, Rudser and Thormodsgard are those of figures in public life, both official and cultural – governors, state officials, artists, etc. – and are well known both inside and outside the Grand Forks area.

Throughout the period of the history of the Department a variety of work was produced by students, who were excellent, good or poor craftswomen/craftsmen; much admirable work in earlier years by Parizek, Barnes, Moe and Halcrow; in the 1920s and 1930s, by Dahl, Robinson, Wilder, Staley, Serum, North, Bready and Rohde; and in the 1940s and 1950s, by Conners, Tollefson, Scott, Miller, Jelliff and Schnell. Artist-identification is often made more difficult by the illegibility of names, initials or monograms contained in the files or incised/painted on the base of vessels, figures, plaques and tiles; also by the number of family members with the same surname who took classes over several generations. Ultimately, information regarding the origination of shapes and designs might not be of paramount importance.

At the beginning of the 1930s, as economic conditions worsened in Grand Forks as throughout the country, Director A. W. Gauger felt obliged to remind Margaret Cable that "the fact be stressed in all the ceramics work that the object is not to make pots to be carried away as souvenirs of the course, but to develop a knowledge of technique and design, and an appreciation." [176] Regrettably, in contrast to the practice at Newcomb College, too many pieces that can only have been considered and possibly "prized" as "souvenirs of the course" [177] bear the mark of the University of North Dakota; the fact that they are so marked does not indicate that they have been examined or judged, in any way, to have attained an appropriate standard of technical or aesthetic quality. It is to be remembered, therefore, that much student work produced at the University -- and currently available in the secondary marketplace -- does not qualify as art objects for acquisition today by art pottery collectors.

This said, those students who produced excellent work can take their place along with their teachers, whose own original, handcrafted work is more often signed in some manner and sometimes dated. Even in the Spencer years the greater number of well-executed decorative schemes are by the instructors themselves on shapes designed by the named students. Consequently, again in contrast to Newcomb Pottery, identification by hands other than those of Cable, Fried, Mattson, Hammers, Taylor, Grantier, Pachl, and such accomplished students, of longer standing in the Ceramics Department, as Ruth Schnell, is not a matter of great concern, since such identification adds little indeed to the aesthetics and desirability of the items themselves.

Endnotes

176 Gauger letter dated August 19, 1931, to Cable.

177 Ibid.

APPENDIX VI

Some Notes on the History of Ceramic Instruction in the United States; and a Further Comparison of the Ceramics Department, University of North Dakota, with three other Ceramics Programs

As a result of the immensely popular exhibits at the Centennial Exposition in Philadelphia in 1876, groups of enthusiasts sought to nurture their awakened interest in ceramics through membership in such clubs as the Women's Pottery Club, founded in 1879, in Cincinnati, and the National League of Mineral Painters and the Atlan Ceramic Art Club, founded in 1891-1892 and 1893 respectively, both in Chicago. Many of those interested in pursuing a knowledge of pottery production and decoration were adult women with some possible previous experience in art, sketching or handicrafts, who were now turning their attention to china painting.[178] Also, during the last two decades of the nineteenth century, the influence of the English Arts and Crafts Movement began to assert itself in the United States, and Arts and Crafts societies were formed, to promulgate crafts for the educated, in Chicago (1897), Boston (1897), Minneapolis (1899), and Detroit (1906). Art academies and museum schools were established to teach an appreciation of design and to provide practical training in handicrafts, and at many universities and colleges, departments of art and design were expanded. During that same period the number of elementary schools giving instruction in manual arts increased from under ten to over four hundred by the turn of the century. Some institutions recognized in this new approach to the applied arts an opportunity to prepare women, particularly, for careers in the arts and crafts other than the vocation of teaching. At the same time state legislatures, eager to develop their regional economies, established schools of ceramic engineering to research the availability and suitability of local resources and to train professionals for potential, future industries.

In the United States, between 1894 and 1907, the first five institutions to establish departments or adjunct schools, where ceramic instruction would be offered, were Ohio State University in Columbus, Ohio, the New York State School of Clayworking in Alfred, New York, Rutgers University in New Brunswick, New Jersey, the University of Illinois, Urbana, Illinois, and Iowa State College in Ames, Iowa. At first – and at some of these schools for some time – the programs were restricted to the commercial/industrial aspects of the ceramics industry and consequently enrollment was limited to men only, as was considered proper at that time in the field of ceramic engineering. It was not until 1926, for instance, 32 years after the establishment of the program there, that the study of ceramic arts was initiated at Ohio State University, with classes, beginning in 1928, under the direction of Arthur Baggs.

Three colleges, whose early ceramics programs can be compared with that at the University of North Dakota, are Newcomb College at Tulane University, in New Orleans, Louisiana, the New York State School of Clayworking at Alfred University, in Alfred, New York, and Iowa State College, in Ames, Iowa.

A. **Newcomb College**

In 1887, the first classes were initiated at Newcomb College, which had been founded the previous year to offer a liberal arts education to women. The Woodward brothers, Ellsworth and William, instructors in the new art department, were joined by Gertrude Roberts Smith, and together they assisted the administrators in establishing the Newcomb Pottery and a program for the production -- for sale -- of art pottery, decorated by design graduates of the College. These women received further practical training in ceramic design, but the emphasis was not on instruction but rather on conducting a viable commercial enterprise which could provide a livelihood for them, while at the same time contributing to an improvement in the economic condition of the city and state. The "administrators felt the commercial success of the Pottery necessitated hiring professional potters" [179] while the decorators, supervised by Mary Given Sheerer from 1894 to 1931, earned commission on sales of their work. Clay and glaze research, as conducted at the University of North Dakota, was of limited interest and significance at Newcomb, and once a "Newcomb style" had been evolved, experimentation in design, technique and motif was not encouraged. This style, instituted by Paul Cox and Mary Sheerer, was based on the process of incising decoration on the ware in the bisque state, sponging the pots to produce an even texture, painting in underglaze blues and greens (occasionally with pink or yellow) and firing under a semi-transparent matt glaze. After more than three decades of official approbation and commercial success, engineered initially by Cox – with assistance from Frederick Walrath – and by Mary Sheerer and Sadie Irvine, the fortunes of Newcomb Pottery, like those of other schools and pottery companies suffered severe reverses as the Depression progressed and public tastes changed.

Plate 218: Newcomb College vases: (left) 1926, by Sadie Irvine; (right) 1929, by Anna Frances Simpson.

At Newcomb College, therefore, in contrast to the program at the University of North Dakota, pottery forms, handcrafted by professional male potters, were decorated by women with considerable training in design, expressly for sale to a national public, in order to provide these women with income. Little other study of ceramic processes was promoted, while high standards of handcraftsmanship in decoration and aesthetic variations of the Newcomb style were sought and maintained, in order to allow the pottery produced to be proudly identified as to its origin. Work inferior in design, execution or glaze was not permitted to be sold, though a small amount of some atypical pottery, especially of a hand-built or experimental nature, or that produced during the struggles of the last years, might nowadays be considered to be unworthy of the Newcomb name.

B. The New York State School of Clayworking, later (from 1932) The New York State College of Ceramics

Established in 1900 at Alfred University in Alfred, New York, with Charles Fergus Binns as its first director (through 1931), this school offered instruction in both ceramic engineering and ceramic arts. Binns believed that studies of both art and science were necessary for a complete course in ceramic processes, and though he was by no means an admirer of china painting and slip-casting, his courses, nonetheless, covered all aspects of pottery making, glazing and firing. Students attended classes in clay technology, clay working and such decorative techniques as over- and underglaze painting, and were also expected to conduct research into the state's mineral resources necessary for their course of study, in addition to gaining knowledge of, and experience in, graphic and decorative arts.

Female students at Alfred, amongst whom five graduated by 1909 with degrees in Ceramic Art and Design, were encouraged to enroll in the regular courses, short courses or summer school sessions along with "special" older students, as at Grand Forks; these included potters and teachers at schools and colleges as well as many others who already had experience in the pottery field. Margaret Cable and Hildegarde Fried studied under Binns, as did also, in the early years, Adelaide Alsop Robineau, Mary Chase Perry and Elizabeth Overbeck, alongside such noteworthy regular students as Arthur Baggs, Paul Cox, Frederick Walrath, Chauncey Thomas and William Bragdon.

Plate 219: (Left) vase by Charles Binns, 1929; (middle) potpourri jar, bearing paper label of "The Ceramic Guild Alfred New York"; (right) vase, marked "NYSS 1901", with unknown artist-cipher.

Binns's teaching, as evidenced in his own work, reflected a respect for materials; the application of a glaze of simple sophistication on an appropriately clean form of classical inspiration obviated the need for any other extraneous ornamentation. Students were given a thorough grounding in the history and development of ceramic art and science to the extent that their own taste and talent under Binns' guidance could be refined and their creative expression richly evolved. Binns was the right teacher at the right time, and his legacy spread as far as North Dakota and beyond.

In 1915, a student branch of the New York State Ceramic Society was formed at Alfred, and in the next two years a "Ceramic Guild" was organized by art students interested in the aims of the Society, under the supervision of a faculty member, to direct activities involved in annual exhibitions and periodic sales of students' work. Membership in the Guild was open to undergraduates and also to alumni and townspeople, who could enroll in special courses at the University; and all pottery produced in class was, initially at least, to belong to the school, prior to the time of sales at Christmas, Easter and commencement week. From these proceeds, a percentage was given to the Guild treasury to be spent on such events as traveling exhibitions invited to Alfred during the year, and also to cover the costs involved in the submission of exhibits to the Arts and Crafts Societies of New York, Boston, and Philadelphia, and to the Smithsonian. Participation in such exhibitions had to be approved by the staff of the Art Department and exhibits marked "not for sale unless a duplicate was available for the college."[180] Pottery by Guild members was offered for sale, inexpensively, at the crafts shop in the Department, and such sales were used for the assistance of poorer students and also to heighten public interest and garner acclaim for the school.

Similarities in the matter of undergraduate instruction and "special" studies exist, therefore, between the programs at Alfred and Grand Forks, though less attention was devoted to slip-casting and painted surfaces at Alfred, and more to the complete process of preparation of materials, throwing, glazing and firing; also far less emphasis was placed, at Alfred, on the importance of sales (in contrast to the practice at the University of North Dakota during the Depression and World War II years). The significant Departmental functions of research and development at Alfred were mirrored, particularly in the early years prior to the mid-1930s, at Grand Forks, while the graduation of future studio potters of note was far more numerous in the program initiated, directed and bequeathed by Binns. By the middle of the twentieth century, Alfred graduates were teaching, full-time, at more than twenty universities, colleges and professional schools in the United States and Canada, and, amongst the others, the numbers of studio potters, ceramic industry executives and industrial designers are legion.

C. **Iowa State College**

Plate 220: Iowa State College: (left) vase, by Mary Yancey; (top right) hand-built and hand-decorated, covered jar, by Schiele (student); (bottom right) bowl, by Mary Yancey.

At the Iowa State College of Agriculture and Mechanical Arts, research and instruction in ceramics was already being conducted by 1899; by 1907, a degree in ceramic engineering was offered; and by 1910-1911, a Department of Ceramics was instituted. Instruction was aimed at graduating ceramic engineers for employment in Iowa's brick, drain tile, sewer pipe and electrical porcelains industries, and students were given the opportunity to attend classes in pottery-modeling, when these were introduced for women in the Home Economics Department. With the appointment of Paul Cox, in 1920, the Department's program was both educational and promotional. Projected sales of pottery on campus, through shops, at exhibitions and at presentations to women's clubs (with prepared lecture material), etc. – similar to those conducted by Margaret Cable at Grand Forks – were intended, from the beginning -- in contrast to the attitude in North Dakota -- to support the program to promote the goals of the Ceramic Engineering Department. These were, as Dean Babcock had earlier mandated at the University of North Dakota, to prove the viability of the state's native clays and to provide economic opportunities for development in the state. Cox, who had graduated from the Alfred course of study under Binns and who had experience in industry and commerce, had been employed for ten years at the Newcomb Pottery, from where he, in turn, recruited Mary Yancey, in 1924, to be instructor and decorator at Iowa State College through 1930. Together they began to produce commercial art pottery in the Newcomb manner, handcrafted and hand-decorated (when not left plain) using indigenous motifs; as at Newcomb, decoration was artistically and carefully applied, through incising, excising and underglaze, inlaid painting, in designs accentuating the various forms. Their Iowa innovation was in the color range and the use of a transparent high-gloss glaze; a palette of vivid, bright red, yellow, blue and green enamels was applied in a complex process to produce a lively polychrome design. Ultimately these colors, in addition to a high price in the local market, resulted in an unsatisfactory reception and poor sales. As a consequence, by 1928, Yancey was spending most of her time teaching ceramic design rather than decorating pottery for sale. Two years later, Yancey left the College. Cox remained there through 1939, after which the emphasis at Ames reverted to engineering ceramics. [181]

Similarities between the two neighboring programs in Ames and Grand Forks can be seen in the institutions' common mission to research and develop native resources and to search for economic opportunities to improve the local economies; to develop a style based on local flora and fauna; and to introduce an exciting palette. Throwing, hand-building and decoration -- though by not as many techniques as practiced by Margaret Cable's students -- were taught in Iowa, and, as in North Dakota, souvenirs were made for visitors to such events as Open House celebrations and the annual Veishea festival. On the other hand, the forms decorated by Yancey were thrown by Cox, and possibly some by Yancey herself, and slip-casting was not a feature of the pottery made for sale in Ames – in contrast to the situation in Grand Forks.

Endnotes

178 "By 1874, many women, including Maria Longworth Nichols and Louise McLaughlin, were painting porcelain to beautify their homes," – *Journal of the American Art Pottery Association*, Vol. 19, No. 5, September/October, 2003: "Cincinnati Ceramics: The Cradle of American Art Pottery," by Anita J. Ellis, excerpted from *The Cincinnati Wing: The Story of Art in the Queen City.*

179 *Journal of the American Art Pottery Association*, Vol. 13, No. 3, May/June, 1997: "Sadie Irvine Potter?" by Maureen A. Donnelly.

180 *Art and Design at Alfred*, by Melvin H. Bernstein.

181 *The Palimpsest*, Vol. 68, No. 3, Fall, 1987: "A Collaboration in Clay: Iowa State's Prairie Pottery," by Susan Russo.

APPENDIX VII

A Guide to Valuation

The difficulties of assigning values to the art pottery of the University of North Dakota are similar to those attendant on assessments of original and unique artwares by other such producers as Rookwood, Newcomb Pottery, Marblehead, etc. This is in contrast to the easier evaluation of the fully documented, collectible, industrial artwares, produced in quantity and in catalogued line-ranges, by such manufacturers as Roseville, Red Wing and Royal Haeger in the middle and later years of the twentieth century. At the University of North Dakota, apart from the mass-produced souvenir items and commemorative medallions, only the standard regular production (for sale in the period 1938-1948/9) of Spencer-list models can in any way be compared -- with an eye to the effect, on value, of mold and color quality -- one against another, since they were produced in multiple copies. Otherwise, the evaluation of the unique wares of the Ceramics Department at Grand Forks has to be considered on the basis of each item's separate, individual merits. Included below are some guidelines which might be of assistance to the collector, buyer or seller in this regard.

The principal considerations for assessing the value of University of North Dakota pottery, in order of priority, are:

A. For Handcrafted / Hand Decorated Vessels / Tiles by Staff Members and Students

1. **Importance, uniqueness and rarity**
The four "North Dakota Products Vases" are arguably the most important pieces of pottery made at the University of North Dakota. The multiplicity, as also the complexity, of design detail was hand-executed on each vase, so each is unique in execution, if not in design. Of the four examples, the most important is the Sorlie vase because it is the first and original version and it is historically significant; the second-most important is the Kane vase since the sgraffito decoration was incised through a brown-stained glaze rather than the blue glaze of the other three examples. Should any of these four ever be available on the open market, each would be valued, if in mint condition, in excess of $25,000.00, with the Sorlie vase, now on exhibit at Oxford House (the Stone Alumni Association Building), if subjected to aggressive offers (by competing purchasers) or spirited bidding (at auction), possibly in excess of even $50,000.00. Other handcrafted presentation pieces would rank in value immediately after the "North Dakota Products Vases," as collectible items of artistic and historic significance, such as the "Queen Marie of Romania Vase and Bowl," the "Lewis and Clark Bowl," the "Scott Vase," the "Crown Princess Martha Vase" and the "President John F. Kennedy Vase."

2. **Aesthetic appeal of decorative scheme and suitability to shape of vessel**
Though certainly subject to the personal preferences of individual collectors, superior examples of larger, more imposing shapes with sophisticated, handcrafted decoration with Art Nouveau resonance or in an Arts and Crafts manner, by Margaret Cable, Hildegarde Fried, Julia Mattson or Freida Hammers could possibly be valued from $15,000.00 to $20,000.00.

3. **Quality of handcraftsmanship and complexity of handcrafted design**
   Unique pieces of somewhat lesser stature/appeal by Cable, Fried, Mattson and Hammers, though still with considerable desirability in terms of design, imagery, color and glaze and with a high standard of craftsmanship in execution, could, at sale, bring a price in the range of $10,000.00 – $15,000.00.

4. **Choice and representation of subject matter in decoration of handcrafted designs**
   Well executed examples – by the four instructors prior to 1950, by Huckfield, and by a few talented students like Ruth Schnell – with especially interesting and regionally significant, if not unique, motifs adapted to handcrafted design, might be estimated at about $7,000.00 -- $10,000.00. Beautifully represented Western themes and other more unusual, though not necessarily regionally significant, motifs in complex decorative schemes, together with larger vases in polychrome bentonite, are to be included in this category. Smaller, and not quite as successful examples by Cable, her colleagues, and a small number of accomplished students would fall in the $4,000.00 -- $7,000.00 range.

5. **Inter-relationship of colors used and blended in handcrafted designs; and**

6. **Glaze effects and treatment and appropriateness to shape and/or design**
   Average-size items with bentonite decoration, with well-executed designs by more than competent students, or work with interesting color combinations, blends and shading, accentuating the shape of the vessel, might be appraised at around $1,000.00 -- $1,500.00, as would also those items with successfully researched and rendered experimental glaze effects. Some simpler, small items designed by talented hands could be estimated at a value of $500.00 - $1,000.00. Average-standard hand-painting on figures, paperweights and small tiles might double the value of the equivalent, plain models, especially when marked and identified, to possibly $400.00 or $500.00.

7. **Unusual items**
   Additional commercial importance can be given to those items which might appear to be extraordinary in terms of construction, technique, glaze and color treatment, imagery or some other consideration which sets the work apart from its contemporary fellows in the production of University of North Dakota art pottery or even of other potteries elsewhere. A vase with sgraffito decoration depicting, for example, giraffes or pre-Columbian, Central or South American figures might be worth twice as much, to an advanced collector, as a similar vessel, of comparable size and quality, with floral imagery ($5,000.00 -- $10,000.00). Again, a student work of individualistic appeal, achieved by throwing or hand-building (coiling or slab technique), though possibly lacking sophisticated execution, might nevertheless be evaluated at $600.00 -- $1,000.00.

8. **Size**
   Generally – all aspects, other than size, being equal – larger pieces are more prized than smaller, as might be expected. Since, in the output of the Ceramics Department, prior to the Pachl era, very few items were produced in a height of more than 10 inches, any vase or pitcher of more than 9 inches in height and any bowl, compote or plate of a diameter greater than 9 inches, would be considered large.

9. **Condition**
   All valuations cited here are based on mint, unrepaired condition without manufacturing or other blemishes, and are conservatively construed at the time of publication.

10. **Maker / decorator identification**
   Other than in those instances where a collector, for personal, family or even eccentric reasons, might collect specifically the work of any one instructor/decorator or student at the University of North Dakota, craftsman-identification adds little to an appreciation or evaluation of a pottery vessel made there. It is indeed doubtful, for example, that any one of the "North Dakota Products Vases" or any of those models in the top echelon of decorative artworks produced at Grand Forks would be deemed of any lesser value, were they not signed by Cable, in the first instance, or by any other of the instructors/decorators or more talented students of the Department, in the second.

11. **Later works**
   Much of the pottery produced after 1950 in the Ceramics Department – including not only the handmade and possibly hand-decorated pieces of a more sculptural nature by Pachl and some students, but also many of those hand-painted/hand-incised items, with abstract decoration, made by Mattson in her last years at the university (plates 221–224) – is more difficult to evaluate than the art pottery of the first half of the twentieth century. Its more restrictive appeal might be considered to be appreciated more by collectors of mid-century design than by art pottery admirers of the earlier styles, and this limitation could presently be reflected in lower estimates of collectible worth.

B. For Pressed Figures, Paperweights, Trays (emblem trays, ashtrays and pin-trays), Souvenir Items, Curtain Pulls, Test Tiles, and for Spencer-List Items (molded, decorated shapes)

1. **Aesthetic appeal of decorative scheme with polychrome addition, and suitability to vessel-shape**
2. **Quality of finishing; crispness/detail of design; enhancement of design detail through color/shading; color contrast**
3. **Choice, representation and placement of design motif**
4. **Color selection and glaze treatment**
5. **Size**
6. **Condition**

Valuations in this category, with special regard for the six listed considerations – depending primarily on aesthetic appeal, quality, importance, color and size – could range from \$75.00+ for a miniature test tile, \$150.00+ for a curtain pull, \$200.00+ for a commemorative medallion, \$300.00 -- \$600.00 for a tray, tea tile, pressed figure or other souvenir item, to \$2,000.00+ for a sizeable vase, bowl or covered vessel (such as a tobacco jar) with successfully executed decoration of special interest. A lamp-vase, or lamp completely fitted and with an original shade of parchment or other material, might be evaluated at about $600.00 -- $800.00 if its surface decoration (even without the advantage of a blended glaze) is enhanced, for example, with in-mold horizontal ribbing or banding.

That sub-group of Spencer-list models whose surfaces received totally unique decorative treatments, such as the previously mentioned planter/bookends (#177) by Haessle and ginger jars (#191) and toasting cup (#222) by Miller, should be considered separately from their more common counterparts. As original variants their values can be estimated at more than twice those of the regular slip-cast models offered by Spencer in the 1940s.

C. For Small, Plain Test Bowls, Jars and Tiles, and for Spencer-List Items (molded, plain shapes)

1. **Aesthetic appeal**
2. **Application of blended, shaded, flowing and drip glazes and suitability to shape**
3. **Color and glaze selection**
4. **Size**
5. **Condition**

In this category, valuations could again vary widely – from $35.00+ for a miniature, plain test tile to $500.00+ for an attractive Spencer-list vase or bowl of some size, or a plain lamp base whose only attribute is a successfully blended glaze treatment applied appropriately to the form.

It cannot be over-emphasized that models appearing on the Spencer list and bearing appropriate identifying numbers should be regarded, for the most part – and consequently evaluated – as the University of North Dakota equivalent of Rookwood's "production" pieces. Without the addition of extensive hand-applied decoration or other original enhancement, their values are essentially those of decorative wares of multiple number and of much lesser ranking in collectible rarity; this should be borne in mind when estimating them vis-à-vis the higher quality, unique works of art pottery by the staff members and the more talented and accomplished students in the Ceramics Department.

Engineering, electrical, structural and other utilitarian wares such as enameled hollow tile, brick, insulators, sewer pipe, cookware and stoneware crocks are items of scholastic and possibly historical value and are not part of this study of art pottery evaluation.

Plates 221–224: Designs by Mattson, 1950s.

Plate 221: Risser/Dilley Coll.

Plate 222: Risser/Dilley Coll.

Plate 223: Risser/Dilley Coll.

Plate 224: Risser/Dilley Coll.

The North Dakota exhibit stand at the Louisiana Purchase Exposition, 1904, St. Louis, Missouri.

Bibliography

Albrecht, Donald, Robert Schonfeld, and Lindsay Stamm Shapiro: *Russel Wright creating American Lifestyle*. New York: Harry N. Abrams, Inc., 2001.

Anderson, Marcia: "Art for Life's Sake: The Handicraft Guild of Minneapolis," published in *Art and Life on the Upper Mississippi, 1890-1915*, edited by Michael Conforti. Newark: The University of Delaware Press, in association with the Minneapolis Institute of Arts, 1994.

Auction catalogs:

North Dakota Pottery, April 22, 1989, Woody Auction;

Ruth R. Schnell North Dakota Pottery, November 22, 1997, Bismarck, ND, Larry J. Barnhardt's Midwest Auction Co.;

Various: David Rago Auctions, Inc./Craftsman Auctions.

Baizerman, Suzanne, Lynn Downey and John Toki: *Fired by Ideals: Arequipa Pottery and the Arts & Crafts Movement*. Rohnert, California: Pomegranate Communications, Inc., with the Oakland Museum of California, 2000.

Barber, Edwin AtLee: *The Pottery and Porcelain of the United States and Marks of American Potters*. New York: Putnam's Sons, 1893, 2nd ed. 1901, 3rd ed. 1909.

Barr, Margaret Libby, Donald Miller and Robert Barr: *University of North Dakota Pottery – The Cable Years*.

Berg, Claudia and Mark J. Halvorson: "A Century of North Dakota Pottery," published in *North Dakota History, Journal of the Northern Plains*, Volume 65, No. 2 & 3.

Bernstein, Melvin H: *Art and Design at Alfred*. Philadelphia: Art Alliance Press, 1986.

Borah, Leo A: "North Dakota Comes Into Its Own," published in *The National Geographic Magazine*, Volume C, No. 3.

Carney, Margaret: *Charles Fergus Binns – The Father of American Studio Ceramics*. New York: Hudson Hills Press, 1998, with the International Museum of Ceramic Art, New York State College of Ceramics at Alfred University.

Clark, Garth and Margie Hughto: *A Century of Ceramics in the United States, 1878-1978*. New York: E. P. Dutton, 1979, with the Everson Museum of Art.

Clef, Roman A, et al: "The Mystery of the Zanesville-Grand Forks Connection," published in the *Journal of the American Art Pottery Association*, Volume 16, No. 5.

Dale, Sharon: *Frederick Hurten Rhead: An English Potter in America*. Erie, Pennsylvania: Erie Art Museum, 1986.

Dommel, Darlene H: *Collector's Encyclopedia of the Dakota Potteries*. Paducah, Kentucky: Collector Books, 1996.

Donnelly, Maureen A: "Sadie Irvine Potter?" published in *The Journal of the American Art Pottery Association*, Volume 13, No. 3.

Eidelberg, Martin: "Myths of Style and Nationalism: American Art Pottery at the Turn of the Century," published in the *Journal of the Decorative and Propaganda Arts*, Volume 20, 1994.

---- : "Art Pottery," published in *The Arts and Crafts Movement in America 1876-1916*, edited by Robert Judson Clark (catalog of an exhibition organized by the Art Museum, Princeton University, and The Art Institute of Chicago, 1972).

Ellis, Anita J: "Cincinnati Ceramics: The Cradle of American Art Pottery," published in the *Journal of the American Art Pottery Association*, Vol. 19, No. 5; excerpted from *The Cincinnati Wing: The Story of Art in the Queen City*, (catalog of an exhibition organized by the Cincinnati Art Museum, 2003), edited by Julie Aronson; Athens, Ohio: Cincinnati Art Museum and Ohio University Press, 2003.

Evans, Paul: *Art Pottery of the United States*. New York: Charles Scribner's Sons, 1974; Feingold and Lewis Publishing Corporation, 1987.

Huxford, Sharon and Bob: *The Collector's Encyclopedia of Roseville Pottery*. Paducah, Kentucky: Collector Books, 1976.

---- : *Weller Pottery*. Paducah, Kentucky: Collector Books, 1979.

Journal of the American Ceramic Society, various issues.

Kaplan, Wendy: *"The Art that is Life": The Arts & Crafts Movement in America, 1875-1920*, (catalog of an exhibition organized by the Museum of Fine Arts, Boston, 1987).

Keen, Kirsten Hoving: *American Art Pottery, 1875-1930*, (catalog of an exhibition organized by the Delaware Art Museum, Wilmington, 1978).

Lehner, Lois: *Encyclopedia of U.S. Marks on Pottery, Porcelain and Clay*. Paducah, Kentucky: Collector Books, 1988.

Miller, Donald: *University of North Dakota Pottery – The Cable Years*.

Murphy, Edward C: "A Brief History of Clay Resources in North Dakota," published in *North Dakota History, Journal of The Northern Plains*, Volume 65, No. 2 & 3.

Nelson, Marion John: *Art Pottery of the Midwest*. Minneapolis, Minnesota: University Art Museum, University of Minnesota, 1988.

Nelson, Scott H: "Two UND Artists," published in the *Journal of the American Art Pottery Association*, Volume 8, No. 1.

Ormond, Suzanne and Mary E. Irvine: *Louisiana's Art Nouveau – The Crafts of the Newcomb Style*. Gretna, Louisiana: Pelican Publishing Company, 1976.

Peck, Herbert: *The Book of Rookwood Pottery*. New York: Crown Publishers, Inc., 1968.

---- : *The Second Book of Rookwood Pottery*. Tucson, Arizona: Herbert Peck, 1985.

Poesch, Jessie: *Newcomb Pottery: An Enterprise for Southern Women, 1895-1940*. Exton, Pennsylvania: Schiffer Publishing Limited, 1984.

Postle, Kathleen R: *The Chronicle of the Overbeck Pottery*. Indianapolis: Indiana Historical Society, 1978.

Russo, Susan: "A Collaboration in Clay: Iowa State's Prairie Pottery," published in *The Palimpsest*, volume 68, No. 3.

Trapp, Kenneth R: *The Arts and Crafts Movement in California: Living the Good Life*. New York: Abbeville Press, with the Oakland Museum, 1993.

Wright, Russel and Mary: *Guide to Easier Living*. New York: Simon and Schuster, 1950.

Xie, Margaret Carney, and Susan R. Strong: *Charles Fergus Binns Stonewares – A Chair Must Invite the Sitter*. Alfred, NY: Museum of Ceramic Art, New York State College of Ceramics at Alfred University, 1992.

About the Author

Ken Forster was educated at New College, Oxford, and attended summer schools at the Universities of Aix-en-Provence and Vienna. He earned an MA degree in modern languages and philology at Oxford University and a diploma in fabric design and weaving technology at the Derby College of Technology. After working in Singapore, Malacca and Kuala Lumpur as a merchant trader for an East India company, and in London producing and recording rock-music programs for BBC radio, he immigrated to the United States in 1968.

The following year he opened his first gallery of American and European decorative arts in Dallas, Texas, with an emphasis on the ceramic, glass and metal design of the late nineteenth and early twentieth centuries and the silver of the Georg Jensen Silversmithy.

He re-located and operated galleries in Alexandria, Virginia (1971-1985), and in Baltimore, Maryland (1985-1991). During those years he exhibited at antiques shows throughout the country, and mounted several nationally advertised exhibitions, including "American Art Pottery - 15 Years of Collecting" and "American Art Pottery - the South;" he curated such other exhibits as "Modern Glass, 1940-1970" and "Tea and Coffee Services - Twentieth Century Design in Silver and Other Metals," and also lectured in Washington for the Smithsonian Institution on various aspects of the Art Nouveau and Art Deco styles.

He resides in the Washington DC area.